IN THE NAME OF

Allah

THE MOST GRACIOUS, THE MOST MERCIFUL

Timeless Seeds of Advice

Hadith on Good Morals

Ibn Kathir

Copyright ©

Noaha - IIPH™

Hadith on Good Morals

Ibn Kathir

Revised (1975)

Revised English Edition 1 (1989)

New Revised English Edition 3 (2023)

All rights reserved. No part of this book may be reproduced or transmitted in any form or by any means, electronic or mechanical, including photocopying, recording, or by any information storage and retrieval system, without written permission from the Publisher.

Table of Contents

Publisher's Note 5

Preface 7

Introduction 9

Chapter One: Honesty 15

Chapter Two: Modesty 21

Chapter Three: Humility 27

Chapter Four: Courage 31

Chapter Five: Steadfastness 35

Chapter Six: Kindness 41

Chapter Seven: Gentleness 45

Chapter Eight: Chastity 47

Chapter Nine: Peacefulness 53

Chapter Ten: Moderation 57

Chapter Eleven: Politeness 65

Chapter Twelve: Contentment 67

Chapter Thirteen: Cheerfulness 73

Chapter Fourteen: Charity 77

Chapter Fifteen: Cooperation 83

Chapter Sixteen: Justice 97

Chapter Seventeen: Forgiveness 97

Chapter Eighteen: Love 103

Chapter Nineteen: Patient perseverance 109

Chapter Twenty: Benevolence 119

Chapter Twenty-One: Mercifulness 123

Chapter Twenty-Two: Respect 131

Chapter Twenty-Three: Generosity 137

Chapter Twenty-Four: Amicability 141

Chapter Twenty-Five: Upholding ties of kinship 145

Chapter Twenty-Six: Caring for the weak 149

Chapter Twenty-Seven: Treating servants well 153

Chapter Twenty-Eight: Hospitality 157

Chapter Twenty-Nine: Protecting people's honour 161

Chapter Thirty: Trustworthiness 165

Chapter Thirty-One: Good neighbourliness 171

Chapter Thirty-Two: Having a good fragrance 175

Chapter Thirty-Three: Forbearance and deliberation 177

Chapter Thirty-Four: Reconciliation 179

Chapter Thirty-Five: Giving gifts 183

Chapter Thirty-Six: Sincerity 185

Chapter Thirty-Seven: Visiting the sick 195

Chapter Thirty-Eight: Thinking well of people 199

Chapter Thirty-Nine: Observing the rights of the street 203

Chapter Forty: Listening and obeying 211

Conclusion 233

Publisher's Note

All praise and thanks belong to Allah alone, the One, the Almighty and All-Merciful. Blessings and peace be upon Prophet Muhammad, the last of His messengers and prophets, and upon his family, his Companions and all those who follow in his footsteps until the end of time.

The statements and actions of our Prophet Muhammad (peace and blessings be upon him) contain much that we need: rules and advice, reminders, examples, warnings and encouragement. The collection of hadiths in *Hadith on Good Morals* by Ibn Kathir is a wonderful anthology of the Prophet's statements on positive ethics and attributes that all people – Muslims and non-Muslims – should strive to adopt in the way we deal with others; we need to work to incorporate these morals and principles into our daily habits.

May Allah accept the efforts of all those who contributed to the production of this book, and may it be acceptable to Him, *âmeen*.

The Editor
al-Imam Noah Ibn Kathir

Preface

All praises and gratitude are due to Allah (Glorified and Exalted is He). We praise Him, seek His help, and ask for His forgiveness. We seek refuge in Allah from the evil in our souls and from our sinful deeds. Whomever Allah guides no one can misguide, and whomever He allows to go astray none can guide. We bear witness that there is no true God worthy of worship except Allah, and we bear witness that Muhammad (blessings and peace be upon him) is His servant and messenger.

O you who believe! Have *taqwâ* of Allah (always being conscious of Allah, loving and fearing Him) as He deserves, and die not except as Muslims. O people! Have taqwâ of your Lord, the One Who created you from a single soul and created from it its mate, and from the two spread forth many men and women. Fear Allah, from whom you demand your mutual rights, and do not cut the ties of kinship. Surely, Allah is ever an All-Watcher over you. O you who believe! Have taqwâ of Allah and speak always the truth. He will make all your works good and will forgive your sins. Whoever obeys Allah and His Messenger (bpuh) has indeed achieved a great success.

To proceed: truly, the best speech is that embodied in the Book of Allah, the glorious Qur'an, and the best guidance is the guidance given by Prophet Muhammad (bpuh) as found in the Hadith[1] and the Sunnah.[2] The most evil affairs are the innovations in religion; and every innovation in religion is an error. (Bukhari and Muslim)

First and foremost, I praise and thank Allah for guiding my family and me to Islam. Had it not been for His grace and mercy on us, we would not have been guided to Islam. Secondly, I praise and thank Allah for giving me the opportunity and ability to complete this compilation. I pray that He accepts this small humble effort, counts it as a good deed for my family and me to make our scales of good deeds heavy on the Last Day, and pardons any errors that may have occurred in it.

I sincerely hope that readers will benefit from this book. Before reading it, you might – after only a perfunctory glance – -pass some kind of judgment. However, let sound logic and precepts taken from revelation arbitrate that judgment. Also, bear in mind that it is indeed a culpable offence for one to judge a work before having read it thoroughly or at least hearing what it is about.

I do hope, though, that you will be just in your judgment and that your bias will be towards true and correct knowledge. Finally, this book is not written for a specific group of people; rather, it is for anyone who wants Allah to enter them into His mercy and make them dwell in His paradise.

The Editor
al-Imam Noah Ibn Kathir

Introduction

Many great and famous Muslim scholars, from the time of the Companions of Prophet Muhammad (bpuh) to this day, have endeavored to compile books of hadiths. Many have made efforts to compile collections of forty hadiths covering different subjects and topics ranging from *'aqeedah* (creed), *akhlâq* (morality, good manners), asceticism, jihad (striving in the cause of Allah), *tarbiyah* (upbringing, moral education), da'wah, and so on, as witnessed in the words of Imam an-Nawawi in the introduction to his compilation of forty-two hadiths, also famously known as *al-Arba'een an-Nawawi* (meaning the forty hadith of an-Nawawi), in which he said:

> The scholars, may Allah be pleased with them, have compiled innumerable works of this nature. The first one that I know of who compiled such a work was 'Abdullâh ibn al-Mubârak. After him came Ibn Aslam aṭ-Ṭoosi, a pious scholar. Then came al-Ḥasan ibn Sufyân an-Nasâ'i, Abu Bakr al-Âjurri, Abu Bakr Muhammad ibn Ibrâheem al-Aṣfahâni, ad-Dâraquṭni, al-Ḥâkim, Abu Nu'aym, Abu 'Abdur-Raḥmân as-Salami, Abu Sa'eed al-Mâleeni, Abu 'Uthmân aṣ-Ṣâbooni, 'Abdullâh ibn Muhammad al-Anṣâri, Abu Bakr al-Bayhaqi, and countless others, both from earlier and later times. I have asked Allah for guidance and prayed to Him while compiling these forty hadiths, following the example of those Imams and guardians of Islam.[4]

Thus, in emulation of these great and famous Muslim scholars, and being inspired by the legacy they left behind, as well as having been greatly encouraged by the positive response to my book *Forty Hadiths on Poisonous Social Habits*, I felt the need to compile yet another collection of forty hadiths covering good moral values. These values are not only taught by Islam but are also respected by all major world religions. By putting these values into practice, humanity once more may gain back long-lost morality and fill up the spiritual and moral emptiness plaguing most world societies. Just as in the collection of *Hadiths on Poisonous Social Habits*, I have included a brief commentary on each of the hadiths for the purpose of understanding, reflection, and implementation. In some chapters, I have included two or more hadiths instead of a single hadith. The overall aim of this book, like the previous compilation, is to remind myself and all others to try to the best of our abilities to practice these good moral values, as embodied in Hadith literature, so that our belief in God may be translated into sincere concrete action rather than remain as empty talk that does not change the moral decadence in our society.

Allah (the Exalted) strongly rebukes this kind of empty belief and talk by saying:

{O you who believe, why do you say that which you do not do? Most hateful it is with Allah that you say that which you do not do.}

(Qur'an 61: 2-3)

Instead, Allah (the Exalted) encourages and motivates us to obey Him to the best of our abilities.

{So keep your duty to Allah and fear Him as much as you can; listen and obey, and spend in charity; that is better for yourselves...}

(Qur'an 64: 16)

Akhlâq is a science of the ethical values of human life. It deals with human conduct and behavior that society either endorses or rejects. Human beings are endowed with the ability to admire what is good and beautiful and to hate and despise what is bad and ugly. Establishing Islamic morality in the language of the glorious Qur'an and Hadith is known as *tahdheeb*, which means moral education that teaches Muslims how to behave well in society. Moral values mainly deal with the dos and the don'ts in human life that make life worth living.[5] Without morality in the daily lives of human beings, a society becomes chaotic and unbearable.

Morality or good behavior is an essential part of human life, especially for those who believe in God. Hence, morality permeates a Muslim's life at home, in school, in the workplace, and in conducting business transactions. As Muslims, we are required to follow the example of Prophet Muhammad (bpuh), the exemplary role model in conduct, manners, and good behaviour.[6] In fact, in praising the excellent moral character and behavior of Prophet Muhammad (bpuh), Allah (the Exalted) said:

{And verily you [O Muhammad] are on an exalted standard of character.}

(Qur'an 68: 4)

Then Allah (the Exalted) commanded us to emulate the Prophet's noble and excellent character and behavior, saying:

{You have indeed in the Messenger of Allah a beautiful pattern [of conduct] to emulate for anyone whose hope is in Allah and the final day, and who engages much in the remembrance [and praise] of Allah.}

(Qur'an 33: 21)

Islam, as a blessing to humanity, emphasizes all the aspects of good manners and morals. Abu Hurayrah (may Allah be pleased with him) narrated that Allah's Messenger (bpuh) said:

«I have only been sent to perfect the most noble character traits.» (A reliable hadith recorded by al-Bayhaqi)

In addition, Prophet Muhammad (bpuh), who was known and respected for his nobility of character and best behavior towards all people, always emphasized the importance of good morals and manners such as honesty, sincerity, kindness, modesty, gentleness, courage, steadfastness, and many other positive values and attitudes. He stressed consideration for others, and a general desire for promotion of the happiness and welfare of society, as will be discussed in the following chapters of this work. In encouraging such noble moral values and character, Abu Umâmah (may Allah be pleased with him) reported that Allah's Messenger (bpuh) said:

«I guarantee a house in the outskirts of paradise for a person who refrains from opinion-based arguing even if he is in the right, and a house in the middle of paradise for the one who refrains from lying even when he is joking, and a house in the highest part of paradise for the one who makes his character good.» (A reliable hadith recorded by Abu Dâwood)

Abu ad-Dardâ' narrated that the Prophet (bpuh) said:

«There is nothing heavier on the believer's scale on the Day of Judgment than good character, for indeed Allah Most High is angered by the shameless, obscene person.» (A sound hadith recorded by Abu Dâwood and at-Tirmidhi)

The chief virtues enjoined by Islam may be classified under two headings: those that prevent a person from injuring the life, property, and honor of others and those that prompt a person to do good to others. Abu Wahb narrated that 'Abdullâh ibn al-Mubârak (may Allah be pleased with him) explained good character by saying, "It is a smiling face, doing one's best in good, and refraining from harm."[7]

Without question, good manners and morals make life worth living. Without them, human life would become unbearable, as has become self-evident in many secular and materialistic societies that have rejected not only Islam but religion together with all that it teaches. For such societies that are at war with religion, especially those at war with Islam, nothing is expected but moral and social corruption, which threatens to destroy them. In addition, they will suffer humiliation on the Day of Judgment.

'Abdullâh ibn 'Umar narrated that Allah's Messenger (bpuh) turned to them and said:

«O *Muhâjireen* (the Muslims who migrated with Prophet Muhammad [bpuh] from Makkah to Madinah), there are five things with which you will be tested, and I seek refuge with Allah lest you live to see them.

[1] Whenever immorality appears among a people to such an extent that they commit it openly, plagues and diseases that were never known among the predecessors spread among them.

[2] Those who cheat in weights and measures will be stricken with famine, severe calamity, and the oppression of their rulers.

[3] If people withhold the *zakâh* (alms tax) of their wealth, rain will be withheld from the sky; and were it not for the (sake of the) animals, no rain would fall on them.

[4] If anyone breaks their covenant with Allah and His Messenger, Allah will enable their enemies to overpower them and take some of what is in their hands.

[5] Unless their leaders rule according to the Book of Allah and seek all good from that which Allah has revealed, Allah will cause them to fight one another.» (A sound hadith recorded by Ibn Mâjah)[8]

Islam emphasizes all good manners and moral values by promising to those who practice and uphold them prosperity and psychological security, happiness in this life, and paradise in the next life. This is taught in the Qur'an and the Sunnah:

{Whoever works righteousness, whether male or female, while he [or she] is a true believer [of Islamic monotheism], verily to him We will give a good life [in this world with respect to contentment, prosperity, psychological satisfaction, and lawful provision], and We shall certainly pay them a reward in proportion to the best of what they used to do [meaning the reward of paradise in the hereafter].}

(Qur'an 16: 97)

«Abu Hurayrah narrated that when Allah's Messenger (bpuh) was asked about that for which people are admitted into paradise the most, he said: Taqwâ of Allah, and good character.[9]

Then he was asked about that for which people are admitted into the fire the most, and he said: The (sins of the) mouth and the private parts.» (A sound hadith recorded by at-Tirmidhi)

When we look at the lifestyle of Prophet Muhammad (bpuh) and his Companions, we find that it is full of amazing excellent behaviors and characteristics. It is this kind of morality that made their society the best and most blessed society – what we would call today a truly civilized society. Allah's Messenger (bpuh) described his society and the first three generations after him as the best of all generations to be emulated. 'Imrân ibn Ḥuṣayn narrated that Allah's Messenger (bpuh) said:

«The best of you are my generation, then those who come after them, then those who come after them, then those who come after them.

('Imrân added: I do not know if the Messenger of Allah [bpuh] mentioned two or three generations.)

Then there will come after them people who will be dishonest and not trustworthy. They will make vows and not fulfil them, and obesity will become widespread among them.» (Muslim)

The main motivating factors that made those three generations the most morally upright generations for posterity to emulate, and which can still make our society the same, are three:

1.
True and sincere belief in Allah (the Exalted) in their everyday lives, coupled with God-consciousness and piety in all that they used to do;

2.
The strong unwavering conviction in their hearts and minds, which was cultivated and inculcated by Allah's Messenger (bpuh), that each of them would stand in the court of Allah (the Exalted) to account for all their actions, manners and behaviors;

3.
The personal psychological serenity and peace of mind, as well as the societal security, that was a consequence of their good morals and behaviors.

That is why when Allah (the Exalted) describes to us the relationship between our duty to Him (which translates as God-consciousness) and our duty to fellow human beings (which implies good behavior towards each other), He says:

{Righteousness is not that you turn your faces toward the east or the west [in prayers]. [True] righteousness is [in] one who believes in Allah, the Last Day, the angels, the Book, and the prophets; and [who] gives wealth, in spite of love for it, to relatives, orphans, the needy, the traveler, those who ask [for help], and for freeing slaves; [and who] establishes prayer and gives zakâh. [Those who] fulfil their promises when they promise, and are patient in poverty and hardship and during battle, those are the ones who have been true, and it is those who are the righteous.} (Qur'an 2: 177)

It was narrated that an-Nawwâs ibn Sam'ân al-Anṣâri said that he asked about righteousness and sin, and the Messenger of Allah (bpuh) explained:

«Righteousness is good character, and sin is that which wavers in your heart and you do not want people to find out about it.» (Muslim)

Chapter One: Honesty

It was narrated from 'Abdullâh ibn Mas'ood that Allah's Messenger (bpuh) said:

«I enjoin you to be truthful, for truthfulness leads to righteousness, and righteousness leads to paradise. A person will continue to tell the truth and endeavor to be truthful until Allah records him as truthful. Beware of lying, for lying leads to wickedness (immorality and evil-doing), and wickedness leads to the fire. A person will continue to tell lies, and endeavor to tell lies, until he is recorded by Allah as a liar.» (Bukhari and Muslim)

Commentary on the hadith

In the above hadith, Allah's Messenger (bpuh) explained to us the characteristics of honesty and the positive consequences and rewards that follow from it, as well as the negative ones that occur in its absence. Honesty and truthfulness are noble characteristics that are increasingly becoming rare in our modern society. Honesty leads to righteousness, and righteousness leads to paradise, whereas lying leads to wickedness and criminality, and wickedness and criminality lead to the fire of hell.

Thus, Islam orders us to be honest and sincere with ourselves and with others. This order comes repeatedly in the noble Qur'an and the sayings of Prophet Muhammad (bpuh). Islam enjoins the Muslims to tell the truth at all times even if it is against our own interest or that of our parents or close relatives. Islam orders that people should not cheat or deceive others; we are ordered to be honest in words and deeds, private and public alike.

{O you who believe! Stand out firmly for justice, as witnesses to Allah, even though it be against yourselves, or your parents, or your kin, be they rich or poor, for Allah is a better protector to both [than you are]. So follow not the lusts [of your hearts], lest you may avoid justice; and if you distort your witness or refuse to give it, verily, Allah is ever Well-Acquainted with what you do.}

(Qur'an 4: 135)

Honesty in words implies telling the truth in all cases and under all conditions. It means fulfilling a promise, whether written or given orally. It also means giving the right advice to one who asks for it. Sincerity in one's work implies carrying out duties as fully as possible, with or without supervision.

Honesty and sincerity mean giving each person his or her due rights without their having to ask for them, doing the right thing in the right way at the right time, objectivity in judgment, objectivity in evaluation, and objectivity in making decisions of all kinds. Honesty also implies the appropriate selection and promotion of personnel according to merit without regard to temperament, favoritism, or personal relationships.

Thus, honesty is a blanket term that covers a wide range of moral and social traits that are requirements for a peaceful and harmonious society. It encompasses telling the truth, sincerity at work, carrying out duties, fulfilling one's word, judging objectively, and making objective decisions. Honesty is indeed the opposite of lying, bluffing, hypocrisy, favoritism, and deceit.[10]

Islam has classified honesty into two types: External honesty is that which is judged by other people, and internal honesty is that which is judged by the person himself or herself.

External Honesty

The rewards for external honesty are twofold, coming from Allah (the Exalted) and coming from the people that one socializes with, and this increases the psychological satisfaction felt by the honest person. When people are honest, Allah (the Exalted) and those people they deal with will like them. Abu Hurayrah (may Allah be pleased with him) narrated that the Prophet (bpuh) said:

«When Allah loves a servant, He calls out: O Gabriel (the angel)! Indeed I love So-and-so, so love him. So Gabriel (peace be upon him) loves him, and then Gabriel also calls out to the inhabitants of the heavens: Allah loves So-and-so; therefore, you should love him also. So all the inhabitants of the heavens will love him, and then he is granted the acceptance (and pleasure) of the people of the earth (as well).» (Bukhari)

Honesty gives a person the social approval that he or she needs, and this is part of the moral and social value of honesty. Moreover, when everyone in the society is honest, social diseases like lying, cheating, stealing, forgery, corruption, and many more, can simply disappear. In other words, honesty is something that you give and take. Others enjoy your honesty, and you enjoy their honesty, and thus the society feels relatively secure.

On the other hand, in the absence of honesty – and it has become increasingly difficult to find honesty in our contemporary society – many social diseases appear, as was foretold by Allah's Messenger (bpuh).

«It was narrated that Ḥudhayfah (may Allah be pleased with him) said: Allah's Messenger (bpuh) related to us two prophetic narrations. One I have seen (realized in this life), and I am still waiting for the other.

He told us: Honesty was preserved in the roots of people's hearts

(one of the narrators, Tanâfisi, said: this means in the core of the human heart)

– and then the Qur'an was revealed, and we learned (honesty) from the Qur'an and from the Sunnah.

Then he told us about its disappearance, saying: A man will go to sleep and honesty will be taken away from his heart, and only its trace will remain, like spots without color. Then he will go to sleep again, and the remainder of honesty will also be taken away (from his heart) leaving a trace like a blister,[11] as when an ember touches your foot and raises a blister that has nothing inside. People will engage in business with one another, but there will hardly be any honest persons among them. Then it will be said that in such-and-such a tribe there is an honest man, and a man will be admired for his intelligence, good manners, and strength, but there will not be even a mustard seed's weight of faith in his heart.

Then Ḥudhayfah said: There was a time when I did not mind dealing with any of you, for if he was a Muslim, his religion would prevent him from cheating, and if he was a Christian, his Muslim ruler would prevent him from cheating, but today I cannot deal except with So-and-so and So-and-so.» (A sound hadith recorded by Ibn Mâjah)

A dishonest person is ready to tell lies, bribe, be bribed, distort the truth, cheat and forge, deceive others, break promises, and corrupt and be corrupted. Thus, a dishonest person is a totality of diseases because any time he or she misbehaves, harm is caused not only to one person or to a group of people but to the whole nation.[12]

Internal Honesty

Internal honesty is that which is judged by the person himself or herself. It cannot be seen by other people, but it can be seen by Allah (the Exalted) and the angels. Internal honesty is a factor in the psychological health of an honest person as well as the health of others who deal with the honest person, and Islam emphasizes internal honesty.

Islam teaches that even though many of our acts are done privately, out of the sight of other people, Allah (the Exalted) is always aware and His angels are constantly watching us. Therefore, a believer in Allah (the Exalted) knows that although no other person is watching him, Allah (the Exalted) the All-Seeing, the All-Hearing, and the All-Knowing is watching him. This continuous and constant oversight by Allah (the Exalted) helps to develop the concept of internal honesty or conscience in a believer; thus internal honesty becomes a person's overall strategy for social security. This is what Prophet Muhammad (bpuh) meant when he advised us through his Companion Abu Dharr (may Allah be pleased with him):

«Fear Allah wherever you are, and follow up a bad deed with a good one, and it will wipe it out, and use good behavior when dealing with the people.» (A reliable hadith recorded by at-Tirmidhi)

This kind of God-consciousness in secrecy merits great rewards, as Allah (the Exalted) says in the glorious Qur'an:

{Indeed, those who fear their Lord unseen will have forgiveness and a great reward. Whether you conceal your speech or publicize it, indeed He knows the secrets of [all] hearts. Should He not know, since He [is the One that] created [all things], and He is the One Who understands the finest mysteries and is Well-Acquainted [with them]?}

(Qur'an 67: 12-14)

When the angel Gabriel came to Prophet Muhammad (bpuh) and asked him a number of questions, he asked about *iḥsân* (good action, sincerity, and excellence of faith). The Prophet (bpuh) answered:

«It is to worship Allah as if you are seeing Him, and while you see Him not, He truly sees you (and all that you do).» (Part of a long hadith recorded by Bukhari and Muslim)

This moral behavior of honesty as taught by Islam makes individuals confident in themselves, in their own behavior, and in their words and deeds. Honesty makes people feel that they trust others and that they can equally be trusted by others. Thus, this mutual confidence builds self-satisfaction, and people generally feel happy and socially secure.

Islam's Way of Building Honesty

Moral values in Islam are not merely theoretical ideals. Islam has various ways by which it builds, and inculcates in humanity, ethical qualities in general and honesty in particular. These practical ways include the following:

1.
The true believers in Allah (the Exalted) are repeatedly ordered to be honest in all cases, in deeds and words, to themselves and others, and to always accompany truthful and honest persons and avoid the company of liars.

{O you who believe! Fear Allah and be with those who are true [in words and deeds].}

(Qur'an 9: 119)

2.
In order to motivate the believers to imbue themselves with honesty, Allah (the Exalted) promises the honest person generous rewards in this life and the hereafter, according to the hadith under discussion.

{O you who believe! Keep your duty to Allah and fear Him, and speak [always] the truth. He will direct you to do righteous good deeds and will forgive you your sins...}

(Qur'an 33: 70-71)

{Allah will say: This is the Day when the truthful will benefit from their truthfulness. For them are gardens [in paradise] beneath which rivers flow, where they will abide forever, Allah being pleased with them, and they with Him. That is the great attainment.}

(Qur'an 5: 119)

3.
To dissuade the believers from practicing dishonesty, Allah (the Exalted) also threatens the dishonest person with severe punishment, in line with the hadith under discussion.

{Allah presents an example of those who disbelieved: the wife of Noah and the wife of Lot. They were under two of Our righteous servants but betrayed them, so [those prophets] did not avail them from Allah at all, and it was said to them: Enter the fire with those who enter.}

(Qur'an 66: 10)

{That [Allah] may question the custodians of truth concerning the truth [they were charged with]; and He has prepared for the unbelievers a grievous penalty.}

(Qur'an 33: 8)

{That Allah may reward the people of truth for their truth, and punish the hypocrites, if that be His will, or accept their repentance; for Allah is Oft-Forgiving, Most Merciful.}

(Qur'an 33: 24)

{The person who brings the truth and the person who confirms [and supports] it, such are the people who fear God. [They are the righteous.] They shall have all that they wish for, in the presence of their Lord; such is the reward of those who do good.}

(Qur'an 39: 33-34)

4. Islam also develops the habit of honesty in Muslims in a practical way, through fasting and prayers.

One who is fasting abstains from any kind of food or drink from dawn until sunset. He or she also abstains from sexual intercourse with his wife or her husband for the same number of hours during daylight. The only observer of a fasting person is Allah (the Exalted) and the person himself. Consequently here comes an actual and real practice of internal honesty exercised during the glorious month of Ramadan, which is the Muslim month of fasting. Therefore, Islam provides a practical training for one to be honest in his life. In fact one of the components of fasting is refusing to submit to temptation and impulses. Thus, in the month of fasting, a Muslim feels thirsty but he does not drink, he feels hungry but does not eat. In Ramadan, the fasting month in Islam, water is spatially close but psychologically far from the Muslim. Water and food is near to the fasting person but far from his desires. Therefore, this is a practical exercise of self-control and internal honesty. Thus Islam builds the social good habit in the Muslim through direct instruction from Allah (the Exalted) and His Messenger, through rational arguments, through the reward and punishment principles, and through real practical practice and experience.[13]

May Allah (the Exalted) help us to be among those who practice honesty in our daily lives and thus to create a morally and socially secure environment and also to gain all the rewards promised by Allah (the Exalted). Âmeen.

Chapter Two: Modesty

Abu Hurayrah (may Allah be pleased with him) narrated that Allah's Messenger (bpuh) said:

«Ḥayâ' (modesty) springs from faith, and faith is in paradise. Obscenity comes from rudeness, and rudeness is in the fire.» (Recorded by at-Tirmidhi and Ibn Mâjah)[14]

«Abu Sawwâr narrated that he heard 'Imrân ibn Ḥuṣayn (may Allah be pleased with him) report that the Prophet (bpuh) said:

Ḥayâ' does not bring anything but goodness.

Bushayr ibn Ka'b said: It is written in the wisdom that it includes dignity and tranquility.

'Imrân said: I narrate to you from Allah's Messenger (bpuh) and you narrate to me from your books (of wisdom)?» (Bukhari and Muslim)

Commentary on the hadiths

Ḥayâ', which is roughly translated as modesty, bashfulness, shame, moral conscience or self-respect, is yet another important moral value taught by Allah's Messenger (bpuh), as seen in these two hadiths. Ḥayâ' is a state of feeling shame and uneasiness in one's heart and mind about doing things that are unpleasant not only to Allah[15] but to fellow human beings, as well as other creatures of Allah (the Exalted). The first one with whom we ought to feel true ḥayâ' is Allah (the Exalted), as the Prophet (bpuh) commanded us.

«'Abdullâh ibn Mas'ood narrated that Allah's Messenger (bpuh) said: Have ḥayâ' for Allah in the correct manner.

We said: O Prophet of Allah, we are bashful towards Allah, and all praise is due to Allah.

He said: That is not what is meant. Rather have the ḥayâ' for Allah that is the true ḥayâ' due to Him. It is for a person to be mindful of the head and what it contains,[16] and to be mindful of the stomach and what it includes,[17] and to remember death and the trial (in the grave), and whoever desires the hereafter abandons the pomp and glitter of this world. The one who does that has ḥayâ' towards Allah in the proper manner.» (Recorded by at-Tirmidhi)[18]

In order to have complete modesty with Allah, we should have more ḥayâ' towards Allah than we have towards any of His creatures. We must not perform any act that is displeasing to Allah when we are alone; instead, we should be too ashamed to act in that manner, realizing that nothing can be hidden from Allah (the Exalted), Who knows and is aware of all our doings.

{They may hide [their crimes] from men, but they cannot hide [them] from Allah, for He is with them [with His knowledge] when they plot by night, in words that He cannot approve; and Allah ever encompasses all that they do.} (Qur'an 4: 108)

According to the modern commentator Zarabozo, the word ḥayâ' is derived from the word ḥayâh, which means life. Just as rain is called ḥayâ because it gives life to the earth and vegetation, so it is said that a person without ḥayâ' (shame and modesty) is like a dead person. The person's heart is considered dead, just like a heart without faith is considered dead. If the people have modesty and shame in their hearts, then their hearts will be sound and healthy because there is faith in them. Zarabozo further notes that 'Umar ibn al-Khaṭṭâb is reported to have said:

If a person has little ḥayâ', he will have little *wara'* (fear of Allah and a feeling of His presence). And the one who has little wara', his heart has died.[19]

Essentially, ḥayâ' is the feeling in the heart that keeps a person away from performing evil deeds. It is directly linked to what is known in the Western world today as one's moral conscience. Therefore, when people have no moral conscience, they will do whatever they please and not care what others may think or say about them. That is because they have reached a state of having dead hearts that have no feeling of shame or prudence. The opposite of this is when people's moral conscience bothers them even if they are alone when doing an act of which they should be ashamed. Their hearts will feel uneasiness, and they will be unhappy because of the nagging shame of what they have done. Accordingly, ḥayâ' is a natural feeling that every human experiences. One aspect of ḥayâ' that is naturally found in almost all cultures of humankind is the feeling of shame when a person has not covered his or her nudity, just as it happened to the first parents, Adam and Eve (in Arabic, Adam and Ḥawwâ') when their enemy, Satan, seduced them.

{Then Satan whispered suggestions to them both in order to uncover that which was hidden from them of their private parts. He said: Your Lord did not forbid you this tree save that you should become like angels or become of the immortals. And He [Satan] swore by Allah to them both [saying]: Verily, I am one of the sincere well-wishers for you both. So he misled them by deception. Then when they tasted of the [forbidden] tree, that which was hidden from them of their shame [of their private parts] became apparent to them, and they began to cover themselves with the leaves of paradise [in order to cover their shame]. Then their Lord called out to them: Did I not forbid you from that tree and tell you: Verily, Satan is an open enemy to you?}

(Qur'an 7: 20-22)

Despite the natural instincts of ḥayâ' endowed in human beings, this moral value can also be nurtured and allowed to grow; if neglected, it may be stunted to the extent that a person loses it completely. This kind of modesty, which increases or decreases, is what the Prophet (bpuh) described as being a consequence of faith. Indeed if we do not believe that Allah (the Exalted) is watching all that we are saying or doing – whether in private or public, whether in the dark of the night or in the light of day – then we are bound to be shameless creatures, probably worse than animals. We would end up doing things that even the lowest of animals would not deign to do, thus stooping to lower than an animal state.

Allah (the Exalted) told us about this situation where human beings reject faith and follow and succumb shamelessly to their wanton desires, causing them to go down to a state worse than that of cattle.

{We have indeed created the human in the best of image. Then do We abase him [to be] the lowest of the low. Except for those who believe and do righteous deeds, for they shall have a reward unfailing [in paradise].}

(Qur'an 95: 4-6)

Al-Muqaddim, as quoted by Zarabozo, says that ḥayâ' is the characteristic that differentiates human beings from animals. In general, animals follow their desires without any concern for whether what they are doing is right or wrong. They do not feel the kind of shame that is expected from human beings. Hence the less ḥayâ' one has, the closer one comes to the level of the animals rather than the level of a moral human being.[20]

Ḥayâ' is a very important moral value because it is a factor in our lives that keeps us from doing whatever our hearts may desire. It plays the role of quality control on our behavior and prevents us from engaging in acts that are regarded as distasteful or lewd.

When we fail to use our God-given faculties of hearing, sight, intelligence, heart, mind, and even the sense of feeling shame in doing certain things that are considered absurdities across nearly all human cultures, then we end up becoming worse than animals because we fail even to make use of our natural abilities and instincts.[21] Allah (the Exalted) again says about this sad situation that many people take it lightly, yet it will be the cause of punishment in the fire of hell:

{Many are the *jinn*[22] and humans We have made for hell. They have hearts with which they do not understand, eyes with which they do not see, and ears with which they do not hear. They are like cattle; no, more misguided, for they are heedless [of warning].}

(Qur'an 7: 179)

Allah's Messenger (bpuh) is reported to have said that among the words that people learned from the earlier prophets is the statement:

«If you feel no shame, then do as you wish.» (A sound hadith recorded by Abu Dâwood and Ibn Mâjah)

This means that if people have no ḥayâ', then they may end up doing things that are totally outside the norms of an upright and productive society. These are things that can be labelled, according to the hadith under discussion, as obscenities and considered rude or harsh. Through these acts, they earn the people's displeasure and Allah's wrath and punishment.

On the other hand, when we behave decently towards each other, with all consideration of the good natural norms in society, and neither hurt people with our tongues, hands, or bad behavior – whether it be in terms of the way we dress in public or offensive manners such as impudence, unkindness, hardheartedness, unfair dealings, and so one – then ḥayâ' brings nothing but goodness to society. This in turn leads to the pleasure of Allah and the great rewards of paradise.

When we endure unpleasant matters, which are not directly contrary to the Sharia (Islamic law) and we do not disclose our hard feelings, then that is considered modesty. However, if the matters in question are contrary to Islamic law, then silence is not considered bashfulness but rather cowardice that is blameworthy. In this respect, Zarabozo says that people do many acts that do not constitute modesty, shyness, or bashfulness. The Islamic concept of ḥayâ' differs slightly from the natural understanding of ḥayâ' in the sense that the Islamic understanding of ḥayâ' leads one to avoid evil deeds, to fulfil obligations, and to give others their due rights. The basic difference between the natural sense of ḥayâ' and the Islamic definition of ḥayâ' is that being silent or afraid of speaking out in the face of evil actions, falsehood, and oppression is not considered part of Islamic ḥayâ'.

According to Ibn aṣ-Ṣalâḥ, such behavior is not ḥayâ' but is a sign of sheer weakness, fear, cowardice, and treachery.[23] Part of the correct modest behavior sanctioned by the Sharia is that we should express our displeasure with matters directly against the norms of Islam, and this should be done in a suitable manner.

Thus, as we said at the beginning, ḥayâ' is a natural disposition that is found in the mind and heart while performing certain deeds or avoiding improper actions that may cause harm to society. Islam fosters and further develops this natural characteristic, since ḥayâ' is a kind of blessing that only brings about good in society. That is why Prophet Muhammad (bpuh) described ḥayâ' as an important and distinct characteristic of Islam. It was narrated from Ibn 'Abbâs (may Allah be pleased with both of them) that Allah's Messenger (bpuh) said:

«Every religion has its distinct characteristic, and the distinct characteristic of Islam is modesty.» (Recorded by Ibn Mâjah)[24]

Since ḥayâ' is the beauty and distinct mark of Islam, we should not allow our shyness to keep us from doing what is correct and loved by Allah just because some people, who have been affected by a secular lifestyle, ridicule our good behavior and our practice of Islam. We should never be embarrassed by our practice of good Islamic traits like dressing modestly, growing a beard for the men, and dressing in the complete hijab (women's dress that covers the whole body except the hands and face) or *niqâb* (face veil) for the women. One should not allow shyness of unwarranted criticism to change one's behavior and actions, as long as they are correct and proper according to the Qur'an and Sunnah.

We should also not allow our shyness to prevent us from asking questions in order to seek knowledge just because we think or feel we are too old to learn from those who are younger than us or because we feel embarrassed that other people might know that we are ignorant about certain matters. It is in line with this that 'Ali ibn Abi Ṭâlib is reported to have said:

The one who does not have knowledge should not be too shy to ask until he gets knowledge. And the one who is asked something he does not know should not be so shy that it keeps him from saying, 'I do not know'.[25]

'Â'ishah (may Allah be pleased with her), the beloved wife of Prophet Muhammad (bpuh), once praised the distinct mark and virtue of the women of the *Anṣâr* (the Muslim citizens of Madinah who gave refuge to the Prophet [bpuh] and the other Muslim emigrants from Makkah) – that their shyness did not prevent them from gaining an understanding of the religion. (Bukhari)

Chapter Three: Humility

It was narrated by 'Iyâḍ ibn Ḥimâr that Allah's Messenger (bpuh) said:

«Allah has revealed to me that you must be humble towards one another, so that no one wrongs anyone else or boasts to anyone else.» (A sound hadith recorded by Abu Dâwood and Ibn Mâjah)

It was narrated by Abu Hurayrah that Allah's Messenger (bpuh) said:

«Charity does not decrease wealth. No one forgives except that Allah increases him in honor, and no one humbles himself for the sake of Allah except that Allah raises him in status.» (Muslim and at-Tirmidhi)

Commentary on the hadiths

Allah's Messenger (bpuh) says in the first hadith above that Allah, the Exalted, revealed to him that people should be humble and down-to-earth with each other, so that there is no boasting or looking down in contempt at others and there is no wronging each other. This is exactly what Allah said to Prophet Muhammad (bpuh):

{Do not pursue that of which you have no knowledge, for every act of hearing, or of seeing, or of [feeling in] the heart will be questioned [by Allah on the Day of Reckoning]. Do not walk on the earth arrogantly and exultantly, for you can neither rend asunder nor penetrate the earth, nor can you attain stature like the mountains in height. All the bad aspects of such things are evil and hateful in the sight of your Lord. These are among the [precepts of] wisdom [good manners and high character] that your Lord has revealed to you [O Muhammad (bpuh)]. Do not set up with Allah any other object of worship, lest you should be thrown into hell, blameworthy and rejected [from Allah's mercy].}

(Qur'an 17: 36-39)

{And be kind and humble to the believers who follow you [O Muhammad (bpuh)].}

(Qur'an 26: 215)

Prophet Muhammad (bpuh) explained these precepts of wisdom by not only enjoining us verbally to be humble but also by being the most humble and lenient person on earth in his daily life. He always ate with the poor, greeted and sat with children, ate his food while sitting on the floor, stitched his own torn clothes, milked his sheep, mended his shoes, and repaired his water bucket. Still, when it was time for prayer, he put aside all worldly activities to devote himself to the worship of Allah.

«Aswad ibn Yazeed (may Allah be pleased with him) narrated that he asked: 'Â'ishah, what would the Prophet (bpuh) do when he entered his house?

She said: He would busy himself with serving his family, then when (the time of) prayer was due, he would stand up for it.» (A sound hadith recorded by at-Tirmidhi)

Humility is a manifestation of our lowering ourselves to our true status in this world – that of mere creatures of Allah (the Exalted) endowed with uncountable blessings. Some of us have been given more than others as a test to see whether we will be grateful to Allah (the Exalted) and treat people of all statuses the same, neither looking down on and despising some nor raising others to levels that only belong to Allah (the Exalted):

{Allah has bestowed His gifts of sustenance more freely on some of you than on others...}

(Qur'an 16: 71)

{It is He Who has made you [His] agents, inheritors of the earth. He has raised you in ranks, some above others, that He may try you in the gifts He has given you. Your Lord is quick in punishment, yet He is indeed Oft-Forgiving, Most Merciful.}

(Qur'an 6: 165)

Allah (the Exalted) admonishes those who do not humble themselves and those who think that they are self-reliant, due to whatever wealth or positions of influence and authority they have been temporarily granted in this short life, and who think they can mistreat and abuse or enslave their fellow human beings as they wish.

{So let the human see from what he is created! He is created from water gushing forth, proceeding from between the backbone and the ribs. Verily, [Allah] is Able to bring him back [to life]! The Day when all the secrets [good and bad, prayers, fasting, ingratitude, arrogance, humility, and so on] will be exposed [as to their truth], then he shall have no power, nor any help.}

(Qur'an 86: 5-10)

{Destroyed is the human [who denies Allah's message]! How ungrateful he is! From what thing did He create him? From a sperm drop He created him, and destined for him [his proportions, provisions, and life span]. Then He eases the way for him.[26] Then He causes his death and provides a grave for him [to conceal his decaying body]. Then when He wills, He will resurrect him. No, but [man] has not yet done what He commanded him.}

(Qur'an 80: 17-23)

All these admonitions, and many more that we have not mentioned, are for people to realize their true status in this world in order to humble themselves for the sake of Allah (the Exalted) and to treat other people with decency as they themselves would like to be treated. (Muslim) When people humble themselves and do not let their egos get the better of them, no one will wrong or hurt the other, as mentioned in the hadith under discussion. People will look at each other as equals in the sight of Allah regardless of their wealth, position of authority, social class, race, tribe, or nationality. There will be no boasting, since there will be no reason or cause for boasting as people treat and see each other as equals in Allah's estimation.

However, when people have little knowledge about the greatness and power of Allah (the Exalted), the supremacy of His Might and Glory, His power to do things that one cannot even dream of doing, and His control over all things in the universe including one's life, and when people have no knowledge about the true, natural disposition of all affairs in this world according to the Sunnah of Allah (the Exalted), then they start suffering from superiority complexes and go around boasting and looking down in contempt on those who are lower than them according to their misguided standards of judgments. This is as Allah (the Exalted) says in the noble Qur'an:

{And among people is one who disputes about Allah without knowledge or guidance or an enlightening book [from Him], twisting his neck [in arrogance] to mislead [people] from the way of Allah. For him in the world is disgrace, and We will make him taste on the Day of Resurrection the punishment of the burning fire.}

(Qur'an 22: 8-9)

In the second hadith under discussion, the Prophet (bpuh) linked charity, the forgiving of faults, and humility for the sake of Allah as the keys to honor and to being raised in status by Allah (the Exalted). Sahl ibn Mu'âdh ibn Anas al-Juhani narrated from his father that Allah's Messenger (bpuh) said:

«Whoever avoids wearing elegant and expensive garments out of humility to Allah, while he is able to (afford them), Allah will call him before the heads of creation on the Day of Judgment so that he can choose whichever garments of faith (garments of paradise for believers) he wishes to wear.» (A reliable hadith recorded by at-Tirmidhi)[27]

When people are not enthralled with wealth and power, they live humble lives, spending their wealth and influence to help the needy for the sake of Allah. They forgive and pardon minor mistakes, so Allah raises them in status, and they gain the love and pleasure of Allah and the love and acceptance of their fellow human beings. That is why Allah (the Exalted) describes such humble people with the following sublime qualities and characteristics:

{And the servants of [Allah] the Most Merciful are those who walk on the earth in humility, and when the ignorant address them [harshly], they say [words] of peace. They are those who spend [part] of the night [in adoration] to their Lord prostrating and standing. And those who say: Our Lord! Avert from us the wrath of hell, for its wrath is indeed a grievous affliction. Evil indeed is it as an abode and as a place to dwell. And they are those who, when they spend, are not extravagant and not miserly, but hold a just [balance] between those [extremes].}

(Qur'an 25: 63-67)

From the understanding of the above description of humbleness, the conclusion made by Muslim scholars is that humility is measured according to the extent of one's glorification of Allah (the Exalted) and how one treats fellow human beings.

Chapter Four: Courage

Abu Hurayrah (may Allah be pleased with him) narrated that Allah's Messenger (bpuh) said:

«The strong believer is better and more beloved to Allah than the weak believer, although in both there is good. Strive to do that which will benefit you (in this world and the hereafter); seek the help of Allah and do not feel helpless (and do not give up). If anything befalls you (like a misfortune), do not say: If only I had done such-and-such, then such-and-such would have happened (instead). Rather say: Allah has decreed, and what He wills He does. For (your saying) 'if only' opens the door to the work of Satan.» (Muslim)

«It was narrated from Ṭâriq ibn Shihâb (may Allah be pleased with him) that a man asked the Prophet (bpuh), when he had put his leg in the stirrup (of his mount): Which kind of jihad is best?

The Prophet (bpuh) answered: A word of truth spoken before an unjust ruler.» (A reliable hadith recorded by at-Tirmidhi, an-Nasâ'i, and Ibn Mâjah)

Commentary on the hadiths

A Muslim is required to be firm and strong in both spirit and willpower. According to the first hadith above, a strong and courageous believer is better and more beloved to Allah (the Exalted) than a weak believer, even though there is good in both.

Life in our time is full of challenges and surprises, and we must be firm and courageous enough to stand by what we believe. We should not feel threatened by a seemingly impossible situation and then give in easily. We must strive hard for what is beneficial in our religion and we must do our best, seeking the help of Allah (the Exalted) in all our endeavors.

Calamities and failures are but a part of our continuous growth and development and a learning process for self-improvement. As Muslims, we are expected to have a firm belief that Allah (the Exalted) has preordained all things according to His perfect wisdom, knowledge, and power, knowing that nothing happens in the universe except according to His will.

{No calamity befalls, on earth or in yourselves, but it is inscribed in a book of decrees before We bring it into existence. Verily, that is easy for Allah, in order that you may not grieve at the things that you fail to get, nor rejoice over that which has been given to you. Allah does not like prideful boasters.}

(Qur'an 57: 22-23)

Of course, this does not mean that we just laze about and leave things to take their due course without our making any effort. The correct understanding of the above verse, which is also in accordance with the hadith under discussion, is that we strive and do our best given the prevailing circumstances. Then we put our full trust in Allah.

Regardless of what we go through in life, if we are patient and firm and never give up easily, then in every situation there will always be good, as long as we stand by the truth and speak out without fear or favor, as is confirmed by another statement of the Prophet (bpuh):

«'Abdur-Raḥmân ibn Abu Laylah narrated from Ṣuhayb that Allah's Messenger (bpuh) said: The ways of a believer are wonderful, for there is good in every affair of his – and this is not the case with anyone else except the believer. If he has an occasion to feel delight, he thanks (Allah), and that is good for him, and if he gets into trouble, he shows resignation (and endures it patiently), and he will be rewarded for that.» (Muslim)

That is why, in the second hadith of this chapter, Allah's Messenger (bpuh) says that the best jihad is a word of truth spoken to a tyrannical ruler. It takes courage and strong willpower to stand up for what we believe is right and to speak out against oppression and immorality with a firm conviction that nothing can harm us as long as we are sincere in our beliefs. This is what the Prophet (bpuh) advised 'Abdullâh ibn 'Abbâs (may Allah be pleased with both of them) when they were riding together on the same mount.

«Ibn 'Abbâs narrated: I was behind the Prophet (bpuh) one day when he said: Son, I will teach you a statement (to benefit you in this life and the hereafter). Be mindful of Allah,[28] and He will protect you. Be mindful of Allah, and you will find Him before you.[29] When you ask, ask Allah, and when you seek aid, seek the aid of Allah. Know that if the entire creation were to gather together to do something to benefit you, you would never get any benefit except what Allah had written for you, and if they were to gather to do something to harm you, you would never be harmed unless Allah had written it for you. The pens have been lifted, and the pages have dried.» (A reliable hadith recorded by at-Tirmidhi)

Courage as a good moral value dictates that we should not become people who agree with everything, being what is called 'yes-men', for in that case many things would go wrong in society. We would then find ourselves swept up by the current of events with regard to whatever is happening, having no firm stand of our own, and simply accepting whatever comes our way. Allah's Messenger (bpuh) expressly forbade this kind of cowardice.

«Hudhayfah (may Allah be pleased with him) narrated that Allah's Messenger (bpuh) said: Do not let yourselves be 'yes-men', saying: If the people are good, then we will be good, and if they are wrong, then we will be wrong. Rather, make up your own minds. If the people are good, then you are good; and if they are evil, then do not behave unjustly (like them).» (A reliable hadith recorded by at-Tirmidhi)

Therefore, we should be courageous enough to help people in their acts of righteousness and piety. If others take the path of sin and immorality, we should not follow them blindly just because they are the people in power and authority. Instead, we should stand up to explain to them the truth of their transgression and bring them back to the right path of morality and good behavior. Allah, the Exalted, says:

{...Help you each other in righteousness and taqwâ; but do not help one another in sin and transgression. And fear Allah. Verily, Allah is severe in punishment.}

(Qur'an 5: 2)

The Messenger of Allah (bpuh) reiterated this point. Abu Sa'eed al-Khudri (may Allah be pleased with him) reported that he heard Allah's Messenger (bpuh) say:

«If anyone of you sees an evil action (taking place), let him change it with his hand (by taking action). If he is not able to do so, then with his tongue (by speaking out), and if he is not able to do so, then with his heart (by hating it and feeling it is wrong) – and that (last option) is the weakest of faith.» (Muslim and Abu Dâwood)

Courage requires that we do not fear other human beings with respect to standing by the truth and speaking the truth. We are to fear none but Allah (the Exalted) alone, at all times:

{...So do not fear the people, but fear Me, and do not exchange My verses for a small price [or worldly gain]...}

(Qur'an 5: 44)

{That is only Satan who frightens [you] of his supporters. So fear them not, but fear Me, if you are [indeed] believers.} (Qur'an 3: 175)

On the same topic, Abu Saʿeed al-Khudri reported that the Messenger of Allah (bpuh) stood up to deliver a sermon, and one of the things he said was:

«No fear of people should prevent a person from speaking the truth if he knows it.» (An authentic hadith recorded by Ibn Mâjah)

There is a similar narration from ʿAbdullâh ibn Masʿood (may Allah be pleased with him), who reported that Allah's Messenger (bpuh) said:

«There is no prophet whom Allah sent to any nation before me who did not have disciples and companions who followed his path and obeyed his commands. Then after them came generations who said what they did not do and did what they were not commanded to do. Whoever strives against them with his hand is a believer; whoever strives against them with his tongue is a believer; whoever strives against them with his heart is a believer. If less than that, then there is not even a mustard seed's worth of faith (in the heart of the person).» (Muslim)

Courage is an important moral value that helps us to meet various challenges in life without fear, while following the guidance of Islam. Courage enables us to venture into unknown territory, whether in business or any other challenging aspect of life, so that we do not just remain aloof, backing out of every promising opportunity simply because we are afraid of possible negative outcomes.

In conclusion to our commentary on these hadiths, we can say that as long as we have done our homework and taken all necessary precautions, then we must just go ahead in life trusting and relying on Allah (the Exalted) for the outcome, whether good or bad. If we do not try and take chances and instead we are always cautious – too afraid of failing and being laughed at or losing out – then we will never learn. We will always be bogged down with our fear and cowardliness.

May Allah (the Exalted) grant us courage in all our endeavors, be they spiritual, moral, social, or political. Âmeen.

Chapter Five: Steadfastness

«Sufyân ibn 'Abdullâh ath-Thaqafi (may Allah be pleased with him) related: I said: O Allah's Messenger, tell me something that I can adhere to.

He said: Say: My Lord is Allah. Then be firm and steadfast (stand straight).

I said: O Allah's Messenger, what is the thing that you fear most for me?

Allah's Messenger (bpuh) took hold of his own tongue, then said: This.» (A sound hadith recorded by Ibn Mâjah)[30]

Commentary on the hadith

Istiqâmah, or firmness and steadfastness, is one of the most challenging moral values and character traits in contemporary times. In this hadith, the Prophet's Companion Sufyân ibn 'Abdullâh ath-Thaqafi (may Allah be pleased with him) requested that Allah's Messenger (bpuh) tell him something that he could hold onto and adhere to, obviously to seek success in this world and salvation in the hereafter. The answer was in a few, but very comprehensive, words: «Say: My Lord is Allah. Then be firm and steadfast.»

This means that the first and most important statement of true conviction (and belief in the heart) that one can utter and hold onto steadfastly is that our Lord is Allah.[31] The meaning of accepting Allah as our Lord is that He is our only Creator and Cherisher, the Controller of all that happens in the cosmos, the only One Who is perfect in His names and attributes, independent of all needs, the one and only Lord Who deserves our worship, the only One Who sustains us and Whom we seek for all our needs, the only One Whose laws are to be implemented in the universe, and the only One Who deserves our unreserved love, fear, obedience, total trust, and devotion.

In other words, the first fundamental principle in having istiqâmah is to have the sound and correct belief in Allah as our only Lord, which implies *tawḥeed* (the oneness of Allah) par excellence. The Prophet (bpuh) then told Sufyân to be firm and steadfast in the correct belief in Allah as our only Lord. The meaning of that, as stated by the Muslim scholars, is for one not to swerve from the proper belief in Allah in any form whatsoever.

Thus, to have istiqâmah we must adhere to that correct belief and understanding – that our only Lord is Allah – by fulfilling all that it entails. This includes obeying all of Allah's commands and staying away from all His prohibitions. It also includes believing in and following the Sunnah of Allah's Messenger, establishing the prayers, fasting in Ramadan, performing the pilgrimage, and embracing the other acts of worship that are enjoined on us.

In the Arabic language, the word istiqâmah is understood to mean: something that is in the right state, a person going right and pursuing a right course, acting rightly or justly, or a person continuing in the way of truth without deviating from it.[32] The word istiqâmah is also derived from the root *qiyâm,* which implies guarding over something constantly or checking a situation and following up to make sure that it is right and good. Allah (the Exalted) used the related term in the same way when He commanded men to be in charge of women, to stand up firmly to take care of them, to guard them, and to ensure that they believe in Islam, practice it correctly, and understand their roles within it.

{Men are the protectors and maintainers of women because Allah has given the one more [strength] than the other and because they support them from their means. Therefore, the righteous women are devoutly obedient and guard in [their husbands'] absence what Allah would have them guard. As to those women on whose part you fear disloyalty and ill-conduct, admonish them [first], [next] refuse to share their beds, [and last] hit them [lightly]; but if they return to obedience, seek not against them any means [of annoyance], for Allah is Most High, Great [above you all].}

(Qur'an 4: 34)

Allah's Messenger (bpuh) alluded to the challenge it is for men to take a leadership position and to guide their women, who have a more delicate nature, in order to enjoy living with them and benefiting from them. The Messenger (bpuh) mentioned that just as each man has his weaknesses, each woman also has her own weaknesses and flaws, and a certain amount of those must be dealt with patiently or overlooked in order to make successful marriages and family relationships, since no one will ever reach perfection.

«Abu Hurayrah (may Allah be pleased with him) narrated that Allah's Messenger (bpuh) said: Indeed, the woman was created from a rib (since Eve was created from the rib of Adam), and (the rib) will never become (completely) straight (*istaqeema*) for you by any means. If you wish to benefit from her then you may benefit from her, along with her crookedness, but if you try to straighten her (completely), you will break her, and breaking her is divorcing her.» (Muslim)

«It was narrated from Abu Hurayrah (may Allah be pleased with him) that the Prophet (bpuh) said: Whoever believes in Allah and the Last Day, if he witnesses something, let him speak good or else keep silent. Deal kindly with women, for the woman was created from a rib, and the most crooked part of a rib is its upper part. If you try to straighten it you will break it, and if you leave it alone it will remain crooked (or imperfect). So deal kindly with women.» (Muslim)

From the root meaning of the word 'istiqâmah,' we come to an understanding that it is not just a mere practice of following the straight path. It also implies adhering firmly and constantly attaching oneself to that straight path, trying one's best to cling to it, and staying within its limits at all times.[33] Thus, this moral value of istiqâmah is not an easy thing to achieve. It is quite challenging, just as it is challenging to straighten and guide women who are created from a bent rib. In fact, istiqâmah was also difficult for Prophet Muhammad (bpuh), as was reported by the Companion Ibn 'Abbâs (may Allah be pleased with both of them) after these verses in Soorat Hood were revealed:

{Therefore, stand firm and steadfast as you have been ordered, you and those who turn in repentance with you; and do not transgress [from that straight path], for indeed He sees well all that you are doing. Do not incline towards those who do wrong, lest the fire should touch you, and you would have no protectors other than Allah, and then you would have no one to help you.}

(Qur'an 11: 112-113)

This verse of the Qur'an was the hardest and most difficult verse on the Messenger of Allah (bpuh). He began to develop a few gray hairs after its revelation; when asked about that, he responded:

«I have been made gray by (Soorat) Hood and her sisters (related chapters in the Qur'an).»[34]

Imam al-Ghazâli also stated that being steadfast along the path in this world is as difficult as being steadfast on the path that is over hellfire. Both paths are finer than a strand of hair and sharper than a sword.[35]

Perhaps the most challenging and difficult aspect of istiqâmah in this world is having control over our tongues and over the desires of our hearts. That is why when Sufyân ibn 'Abdullâh ath-Thaqafi asked the Prophet (bpuh), in the hadith under discussion, about what he feared most for him, the Prophet (bpuh) directly demonstrated by holding his own tongue and saying: «This.»

Similarly, it was reported by the Companion Anas ibn Mâlik (may Allah be pleased with him) that the Prophet (bpuh) said:

«The faith of a servant (of Allah) will not be firm and steadfast (straight and sound) until his heart is firm and steadfast, and his heart will not be firm and steadfast until his tongue is made firm and steadfast. A man will not enter paradise if his neighbors were not safe from his troublesome disturbances.» (A reliable hadith recorded by Aḥmad)

Because of the difficult and challenging nature of istiqâmah, the rewards promised by Allah (the Exalted) in the glorious Qur'an are enormous:

{Verily, those who say: Our Lord is Allah [alone] – and then they stand firm and steadfast – on them the angels will descend [at the time of their deaths, saying]: Fear not nor grieve, but receive the glad tidings of paradise that you have been promised! We have been your friends in the life of this world and are [so] in the hereafter. In [the hereafter] you will have [all] that your inner-selves desire, and you will have [all that] for which you ask, an entertainment from [Allah], the Oft-Forgiving, Most Merciful.}

(Qur'an 41: 30-32)

{Verily, those who say: Our Lord is Allah [alone] – and then they stand firm and steadfast – on them shall be no fear, nor shall they grieve. Such shall be the dwellers of paradise, abiding in it [forever as] a reward for what they used to do.}

(Qur'an 46: 13-14)

{If only they would have remained firm and steadfast on the [right] path, We would certainly have bestowed on them water [rain, and other blessings] in abundance.}

(Qur'an 72: 16)

Prophet Muhammad (bpuh) also gave a guarantee of paradise to those who can control their tongues and private parts from evil action; this implies being firm and steadfast in avoiding the temptation to follow our evil desires. Sahl ibn Sa'd (may Allah be pleased with him) narrated that Allah's Messenger (bpuh) said:

«If anyone can guarantee (the chastity of) what is between his two jawbones (meaning his tongue) and what is between his two legs (namely, his private parts), I guarantee paradise for him.» (Bukhari)

The way to attain istiqâmah – and by Allah's mercy we are not required to have perfect istiqâmah – is to live according to the teachings of the glorious Qur'an to the best of our ability, as Allah (the Exalted) says:

{Verily, this [Qur'an] is no less than a reminder to all the worlds for those who will to be firm and steadfast on the right course; and you cannot will unless [it be that] Allah, the Lord of the worlds, wills it to be.}

(Qur'an 81: 27-29)

Allah and His Messenger Muhammad (bpuh) clarified to us that due to the mercy of Allah, perfect istiqâmah is not what is required of humankind. Perfect steadfastness would mean perfect obedience to the commandments of Allah at all times, and this is beyond practical human capabilities. Rather, what is expected of us are the intention and willpower to do our best in fulfilling Allah's commandments and in abstaining from all that He has forbidden us, and to strive in that effort. Whenever we fall short of that, then we should immediately repent to Allah (the Exalted), seeking His pardon and forgiveness.

{So keep your duty to Allah and fear Him as much as you can; and listen and obey, and spend in charity; that is better for your-selves...}

(Qur'an 64: 16)

{Say [O Muhammad]: I am but a human being like you. It is revealed to me, by inspiration, that your God is One God. So stand firm and true to Him, and ask for His forgiveness; and woe to those who join gods with Allah.}

(Qur'an 41: 6)

«Shu'ayb ibn Ruzayq said: I sat by a Companion of the Messenger of Allah (bpuh) named al-Ḥakam ibn Hazn al-Kulafi (may Allah be pleased with him), and he began to narrate to us.

He said: I went as part of a delegation to Allah's Messenger (bpuh), and I was the seventh of seven people (or the ninth of nine). We visited him and said: O Messenger of Allah! We have come to visit you, so pray to Allah to bless us with good.

So he ordered that some dates be given to us – and the situation at that time was not good (because the Muslims were poor). We stayed a few days with him, and attended the Friday prayer with Allah's Messenger (bpuh). He stood up, supporting himself on a stick, or bow, and praised Allah and glorified Him with words that were concise, pure, and blessed.

Then he said: O people, you will not be able to handle, or you will not do, all that you have been commanded to, but aim to achieve righteousness (uprightness or come close to it) and receive glad tidings (that Allah will reward you for it).» (A reliable hadith recorded by Abu Dâwood)

The great scholar Ibn Rajab, in his *Jâmi' al-'Uloom wal-Ḥukam,* says that the above verse is a sign that everyone will somehow fall short in istiqâmah. That is why, immediately after Allah (the Exalted) gives the command to be steadfast, He orders us to seek His forgiveness. Thus, Allah's forgiveness is to be sought with respect to all our shortcomings, especially in istiqâmah.

May Allah (the Exalted) help us all in our constant struggle to obey Him to the best of our abilities, and may He accept us with all our faults and shower us with His abundant mercy and forgiveness. Âmeen.

Chapter Six: Kindness

\«It was narrated that 'Â'ishah (may Allah be pleased with her) said: A group of Jews asked permission to come in to see the Messenger of Allah (bpuh), and they said: *As-sâmu 'alaykum* (Death be upon you).

'Â'ishah replied: Rather may death be upon you, and curses!

The Messenger of Allah (bpuh) said: O 'Â'ishah, Allah has enjoined kindness in all things.

She responded: Did you not hear what they said?

He replied: (I did and) I answered: *Wa 'alaykum* (and also upon you).» (Bukhari and Muslim)

It was narrated from 'Â'ishah, the wife of the Prophet (bpuh), that Allah's Messenger (bpuh) said:

«O 'Â'ishah, Allah is kind and He loves kindness. He confers upon kindness what He does not confer upon harshness and what He does not confer upon anything else besides (kindness).» (Muslim)

Commentary on the hadiths

Another important moral value common to all cultures and religions, and inseparable from Islam, is kindness. In the first hadith, some Jews sought an audience with the Prophet (bpuh), and due to their jealousy and hatred of the last and final Prophet and Messenger, Muhammad (bpuh), they twisted the beautiful greeting of peace[36] into a wish for the Prophet's death. Allah's Messenger (bpuh), being the pinnacle of morality and character, simply replied in a very kind but straightforward manner:

«And also upon you.» (Bukhari)

His beloved wife 'Â'ishah (may Allah be pleased with her) naturally was not amused by the Jews' behavior towards the Messenger of Allah (bpuh). She was harsh and coarse in her response to them, wishing them not only death but also many curses. The Prophet (bpuh) immediately interrupted and corrected that rough and harsh behavior, even though the Jews were the ones in the wrong. He told his beloved wife 'Â'ishah that Allah (the Exalted) has prescribed kindness in every matter.

Due to this magnanimous behavior of Allah's Messenger towards the Jews, Allah (the Exalted) defended the personality of the Prophet (bpuh) and revealed a number of verses exposing the Jews and their uncouth behavior towards the Prophet (bpuh):

{Have you not seen those who were forbidden to hold secret counsels, yet they revert to that which they were forbidden [to do]? They hold secret counsels among themselves and conspire for iniquity and hostility and disobedience to the Messenger. When they come to you, they greet you, not as Allah greets you, and they say to themselves: Why does Allah not punish us for what we say? Enough for them is hell. In it will they burn, and evil is that destination!}

(Qur'an 58: 8)[37]

Such wicked and unwarranted behavior as belittling Allah's Messenger (bpuh) deserved a severe punishment in hellfire, as Allah (the Exalted) revealed in the verses of the Qur'an quoted above.

Further, in the second hadith, Allah's Messenger (bpuh) made it clear to his wife 'Â'ishah, and to all believers and all humankind in general, that Allah (the Exalted) is Most Kind. He loves kindness, and He rewards kindness with rewards that He does not give for harshness or anything else. 'Iyâḍ ibn Ḥimâr narrated that one day, in a sermon, Allah's Messenger (bpuh) said:

«The people of paradise are of three types: a person of authority who is fair and just, who gives charity and does good; a person who is compassionate and kind to every relative and Muslim; and a person who refrains from asking for help even though he has dependents.» (Muslim)

Allah (the Exalted) encourages us to be kind in the way we respond to people, even when we have been wronged.

{Kind speech and forgiveness are better than charity followed by injury. Allah is free of all needs and Forbearing.}

(Qur'an 2: 263)

Therefore, showing kindness is not a point of weakness or cowardice. Rather, harsh and coarse behavior towards fellow human beings is certainly weakness of character and only shows that we cannot control our anger when wronged. Abu Hurayrah (may Allah be pleased with him) narrated that Allah's Messenger (bpuh) said:

«The strong one is not the one who overcomes the people in wrestling by his strength, but the strong one is the one who controls himself while angry.» (Bukhari)

Islam discourages revenge even if one has been wronged, because good and evil are never the same. Repelling evil with evil only begets more evil, whereas following up evil with good will surely calm the situation, bringing much good between individuals and creating a better society. Thus, the high moral ground taught by Islam is not to take revenge, even though we are allowed to do so; a better option is to forgive and meet evil with good. Allah (the Exalted) captures this kind and magnanimous behavior in very pure and sublime words:

{The good deed and the bad are not equal. Repel [evil] by that [deed] which is better; then the one whom between you and him is enmity [will become] as though he was a devoted friend. However, none is granted [the ability to do] it except those who are patient; and none is granted it except one having a great portion [of good].}

(Qur'an 41: 34-35)

In the same light, the Prophet (bpuh) made another statement with respect to the good that accrues from behaving kindly towards fellow human beings and other creatures. It was narrated from his wife 'Â'ishah (may Allah be pleased with her) that he said:

«Kindness is not to be found in anything but that it adds beauty to it, and it is not withdrawn from anything but it makes it defective (and ugly).» (Muslim)

The Prophet (bpuh), with his shining and perfect model of good behavior, exemplified in his own personal life the qualities of forbearance, patience, forgiveness, and tenderness of heart when he told his wife not to be harsh and coarse in her reply to the Jews who had wished the Prophet (bpuh) death in their crooked and twisted way of greeting. Thus, we are taught through this quality of kindness to restrain ourselves, to forgive the mistakes and failures of other people, and not to take revenge – even though we are entitled to revenge if we choose.

Kindness to human beings must start with the way we behave and treat our parents. Quite naturally, kindness towards parents should come first. How can a person like other people and be kind to them ahead of treating his or her own parents kindly, when it is they who gave birth to, cared for, and brought the person up into maturity? That is why our close relations have the first rights to our kindness before it is extended to others outside family relationships.

Therefore, the simple and logical starting point in our good moral behavior is kindness and obedience to our parents and to other elders in the family. Beyond that, this good social behavior should be extended to people outside the family. This is why Allah (the Exalted), after enjoining us to worship Him alone, immediately directed us to be kind and obedient to our parents:

{And your Lord has decreed that you worship none but Him, and that you be kind and dutiful to your parents. If one of them or both of them attain old age in your lifetime, do not say to them a word of disrespect, nor shout at them, but address them in terms of honor. Lower unto them the wing of submission and humility through mercy, and say: My Lord! Bestow on them Your mercy as they did bring me up when I was small. Your Lord knows best what is in your inner selves. If you are righteous, then, verily, He is ever Most Forgiving to those who turn unto Him again and again in obedience and in repentance.}

(Qur'an 17: 23-25)

Chapter Seven: Gentleness

Abu ad-Dardâ' (may Allah be pleased with him) narrated that the Prophet (bpuh) said:

«Whoever is given his (generous) share of gentleness, he has been given a share of good; whoever has been denied his share of gentleness, he has been denied his share of good.» (A reliable hadith recorded by at-Tirmidhi)

'Abdullâh ibn Mas'ood narrated that Allah's Messenger (bpuh) said:

«Shall I not inform you for whom the fire is unlawful and he is unlawful for the fire? (It is) every person who is gentle, kind, and easy (to deal with).» (A reliable hadith recorded by at-Tirmidhi)

Commentary on the hadiths

Anyone who has been given his or her portion of gentleness has been given much good. Indeed it does not cost us much to be gentle and amicable to our fellow human beings even if they have wronged us, whereas the rewards are so great. The reward of gentleness is that one is screened from the fire of hell, and that means being admitted to paradise by Allah's mercy.

Human beings are social creatures who interact with each other freely on a daily basis. When we act towards and speak to our fellow human beings in a gentle and polite manner, this creates a warm and lasting relationship among us and leaves a good impression on them, consequently earning us credit and opening other doors of opportunities.

On the other hand, when we speak and deal harshly with our fellow human beings, it only produces bad results and leaves bad impressions on people. Consequently, that closes many doors of opportunities which might have followed in the future, as alluded to by Allah's Messenger (bpuh) when he said that the person without gentleness would be denied goodness.

Allah's Messenger (bpuh) was very gentle with everyone – even his enemies, as we have seen in the hadith in the previous chapter – but he was especially gentle to women. In the following hadith, he told Anjashah (may Allah be pleased with him) to drive the camels slowly because women were riding with him:

«It was narrated that Anas ibn Mâlik (may Allah be pleased with him) said: Umm Sulaym (may Allah be pleased with her) was with the wives of the Prophet (bpuh), and a camel-driver was driving the camels on which they were riding.

The Messenger of Allah (bpuh) said: O Anjashah, go slowly when driving mounts that are carrying glass vessels.» (Muslim)

In the noble Qur'an, Allah (the Exalted) has repeatedly exhorted us to be gentle and polite in speech and the way we treat others, regardless of their socio-economic status.

{...and speak nicely to people...}

(Qur'an 2: 83)

Part of gentleness is to avoid speaking harshly and acting arrogantly to fellow human beings, however low in social class they may seem. We should not mistreat people because they are our servants at home or laborers at work, abusing and mistreating them harshly by shouting and barking at them as we wish just because they are our employees. Likewise, husbands and wives must not mistreat, or shout or bark at, each other just because one feels that he or she is at a higher level than the other. Allah (the Exalted) criticized such behavior in very strong terms, saying that He does not love people who show no manners or gentleness.

{And do not turn your face away from people in contempt, nor walk in insolence through the earth, for Allah does not love arrogant boasters. Be moderate in your pace when walking [showing no sense of arrogance] and lower your voice, for the harshest of all the voices, without doubt, is the braying of the donkey.}

(Qur'an 31: 18-19)

Maintaining gentle and amicable relationships between spouses, people and their servants, employers and employees, even friends and foes is an important virtue and moral value in society, one that helps the society to be calm and at peace. May Allah bless us with an easygoing nature towards our fellow human beings. Âmeen.

Chapter Eight: Chastity

Abu Hurayrah (may Allah be pleased with him) narrated that Allah's Messenger (bpuh) said:

«There are three who have a right to help from Allah: the one who fights in the cause Allah, the one getting married who intends to guard his or her chastity, and the slave who has made a covenant of manumission from his master, intending to buy his own freedom.» (A reliable hadith recorded by at-Tirmidhi and an-Nasâ'i)

Commentary on the hadith

Chastity today has become an increasingly rare moral virtue in many societies around the world, due to the influence of secular materialistic cultures and a mentality that gives human beings a false freedom to do whatever they wish with their sexual lives.

In Islam, however, sexuality and fulfilling sexual desires in the right manner is a very important and sacred virtue. Islam is not against all manners of fulfilling sexual desires, but Islam provides the correct and moral perspective on sex; this guards the legitimacy of family relations and saves not only individuals but the whole society from the great harm that results when few or no restraints apply to sexual relations.[38]

Islam puts sex and its proper fulfilment in its right and true perspective, presenting it as an urge that is created, ordained, and blessed by God, but which has limits imposed on it so that it may not be misused. Thus, the limits that are placed on this pure, natural urge are not aimed at taking the joy out of life but at providing humanity with guidelines for protecting our happiness and making our journey through this life as safe as possible.[39]

That is why, as explained in the above hadith, when a person marries to preserve his or her chastity, Allah (the Exalted) has made it an obligation upon Himself to help the person out when he or she encounters any difficulty regarding married life. In fact, in this hadith, the Prophet (bpuh) has put the person who marries to keep chaste from all forms of sexual immorality at the same level as the one who fights in the cause of Allah. This is especially relevant today, since the moral situation is not getting better but rather worse.

It has become a form of jihad for one to avoid gazing at indecently dressed women or at nude pictures full of immorality that are constantly bombarding us through the main mass media via television, newspapers, magazines, billboards, and the Internet. This is just as Allah's Messenger (bpuh) foretold when he said that nearing the end of the time of this world, sexual immorality will be widespread, and that it will be linked with the pervasive presence of alcohol and music, an increase in ignorance of religion, and an increase in the number of women that each responsible man will need to care for:

«Anas ibn Mâlik (may Allah be pleased with him) said: I will narrate to you a hadith that no one else can tell you about. I heard Allah's Messenger (bpuh) say that among the signs of the (coming of the) Hour (of Judgment) are that knowledge will decrease, ignorance will prevail, open illegal sexual intercourse will be prevalent, and women will increase in number and men will decrease in number so much so that fifty women will be looked after by one man.» (Bukhari)

Another narration states:

«A group of people of my Ummah (the Muslim nation) will drink wine, calling it by another name. Merriment will be made for them through the playing of musical instruments and the singing of female singers. Then Allah will cause the earth to swallow them up, and He will turn them into monkeys and pigs.» (A reliable hadith recorded by Ibn Mâjah)

It was narrated by Abu Hurayrah (may Allah be pleased with him) that Allah's Messenger (bpuh) said:

«There are two types of the people of hell whom I have not seen (yet): people with whips like the tails of cattle with which they strike the people, and women who are clothed yet naked, walking with an enticing gait, turning away from righteousness and leading others astray, with something on their heads that looks like the humps of camels, leaning to one side. They will not enter paradise, and they will not smell its fragrance, even though its fragrance may be detected from a great distance.» (Muslim)

The Prophet (bpuh) spoke the truth when he foretold how difficult it was going to be to practice chastity, especially as we near the Day of Judgment, when it will be as if all taps of sexual immorality are opened. The Companion 'Abdullâh ibn Abbâs (may Allah be pleased with both of them) said he had not seen a thing more resembling 'minor faults'[40] than what Abu Hurayrah (may Allah be pleased with him) narrated from the Prophet (bpuh):

«Allah has written for the children of Adam their share of *zinâ* (adultery or fornication), which they inevitably commit. The zinâ of the eyes is the sight (and gazing at forbidden things); the zinâ of the tongue is the speaking, and the zinâ of the mind is one's inner wishes and desires. Then the private parts either act upon this or deny it.» (Bukhari)

It is understandable that people who wish to marry in order to maintain their chastity deserve the help of Allah (the Exalted). In the time of Prophet Muhammad (bpuh) over 1400 years ago, a lady came to offer herself for marriage to the Prophet (bpuh). When he indicated to her that he was not in need of marriage at that time, the lady sat down and said she would not leave the place until she was married. How about today when, as we have pointed out, it is as if all kinds of advertisements are calling people to sexual immorality? Look at the situation and how difficult has it become for young men and women to keep their chastity! Striving to guard one's chastity today is definitely a form of jihad that surely requires Allah's help.

It is for this reason that Prophet Muhammad (bpuh) married off this woman, who had offered herself to him in marriage, to another man among the Companions, even though he did not have anything to give for a dowry, not even a ring made of iron, as reported in the following hadith:

«It was narrated that Sahl ibn Sa'd as-Sâ'idi (may Allah be pleased with him) said: A woman came to the Messenger of Allah (bpuh) and said: I have come to give myself to you (in marriage).

The Messenger of Allah (bpuh) looked her up and down, and then the Messenger of Allah (bpuh) lowered his head.

When the woman saw that he had not made any decision about her, she sat down.

A man among his Companions stood up and said: O Messenger of Allah, if you have no need of her, then marry me to her.

He said: Do you have anything (to offer her as a dowry)?

He said: No, by Allah, O Messenger of Allah.

He said: Go to your family and see if you can find something.

So he went. Then he came back and said: No, by Allah, O Messenger of Allah, (I could) not (find) even a ring of iron, only this lower garment of mine – Sahl added: He did not have an upper garment – and she may have half of it.

The Messenger of Allah (bpuh) said: What will she do with your garment? If you wear it, she will not have anything of it, and if she wears it, you will not have anything of it.

The man sat down, and after he had sat for a long time, he got up (to leave).

The Messenger of Allah (bpuh) saw him turning away, and he ordered that he come close to him. When the man came, he said: What do you know of the Qur'an?

He said: I know Soorat such-and-such and Soorat such-and-such – and he listed them.

The Messenger (bpuh) said: Do you recite them by heart?

He answered: Yes.

He said: Go. You have been given her (in marriage) for what you know of the Qur'an.

(In another narration, there is an addition in which the Messenger of Allah [bpuh] said: Go, for I have married her to you, so teach her what you know of the Qur'an.)» (Bukhari and Muslim)

The Muslim scholars have concluded from this hadith, and the hadith under discussion in this chapter, that even though this Companion did not have anything to give as a dowry, the Prophet (bpuh) gave him the woman in marriage because the Prophet (bpuh), as well as the man himself, had sincere faith and full trust in and reliance on Allah (the Exalted). Since both the Companion and the woman desired marriage and feared committing unlawful sexual intercourse, Allah (the Exalted) would surely help them and provide a lawful way out for them, for indeed Allah, the Exalted, says:

{And marry those among you who are single, and the virtuous ones among your slaves, male or female. If they are in poverty, Allah will enrich them from His bounties, for Allah encompasses all, and He knows all things.}

(Qur'an 24: 32)

{...Whoever fears Allah and keeps his duty to Him, He will make a way for him to get out [from every difficulty], and He will provide for him from [sources] he never could imagine. Whoever puts his full trust in Allah, Allah will suffice him. Verily, Allah will accomplish His purpose. Indeed Allah has set a measure for all things.}

(Qur'an 65: 2-3)

Other ways of keeping ourselves chaste from sexual immorality in all its forms include: keeping ourselves busy with lawful games, sports, and recreational activities, such as swimming, running, wrestling, football, basketball; reading Islamic books and other good educational materials; watching Islamic documentary programs; attending Islamic study circles; reciting the Qur'an; and *dhikr* (remembrance of Allah). The Messenger of Allah (bpuh) also advised fasting many days of every month:

«It was narrated that 'Alqamah said: I was walking with 'Abdullâh in Minâ when he was met by 'Uthmân. He stood and talked with him, and 'Uthmân said to him: Abu 'Abdur-Rahmân, shall we not marry you to a young girl who can remind you of the times past?

'Abdullâh said: If that is what you are telling me, let me tell you that Allah's Messenger (bpuh) said to us: O young men! If anyone among you can afford it, let him get married, for it is more effective in lowering the gaze and guarding one's chastity; whoever cannot afford it should fast, for the fasting will be a shield for him.» (Bukhari and Muslim)

May Allah (the Exalted) give all young men and women the means and ability to marry and to be faithful to their spouses and thus maintain their chastity. May Allah help us to fear Him and fear the consequences of sexual immorality, and to be content with our situation just like the Prophet (bpuh), who used to beseech Allah with the following supplication, narrated by 'Abdullâh (may Allah be pleased with him):

«*Allâhumma inni as'alukal-hudâ wat-tuqâ wal-'afâfa wal-ghinâ.* (O Allah, indeed I ask You for true guidance, piety, chastity and self-sufficiency (or contentment in my heart with Your lawful bounties.)» (Muslim, at-Tirmidhi and Ibn Mâjah)

Chapter Nine: Peacefulness

«'Abdullâh ibn Salâm (may Allah be pleased with him) said: When the Messenger of Allah (bpuh) arrived in Madinah, the people came out to meet him. It was said that the Messenger of Allah (bpuh) had arrived, so I went among the people to get a look at him. When I gazed upon the face of the Messenger of Allah (bpuh), I knew that his face was not the face of a liar.

The first thing that he said was: O people! Spread the *salâm* (peace and the greeting of peace), feed (others who are hungry), and perform prayers while the people are sleeping, and you will enter paradise with ease.» (An authentic hadith recorded by at-Tirmidhi)

Commentary on the hadith

Peacefulness (and spreading peace in society) is another virtue taught by Allah's Messenger (bpuh) which the whole world is craving. It has often been falsely claimed by the enemies of Islam that Islam is a religion of war and violence; however, that is not true. We can clearly see in the above hadith that the first thing that came out of the lips of Allah's Messenger (bpuh) when he arrived in Madinah to be its leader was that people should be peaceful and spread peace among themselves. He also advised them to feed the needy and offer the prayers in the night so that they might hope for Allah's mercy and enter paradise with ease.

It is obvious that meeting people with greetings full of peace, love, affection, sympathy, and well wishes promotes peace in a society. If they couple this with sincere hearts, devoted to the obedience and worship of Allah (the Exalted), people will earn the pleasure of Allah and an unimpeded smooth entry into paradise. On the Day of Judgment, Allah (the Exalted) will address His devoted and loyal friends who consistently feared Him in their worldly life:

{[To the righteous soul will be said:] O [you] soul, in [complete] rest and satisfaction! Come back to your Lord, well pleased [yourself], and well-pleasing to Him! Enter, then, among My devoted [and honored] servants. Enter My paradise!}

(Qur'an 89: 27-30)

Peacefulness, be it within an individual's mind and soul or within society in general, has become a very rare virtue in today's world. The current times are full of all sorts of unrest, ranging from insecurity, theft, robbery with violence, domestic violence, oppression and injustice, to uncalled for national and international wars motivated by uncontrolled materialistic greed and desires to own more and more of the pomp and glitter of this world.

The truth of the matter is that Islam is a religion of peace; it does not advocate perpetual war or violence. Islam advocates peace because it is a religion of peace. The name Islam itself means peace. This implies that when we consciously choose to submit totally to Allah (the Exalted), by obeying him and living according to His laws and regulations, Allah (the Exalted) grants us peace in our hearts and minds, peace between us and our fellow human beings, peace between us and other creatures and the environment, and foremost peace between us and Himself.

Another hadith – one phrase of which is often quoted out of context by Orientalists to affirm their false claim that Islam advocates perpetual war and violence – clarifies that peace and peacefulness were advocated by Allah's Messenger Muhammad (bpuh):

«Sâlim Abu an-Nadr, the freed slave of 'Umar ibn 'Ubaydullâh, narrated: I was 'Umar's clerk. Once 'Abdullâh ibn Abi Awfâ wrote a letter to 'Umar ibn 'Ubaydullâh while he proceeded to al-Haruriyah. I read in it that during some of his military expeditions against the enemy, Allah's Messenger (bpuh) waited until the sun declined, and then he got up among the people and said: O people! Do not wish to meet the enemy, but (instead) ask Allah for safety (peace and security). Still, when you (must) come face to face with the enemy, be patient, and know that paradise is under the shade of swords.

Then he said: O Allah, the One Who revealed the Book (the Qur'an), the Mover of the clouds, and the defeater of the Aḥzâb (Confederates), defeat them, and grant us victory over them.» (Bukhari)

It seems that everyone is wishing for and wanting peace, yet it is becoming increasingly difficult to find this noble virtue, in spite of the high standard of living that many people enjoy today. Though they live an easy life full of all kinds of material comfort, most people have neglected the true source of peace and are looking for it elsewhere. They look for inner peace in music, sports, movies, wealth, power and positions of influence, promiscuity, alcohol, drugs, and other things, all in vain. The true source of inner peace and peacefulness is in understanding the purpose of our creation; knowing and believing in our sole Creator, Cherisher, and Sustainer; and calling on Him constantly, seeking peace from Him as the Prophet (bpuh) used to do:

«It was narrated that Thawbân (may Allah be pleased with him) said: When the Messenger of Allah (bpuh) had finished the prayer, he would ask for forgiveness three times and then say: *Allâhumma antas-Salâmu wa minkas-salâmu, tabârakta yâ dhal-jalâli wal-ikrâm*. (O Allah, You are the Source of Peace and Perfection and from You is all peace. Blessed are You, O Owner of Majesty and Honor.)

Al-Waleed said: I asked Awzâ'i: How does one ask for forgiveness?

He replied: Say, *Astaghfirullâh, astaghfirullâh*. (I ask Allah for forgiveness, I ask Allah for forgiveness.)» (Muslim)

In the glorious Qur'an, Allah (the Exalted) confirmed that hearts will find inner peace and tranquility from believing in Him, always remembering Him with words of glorification, supplicating to Him, being grateful to Him, and seeking His mercy, forgiveness, and bounties.

{Those who believe, and whose hearts find satisfaction [inner peace] in the remembrance of Allah; for without doubt in the remembrance of Allah do hearts find satisfaction [inner peace].}

(Qur'an, 13: 28)

O Allah! You are the true source of peace and mercy. Grant us inner peace in our hearts, minds, and souls, and make us peaceful people who love peace and spread peace. Âmeen.

Chapter Ten: Moderation

It was narrated from Abu Ḥumayd as-Sâ'idi (may Allah be pleased with him) that the Messenger of Allah (bpuh) said:

«Be moderate in seeking worldly things, because that for which each (creature) was created will be facilitated for them.» (A sound hadith recorded by Ibn Mâjah)

It was narrated from Jâbir ibn 'Abdullâh (may Allah be pleased with both of them) that the Messenger of Allah (bpuh) said:

«O people, fear Allah and be moderate in seeking a living, for no soul will die until it has received all its provision, even if it is slow in coming. So fear Allah and be moderate in seeking provision. Take that which is permissible, and leave that which is forbidden.» (A sound hadith recorded by Ibn Mâjah)

Commentary on the hadiths

Not only did Allah's Messenger (bpuh) direct us to be moderate in seeking our livelihood[41] in this world, but in a number of passages in the noble Qur'an, Allah (the Exalted) repeatedly commands us to be moderate and balanced in all affairs; this includes our food, clothes, speech, property, fasting, prayers, and so on. Allah, the Exalted, says:

{Thus have We made you a community justly balanced [and moderate] that you may be witnesses over humankind, and the Messenger a witness over you...}

(Qur'an 2: 143)

Abu Hurayrah (may Allah be pleased with him) narrated that the Prophet (bpuh) said:

«The religion (of Islam) is very easy, and whoever overburdens himself in his religion will not be able to continue in that way. So you should not be extremists, but try to be moderate and near to perfection. Receive the good tidings that you will be rewarded, and gain strength by worshipping in the mornings and during the night.» (Bukhari)

Thus, being moderate and balanced in obeying Allah and His Messenger (bpuh) by living an Islamic way of life is the best way to live without being overburdened. It enables a person to be consistent in his or her duties to Allah and to other human beings. It is a life without the extremes of being lazy or overzealous, the latter of which is usually followed by fatigue that causes one to stop worshipping Allah or to stop being dutiful to fellow human beings.

Furthermore, moderation and balance motivate us to continue with all forms of worship and obedience of Allah (the Exalted). That is why it is the most beloved way to worship Allah (the Exalted) and hence earns His pleasure and great rewards, according to the two narrations under discussion. In yet another statement, Allah's Messenger (bpuh) is reported to have said that the best of deeds are continuous and consistent ones, even if they are little.

«'Â'ishah (may Allah be pleased with her) narrated that the Prophet (bpuh) was asked: What deeds are loved most by Allah?

He answered: The most regular, consistent deeds, even though they may be few.

Then he added: Do not take upon yourselves except the deeds which are within your ability.» (Bukhari)

Likewise, when it comes to wealth in Islam, one should be neither extravagant nor a miser but should take a moderate and balanced path in regard to daily expenditure. Allah, the Exalted, says:

{Give the relatives their rights, and [also] the poor and the traveler, and do not spend wastefully.[42] Indeed, the wasteful people are brothers of the devils, and Satan is ever ungrateful to his Lord. If you [must] turn away from them [the needy] awaiting a mercy from your Lord which you expect,[43] then speak to them a gentle word. Do not make your hand [as if it is] chained to your neck [refusing to spend] or extend it completely [by being extravagant] and [thereby] become blamed and insolvent. Indeed, your Lord extends provision for whom He wills and restricts [it for whom He wills]. Indeed, concerning His servants, He is ever Acquainted [with all their affairs] and All-Seeing.}

(Qur'an 17: 26-30)

{[The blessed servants of Allah are] those who, when they spend, do not do so excessively or sparingly but hold a just [balance] between those [two extremes].}

(Qur'an 25: 67)

Abu Hurayrah (may Allah be pleased with him) narrated that the Prophet (bpuh) said:

«Every day, two angels come down from heaven, and one of them says: O Allah, compensate every person who spends in Your cause!

The other angel says: O Allah, destroy every miser!» (Bukhari)

With regard to food and drink, we are also taught, according to the hadiths under discussion, that people should not be wasteful and extravagant, nor should they deny themselves to the extent of starving themselves. Furthermore, they should only eat and drink that which is lawful and pure, as Allah (the Exalted) says:

{O people, eat of what is on earth that is lawful and good [and pure], and do not follow the footsteps of the Evil One. Indeed he is to you an avowed enemy.}

(Qur'an 2: 168)

{O Children of Adam, wear your beautiful apparel at every time and place of prayer. Eat and drink, but waste not by excess, for Allah does not love those who are wasteful. Say [O Muhammad]: Who has forbidden the beautiful [gifts] of Allah, which He has produced for His servants, and the things, clean and pure [which He has provided] for sustenance? Say: They are, in the life of this world, for those who believe, and purely for them on the Day of Judgment. Thus do We explain the signs and verses in detail for those who understand. Say: The things that my Lord has indeed forbidden are shameful deeds, whether open or secret; sins and trespasses against truth or reason; assigning partners to Allah, for which He has given no authority; and that you say about Allah that which you do not know.}

(Qur'an 7: 31-33)

{O you messengers! Eat [all] things good and pure, and work righteousness. I am Knowledgeable about [all] that you do.}

(Qur'an 23: 51)

The Prophet (bpuh) gave us all the guidance we need with his statements on what food to eat and what not to eat. Therefore, even though we are encouraged to eat of the good and wholesome things that Allah has provided for us, the Prophet (bpuh) also stressed that overeating and gluttony are harmful.[44] Miqdâm ibn Ma'dikarib (may Allah be pleased with him) narrated that he heard the Messenger of Allah (bpuh) say:

«A human being fills no worse vessel than his stomach. It is sufficient for a human being to eat a few mouthfuls to keep his spine straight; but if he must (fill it), then one-third for food, one-third for drink, and one-third for air.» (A sound hadith recorded by at-Tirmidhi and Ibn Mâjah)

Not being moderate with regard to food and drink results in overeating, gluttony, and extravagance, which leads to obesity, self-indulgence, and thereafter laziness and lethargy. It can even lead to inactivity and the abandonment of work, which is very detrimental from a number of perspectives. That is why our righteous predecessors recognized the evil effects of gluttony and extravagance and voiced their concern, warning strongly against it. 'Â'ishah, the Mother of the Believers (may Allah be pleased with her), said:

The first tribulation that befell this Muslim Ummah after its Prophet (bpuh) [had died] was gratification. For when people felt gratified, they became fat; therefore, their hearts became weak and their desires overgrew.[45]

'Umar ibn al-Khattâb (may Allah be pleased with him) also said:

Beware of overeating and drinking too much, for they spoil the body, cause disease, and discourage one from performing the prayer. Show moderation in both eating and drinking, for moderation is more beneficial to the body and farther from extravagance. Surely, Allah the Almighty detests the fat scholar, and humans will never be destroyed until they give preference to their desires over their religion.[46]

On the other hand, excessive abstinence from food, lawful drinks, and other worldly affairs is also against the Islamic principle of moderation. Excessive abstinence is also discouraged because it leads to weakness and incapacity. The incident of the two Companions of Prophet Muhammad (bpuh) who were joined together as brothers,[47] Abu ad-Dardâ' and Salmân al-Fârisi (may Allah be pleased with both of them), is sufficient for us to reflect on:

«Abu Juḥayfah (may Allah be pleased with him) narrated that the Prophet (bpuh) established a bond of brotherhood between Salmân and Abu ad-Dardâ'. Salmân paid a visit to Abu ad-Dardâ' and found (his wife) Umm ad-Dardâ' dressed in shabby clothes, so he asked her why she was in that state.

She replied: Your brother, Abu ad-Dardâ', is not interested in the luxuries of this world.

In the meantime, Abu ad-Dardâ' came (back), prepared a meal for (Salmân), and said to him: (Please) eat, for I am fasting.

Salmân said: I am not going to eat unless you eat.

Abu ad-Dardâ' ate.

When it was night, Abu ad-Dardâ' got up (for the night prayer).

Salmân said (to him): Sleep.

So he slept.

Again Abu ad-Dardâ' got up (for the prayer), and Salmân said (to him): Sleep.

When it was the last part of the night, Salmân said to him: Get up now (for the prayer).

Both of them offered their prayers, and Salmân said to Abu ad-Dardâ': Your Lord has a right on you, your soul has a right on you, and your family has a right on you – so you should give the rights to all those who have a right on you.

Later on, Abu ad-Dardâ' visited the Prophet (bpuh) and mentioned that to him.

The Prophet (bpuh) said: Salmân has spoken the truth.» (Bukhari and at-Tirmidhi)

Even when it comes to our acts of worship, such as prayers and fasting, we are advised by Allah's Messenger (bpuh) to be moderate and balanced. In this regard, there are two incidents in the life of Prophet Muhammad (bpuh) that are quite revealing.

The young 'Abdullâh, son of the famous Companion 'Amr ibn al-'Âṣ, had become known for his extreme self-denial, and the Prophet (bpuh) learned of the punishing routine to which he had resorted.

«'Abdullâh reported that the Prophet (bpuh) came to him and asked: 'Abdullâh, have I not been informed that you fast during the day and offer prayers all the night?

'Abdullâh replied: Yes, Allah's Messenger!

The Prophet (bpuh) said: Do not do that. Fast for a few days, and then give it up for few days. Offer prayers and also sleep at night. Your body has a right on you, and your wife has a right on you, and your guest has a right on you. It is sufficient for you to fast three days in a month, for the reward of a good deed is multiplied ten times, so it will be like fasting throughout the year.

I ('Abdullâh) insisted (on fasting), so I was given a hard instruction. I said: O Messenger of Allah, I have strength (to do more than that).

The Prophet (bpuh) said: Then fast like the fasting of the Prophet David, and do not fast more than that.

I asked: How was the fasting of David, Prophet of Allah?

He replied: Half of the year. He used to fast on alternate days, and he used not to flee on meeting the enemy.» (Bukhari)

«Anas ibn Mâlik (may Allah be pleased with him) narrated that a group of three men came to the houses of the wives of the Prophet (may Allah be pleased with all of them) asking about how the Prophet (bpuh) worshipped (Allah).

When they were informed about that, they considered their worship insufficient and said: Where are we compared to the Prophet (bpuh), as his past and future sins have been forgiven?

Then one of them said: I will offer the prayer throughout the night forever.

The other said: I will fast throughout the year and will not break my fast.

The third said: I will keep away from women and will not ever marry.

Allah's Messenger (bpuh) came to them and said: Are you the same people who said such-and-such? By Allah, I am more fearful of Allah and more conscious of Him than you; yet I fast and break my fast, I pray and sleep, and I also marry women. Therefore, whoever turns away from my way of life is not from me (not one of my true followers).» (Bukhari)

Even with regard to enmity and friendship, Prophet Muhammad (bpuh) advised us to be balanced and moderate. He instructed that we should neither befriend people to the extent that we give them our total love nor hate our enemies such that we leave no space for possible friendship. Instead, we should love our friends moderately and hate our enemies moderately. Muhammad ibn Seereen narrated from Abu Hurayrah – whom he believed narrated from the Prophet (bpuh):

«Love your beloved moderately, for perhaps he may become hated to you someday; and hate whom you hate moderately, for perhaps he may become your beloved someday.» (A reliable hadith recorded by at-Tirmidhi)

May Allah (the Exalted) help us to be people of moderation and balance in our everyday lives. Âmeen.

Chapter Eleven: Politeness

«'Urwah ibn Zubayr narrated that 'Â'ishah (may Allah be pleased with her) said: A man sought permission to meet the Messenger of Allah (bpuh).

So the Messenger (bpuh) said: Grant him permission. What an evil brother of his tribe he is – or (he said) what an evil son of the tribe.

When the man entered, the Messenger (bpuh) spoke politely to him.

I said: Messenger of Allah, you said what you said about him, then you spoke politely to him?

He said: O 'Â'ishah! Indeed among the evilest of people is he whom the people avoid, or whom the people leave, fearing his filthy speech.» (Bukhari and Muslim)

Commentary on the hadith

Politeness is a moral virtue that helps us to reduce the number of our enemies and to guard ourselves from the evil and harm that can be avoided from simple-minded people when we behave politely to them. According to these words of Allah's Messenger (bpuh), we should avoid evil people who are well known for their vile and evil speech.

It does not cost us much to be gentle and amicable to our fellow human beings, even if they have wronged us. Similarly, it would not cost us anything to be polite and avoid embarrassment and vile behavior from rude and uncouth people, who are always looking for any excuse to cause trouble and create a mountain out of a molehill.

If we do not avoid such people, or guard against them by behaving politely to them, they may become a great source of pain and discomfort in our lives. Hence, Allah's Messenger (bpuh) gave us the apt advice to avoid them by all means. This is also what Allah (the Exalted) says in praising his devout righteous servants who are humble, polite, and amicable to people:

{Those who witness no falsehood and, if they pass by some ill speech, they pass by it honorably [and avoid it].}

(Qur'an 25: 72)

Politeness is not a manifestation of weakness or cowardice, although some may misinterpret it that way. In reality, it is a sign of maturity and strength in dealing with fellow human beings. This is why the Prophet (bpuh) promised great rewards for those who leave off arguing with people once they realize that continuing will not bring any good results, even if they think they are right and even when they have a better or stronger argument. The Prophet (bpuh) said:

«I guarantee a house in the outskirts of paradise for a person who refrains from opinion-based arguing, even if he (or she) is in the right…» (A reliable hadith recorded by Abu Dâwood)

Moreover, Allah's Messenger (bpuh) promised paradise to those who speak nicely to their fellow human beings, who feed people, and who are concerned with their own devotional prayers and fasting.

«'Ali (may Allah be pleased with him) narrated that the Messenger of Allah (bpuh) said: Indeed in paradise there are chambers whose outside can be seen from their inside and whose inside can be seen from their outside.

A Bedouin stood up and asked: Who are they for, Messenger of Allah?

He said: For those who speak well, feed others, fast regularly, and perform prayer during the night while the people are asleep.» (A reliable hadith recorded by at-Tirmidhi)

Chapter Twelve: Contentment

It was narrated from Abu Hurayrah (may Allah be pleased with him) that the Prophet (bpuh) said:

«Richness is not an abundance of worldly goods; rather, richness is contentment with oneself (and one's lot in life).» (Bukhari, Muslim, at-Tirmidhi, Ibn Mâjah, and Aḥmad)

Commentary on the hadith

Contentment, or satisfaction, is yet another moral virtue that seems to be scarce in our modern age, and Prophet Muhammad (bpuh), in very few concise words, has summed up what it entails. Contrary to what many people think, contentment is not brought about through worldly possessions but rather through satisfaction in our hearts with whatever Allah (the Exalted) has blessed us with of His bounties – be it health, beauty, good companionship, a day's provision of food, a secure home and shelter, or something else. Salamah ibn 'Ubaydullâh ibn Miḥṣan al-Khaṭmi narrated the following from his father, who was a Companion of the Prophet (bpuh):

«Whoever among you wakes up in the morning secure in his dwelling, healthy in his body, and having food for the day, then it is as if the world has been gathered for him.» (A reliable hadith recorded by at-Tirmidhi)

In a similar narration collected in *Sunan Ibn Mâjah*, it is reported that Allah's Messenger (bpuh) said:

«Whoever among you wakes up physically healthy, feeling safe and secure within himself, with food for the day, it is as if he acquired the whole world.» (A reliable hadith recorded by Ibn Mâjah)

Is it possible to have more wonderful, sweet, and beautiful words than these for contentment and satisfaction that brings peace of mind? Remember, dear brothers and sisters (may Allah have mercy on you), that the Prophet (bpuh) did not speak from his own desires. These words are only a revelation sent down to him from Allah, the Exalted:

{Nor does he [Muhammad (bpuh)] say [anything] of [his own] desire. It is no less than a revelation sent down to him.}

(Qur'an 53: 3-4)

This concept of contentment is very important as a factor in the psychological health of the human being because without some kind of contentment, human life would be a real torture. If one is always dissatisfied in life, no matter what, then there can never be any feeling of happiness. Each human being needs some kind of contentment in order to feel satisfied, at ease, and happy, and thus continue with life.

Allah (the Exalted) and His Messenger Muhammad (bpuh) therefore provided a way for every individual to feel calmness, with these beautiful words of advice that contain ways and means of controlling one's feelings and desires. Thus, a person becomes a master of his or her desires rather than a slave to them. Allah, the Exalted, says:

{Do not wish [or desire] for that by which Allah has made some of you exceed others. For men is a share of what they have earned, and for women is a share of what they have earned, so ask Allah of His bounty. Indeed Allah is ever All-Knowing of all things.}

(Qur'an 4: 32)

{Have you seen him who takes as his god his own vain desire? Allah has, knowing [him as such], left him astray, and sealed his hearing and his heart [and understanding], and put a cover on his sight. Who, then, will guide him after Allah [has withdrawn guidance]? Will you not then receive admonition?}

(Qur'an 45: 23)

Without contentment, people will destroy themselves, and this has become common today. People who are never content with their positions, or their wealth, or their knowledge, or their jobs can never hope for any kind of true self-satisfaction or happiness. That is why Allah's Messenger (bpuh) urged the believers to be content with however little they might possess. Prophet Muhammad (bpuh) is reported to have encouraged a positive attitude with regard to self-satisfaction in these narrations from Abu Hurayrah (may Allah be pleased with him):

«If any one of you looked at a person who was made superior to him in property and appearance, then he should also look at the one who is inferior to him and to whom he has been made superior.» (Bukhari)

«Look at those who stand at a lower level than you, and do not look at those who stand at a higher level than you; for that may keep you from scorning the blessings of Allah.» (Muslim)

In other words, when it concerns worldly affairs and the pomp and glitter of worldly belongings, people should always look at those who are below them, those who are in far worse situations, so as to be appreciative of the bounties of Allah. However, when it comes to spiritual matters such as prayers, fasting, or righteousness, people must always look to those above them, those who exceed them in these good qualities, so as to strive for self-improvement.

This does not in any way mean that we should be lazy, not working hard for our worldly affairs and then begging and depending on others for our livelihood. Abu Hurayrah reported that he heard the Messenger of Allah (bpuh) say:

«For one of you to go out and gather firewood on his back (and sell it), then make himself independent of people and give charity with it, is better than asking the people (for assistance), who may give to you or withhold (it) from you. The upper hand (that gives) is better than the lower hand (that receives), and start (giving in charity) with those who are under your care.» (Muslim)

Moreover, Allah (the Exalted) commands the believers in the Qur'an to work hard, for work is a form of worship:

{Say: Work [righteousness]. Allah will observe your work, and [so will] His Messenger and the believers. Soon you will be brought back to the Knower of what is hidden and what is open. Then will He [Allah] show you the truth of all that you used to do.}

(Qur'an 9: 105)

{When the prayer is finished, then you may disperse through the land and seek of the bounty of Allah, and celebrate the praises of Allah often [and without stint] that you may prosper.}

(Qur'an 62: 10)

Thus, Islam strikes a just balance between self-dependence and reliance on Allah (the Exalted). Allah orders us to work hard and depend on our own efforts because the sky will not rain down gold or silver upon us. At the same time, He instructs the believers to trust and depend on Him and to ask for His inspiration, strength, and blessings in all that they do.

This kind of balance creates in the hearts and minds of the believers a sense of internal security, which brings about contentment and self-satisfaction. Logically speaking, since a person's abilities are limited in many ways, one is not expected to achieve everything or to overcome all difficulties in life. To a Muslim, failure does not mean despair, because a believer is strongly and continuously connected to Allah (the Exalted), trusting Him fully in all circumstances and situations without losing hope in Him.

{...Whoever puts his full trust in Allah, then He is sufficient for him...}

(Qur'an 65: 3)

Having our full trust in and reliance on Allah (the Exalted), after taking all possible necessary and lawful means of gaining the sustenance available to us, brings contentment. In another beautiful hadith, 'Umar ibn al-Khaṭṭâb (may Allah be pleased with him) narrated that the Messenger of Allah (bpuh) said:

«If you were to truly rely upon Allah with the required reliance, then He would provide for you just as the bird is provided for. It goes out in the morning (with its stomach) empty and returns full.» (A reliable hadith recorded by at-Tirmidhi)

Abu Hurayrah (may Allah be pleased with him) narrated that the Prophet (bpuh) said:

«Indeed Allah, Most High, said: O son of Adam! Devote yourself to My worship, and I will fill your chest with riches and alleviate your poverty. If you do not do so, I will fill your hands with problems and leave you in your poverty.» (A reliable hadith recorded by at-Tirmidhi)

The English translators of *Jâmi' at-Tirmidhi* commented on the above hadith, saying:

If a man engages himself in worshipping Allah and in the doing of His commands, Allah grants him contentment and exemption from wants and drives penury and need away from him. In case the man is heedless of Allah's commands and neglects His worship, He divests him of the wealth of contentment and fills his heart with avarice and greed, and robs him the tranquility and peace of mind.[48]

This is contrary to what secular, materialistic living has made us believe: that the more time we spend in seeking material wealth, the more riches and wealth we will gain and the more contentment, satisfaction, and happiness we will have. The reality is the exact opposite, as was explained by the words of Allah's Messenger (bpuh).

The truth is that Allah is the true owner of all that is in the heavens and the earth. Therefore, the more time we dedicate to worshipping Him and asking for His bounties, the more sustenance and satisfaction we will derive from the little time we spend working. More than twenty times in the glorious Qur'an, Allah (the Exalted) has explained this reality so that we may comprehend it. What follows is a sample of eight passages from the Qur'an that tell us with certainty that He is the One Who grants provision in due measure, according to His knowledge and wisdom.

{And there is not a thing but its [sources and] treasures are with Us [Allah]; but We only send it down in known measures.} (Qur'an 15: 21)

{...To Allah belong the treasures of the heavens and the earth, but the hypocrites understand not.}

(Qur'an 63: 7)

{Allah extends, or grants by [strict] measure, the sustenance [which He gives] to whomever He pleases. And they rejoice in the worldly life, while the worldly life is not, compared to the hereafter, except a [brief] enjoyment.}

(Qur'an 13: 26)

{Indeed, your Lord extends provision for whom He wills and restricts [it for whom He wills]. Indeed He is ever Aware and Seeing of [all that concerns] His servants.}

(Qur'an 17: 30)

{That Allah may reward them [according to] the best of what they did and increase them from His bounty. And Allah gives provision to whom He wills without account [or limit].}

(Qur'an 24: 38)

{Allah extends the provision for whom He pleases of His servants, and He [similarly] restricts for him [as He pleases]. Indeed Allah has full knowledge of all things.}

(Qur'an 29: 62)

{Do they not see that Allah extends the provision and restricts it, to whomever He pleases? Verily in that are signs for a people who believe.}

(Qur'an 30: 37)

{Allah is the One Who created you, then provided for you sustenance. Then He will cause you to die, and then He will give you life. Are there any of your [false god] 'partners' who can do any of these things? Glory be to Him, and High is He above the partners they associate [with Him]!}

(Qur'an 30: 40)

{Say [O Muhammad]: Verily my Lord enlarges and restricts the provision to whom He pleases, but most men know not.}

(Qur'an 34: 36)

{To Him [Allah] belong the keys of the heavens and the earth. He extends and restricts the provisions for whom He wills, for He knows full well all things.}

(Qur'an 42: 12)

As we said, all these verses have been quoted to bring certainty about this reality that sustenance is in the Hands of Allah (the Exalted) and that He distributes it as he pleases. Once we comprehend and understand this important reality, we will find contentment. We will dedicate much of our precious time to trying to worship, obey, and please Him – rather than spending so much of our time working tirelessly until we are exhausted and have no energy to worship and please Allah (the Exalted). Contentment is found only when hard work is coupled with giving Allah the rights due to Him.

Chapter Thirteen: Cheerfulness

«It was narrated from Mu'âdh ibn 'Abdullâh ibn Khubayb, from his father, that his paternal uncle said: We were sitting in a gathering, and the Prophet (bpuh) came with traces of water on his head.

One of us said to him: We see that you are of good cheer today.

He said: Yes, praise be to Allah.

Then he spoke to the people about being rich.

He said: There is nothing wrong with being rich for one who has piety, but good health is better than riches, and being of good cheer is a blessing.» (A sound hadith recorded by Ibn Mâjah)

Commentary on the hadith

According to this hadith, cheerfulness in life is a great boon from Allah (the Exalted), and it does not come about because of riches. Even though there is nothing wrong with looking for riches, the Prophet (bpuh) put the issue of wealth in the right perspective by declaring that without piety, an abundance of riches is dangerous. In most cases, wealth without righteousness leads to pride, showing off, lavish spending, and living an unreasonable lifestyle of extravagance and wastefulness. Thus, the effort people put in to gain such wealth becomes a source of sin for them, and the spending of it multiplies their sins even more. For people who have riches but no piety, the wealth becomes a test and a cause of their destruction. Their wealth and children will not avail them in this world or in the hereafter.

{The day when wealth or children will not benefit [anyone] except the person who comes to Allah with a sound heart.}

(Qur'an 26: 88-89)

In the hereafter, those who had wealth but did not fear Allah or the Day of Judgment enough to spend their riches in the right way will cry with loads of worthless regrets, as Allah, the Exalted, says:

{But as for he who is given his record in his left hand, he will say: Oh, I wish I had not been given my record and had not known what my account is. I wish it [my death] had been the decisive one.[49] My wealth has not availed me; gone from me is my authority. [Allah will say]: Seize him and shackle him, then into hellfire drive him. Then insert him into a chain whose length is seventy cubits. Indeed, he did not used to believe in Allah, the Most Great, nor did he encourage the feeding of the poor. So there is not for him here this day any devoted friend, nor any food except from the discharge of wounds [pus]; none will eat it except the sinners.}

(Qur'an 69: 25-37)

On the other hand, the Prophet (bpuh) said that having wealth is not bad for those who have piety, because their fear of God urges them and motivates them to spend in the path of Allah (the Exalted) in taking care of the poor, the destitute, and all the needy in society. Still, health is better than riches for a person who has piety, because being rich is not a direct ticket to cheerfulness and happiness, as many people wrongfully think. The rich also cry, and they will really cry a lot when they realize that possessions that are void of blessings fail to bring them the happiness and cheerfulness that they earnestly yearn for in life.

As Prophet Muhammad (bpuh) says in this hadith, health is a better blessing than wealth, since being in a good state of health, despite being less fortunate in terms of wealth, gives one a chance to do many righteous deeds that bring happiness to his or her life. A sick person, no matter how much wealth he or she may have, is always unwell and complaining – unable to enjoy even the best of foods, sleep, companionship, and other amenities of life. A sickly person will not have a good time with his or her family and children. Many sick people have even wished they could give away all their wealth and riches in exchange for good health.

Prophet Muhammad (bpuh) was always conscious of appreciating and thanking Allah (the Exalted) for good health. Every day, after the formal prayers in the early morning and late evening, it was his habit to supplicate to Allah (the Exalted) to continue granting him good health, and he advised us to do the same:

'Abdur-Raḥmân ibn Abi Bakrah said that he told his father: O my father, I hear you repeating this supplication three times every morning and three times every evening: O Allah, grant me health in my body! O Allah, grant me health in my hearing! O Allah, grant me health in my sight! None has the right to be worshipped except You.

His father replied: I heard Allah's Messenger (bpuh) using these words as a supplication, and I like to follow his practice.[50]

Cheerfulness in our daily lives is a very healthy and important moral virtue, for it adds to our peace of mind. Plus, we get more rewards; the Messenger of Allah (bpuh) indicated that meeting our fellow human beings with a cheerful countenance is a form of charity. Abu Dharr (may Allah be pleased with him) narrated that the Prophet (bpuh) said to him:

«Do not regard any act of kindness as insignificant, even if it is only meeting your brother with a cheerful countenance.» (Muslim)

Part of the beauty of the teachings of Islam with respect to cheerfulness is that any gesture of kindness, well-wishing, and sympathy – however minute and seemingly insignificant – earns rewards from Allah (the Exalted), especially when it brings joy and happiness to a fellow human being and in particular a Muslim brother or sister. Jâbir ibn 'Abdullâh narrated that the Messenger of Allah (bpuh) said:

«Every good (deed) is a charity. Indeed among the good (deeds) is to meet your brother with a smiling face and to pour what is left in your bucket (beyond your needs) into the vessel of your brother.» (A sound hadith recorded by at-Tirmidhi)

May Allah (the Exalted) cheer up our lives with His unlimited favors and bounties and bless us with good health and inner peace. Âmeen.

Chapter Fourteen: Charity

«Abu Burdah narrated from his father, from his grandfather, that the Prophet (bpuh) said: Every Muslim has to give charity.

The people asked: O Prophet of Allah, if he cannot find that?

He said: He should work with his hands and benefit himself and also give in charity (from what he earns).

The people further asked: If he cannot find even that?

He replied: He should help the needy who appeal for help.

Then the people asked: If he cannot do even that?

He replied: Then he should perform good deeds and keep away from evil deeds, and this will be (regarded as) charity for him.» (Bukhari and Muslim)

Commentary on the hadith

Charity is not only a pillar of Islam but a moral obligation that ensures that the less fortunate – such as the weak, needy, poor and destitute, widows, and the like – are taken care of by those more fortunate. In this way, the Muslim society remains happy and secure from much of the social malaise affecting many societies that have neglected and forgotten this important duty and moral virtue.

Prophet Muhammad (bpuh) made it an obligation for every Muslim to give charity, to the extent that he said that one who has nothing to give should continuously do good deeds and refrain from evil deeds; by the mercy of Allah, that will be counted as charity.

This command that everyone must give charity is a strong encouragement for everyone to work hard and not depend on handouts. Relying on handouts can make a person so dependent on others that it can lead to obeying them instead of obeying Allah (the Exalted). As the saying goes, one cannot bite the hand that feeds him or her. This is why, when the Companions of Prophet Muhammad (bpuh) complained that the wealthy seemed to take all the rewards, he gave them a veritable solution.

«Abu Dharr (may Allah be pleased with him) reported: Some of the people from among the Companions of the Messenger of Allah (bpuh) said to him: Messenger of Allah, the rich have taken away (all) the rewards. They observe prayer as we do; they fast as we do; and they also give in charity out of their surplus wealth.

Upon hearing this, the Prophet (bpuh) said: Has Allah not prescribed for you (a means) by following which you can (also) get (the reward of) charity? In every declaration of the glorification of Allah (saying *Subḥân Allâh*, meaning "Glory be to Allah") there is a charity, and every *takbeer* (saying *Allâhu akbar*, meaning "Allah is the Greatest") is a charity, and every praise of Him (saying *Alḥamdulillâh*, meaning "all praise is for Allah") is a charity, and every declaration of faith that He is One (saying *Lâ ilâha illâ Allâh*, meaning "There is none worthy of worship other than Allah") is a charity. Enjoining what is good is a charity, forbidding what is evil is a charity, and in sexual intercourse (with one's spouse) there is a charity.

The Companions asked: Messenger of Allah, is there a reward for the person among us who satisfies his sexual passion?

He replied: Tell me, if he were to satisfy it in a forbidden way, would it not be a sin on his part? If he satisfies it in a lawful way, he shall have a reward.» (Muslim)

Charity is a very important moral virtue in a world where nearly everyone is indoctrinated – by materialism and secularism – to mind his or her own business. In many passages of the Qur'an, Allah (the Exalted), Who is All-Knowing of our behaviors and of how humanity is affected by materialism and miserliness, has enjoined us to give charity.

In the glorious Qur'an, almost every time Allah (the Exalted) commands the establishment of the prescribed prayers, He links it with the establishment of zakâh (the alms tax that is compulsory upon Muslims who have the means). Allah (the Exalted) simultaneously commands the believers to establish prayer and zakâh; these two terms are linked together in eighty-two verses. This is to emphasize an important point: that only by the sincere establishment of these two great pillars of Islam can society become morally upright.

{And they were not commanded except to worship Allah, [being] sincere to Him in religion, inclining to truth, and to establish prayer and to give zakâh; and that is the correct religion.}

(Qur'an 98: 5)

{People whom neither commerce nor merchandise can divert from the remembrance of Allah, or from regular prayer, or from the giving of zakâh. They fear a day when hearts and eyes will turn about.}

(Qur'an 24: 37)

{And establish regular prayer, and give zakâh, and obey the Messenger – that you may receive mercy.}

(Qur'an 24: 56)

{Indeed those who believe, and do deeds of righteousness, and establish regular prayers and give zakâh, will have their reward with their Lord. On them shall be no fear, nor shall they grieve.}

(Qur'an 2: 277)

{Perform prayer and give zakâh, and whatever of good [deeds] you send forth for yourselves before you, you shall find it with Allah. Certainly, Allah is All-Seeing of what you do.}

(Qur'an 2: 110)

This means that if we do good to others, Allah will in turn reward us in this life by having others do good to us; in the hereafter, Allah (the Exalted) by His grace will grant us entry into paradise, a place of eternal bliss and enjoyment.

Allah (the Exalted) has emphasized the practice of charity many times. Not only have prayers and charity been mentioned side by side eighty-two times in the Qur'an, but charity has been mentioned another sixty-two times by itself, with a promise of great rewards. Allah, the Exalted, says:

{Believe in Allah and His Messenger [Muhammad (bpuh)], and spend of that of which He has made you trustees. For those of you who believe and spend [to please Allah], there will be a great reward.}

(Qur'an 57: 7)

Similarly, Allah's Messenger (bpuh) did not encourage charity on this one occasion only. In many instances, he encouraged the practice of giving charity to the poor and needy, and he discouraged greed and miserliness in different situations and at different levels among individuals and at a societal level, as reported in Hadith literature.

«'Adiy ibn Ḥâtim (may Allah be pleased with him) narrated that he heard the Prophet (bpuh) say: Save yourself from the hellfire even if it is by giving half a date-fruit in charity.

(The narration in *Ṣaḥeeḥ Muslim* adds: And if you do not have that, then with a kind word.)» (Bukhari and Muslim)

«It was narrated that Abu Hurayrah (may Allah be pleased with him) said: A man came to the Prophet (bpuh) and asked: O Allah's Messenger, what kind of charity is the most superior in rewards?

He replied: The charity that you practice while you are healthy and inclined to stinginess, you are afraid of poverty, and you wish to live long and become wealthy. Do not delay it to the time of approaching death and then say: Give so much to such-and-such, and so much to such-and-such; by then it already belongs to So-and-so (his heirs).» (Bukhari and Muslim)

«'Â'ishah (may Allah be pleased with her) reported that Allah's Messenger (bpuh) said: When a woman gives in charity some of the foodstuff (that she has in her house) without causing any harm, she will receive the reward for what she has spent, and her husband will receive the reward because of his earning, and the storekeeper will also have a reward similar for it. The reward of one will not decrease the reward of the others.» (Bukhari)

«Ḥakeem ibn Ḥizâm (may Allah be pleased with him) narrated that the Prophet (bpuh) said: The upper hand is better than the lower hand (meaning that the person who gives charity is better than the one who takes it). One should start giving to his dependents first, and the best object of charity is that given by a wealthy person. If a person abstains from asking others for some financial help, Allah will provide for him and save him from asking others; Allah will make him self-sufficient.» (Bukhari)

«Asmâ' bint Abu Bakr (may Allah be pleased with both of them) narrated that she had gone to the Prophet (bpuh) and he told her: Do not shut your purse; otherwise Allah too will withhold His blessings from you. Spend (in Allah's cause) as much as you can afford.» (Bukhari)

In all these statements from the Prophet (bpuh), we can clearly see that Allah (the Exalted) and His Messenger (bpuh) regard charity as a visible expression of a person's love of God. Giving charity signifies that we are prepared to sacrifice every cherished thing or desire for the sake of Allah (the Exalted).

Thus, giving charity becomes a symbol or proof of our devotion to God Almighty. Since charity is an expression of a devoted and pious heart, it can therefore manifest itself in every act of piety, such as remembering Allah, performing religious duties with sincerity and a full sense of responsibility, doing good acts and encouraging others to do the same, refraining from evil and persuading others to shun it, and observing the limits imposed by Allah (the Exalted) on what is lawful and unlawful. In Islam, all these are considered as acts of charity.

In fact, the whole lifespan spent in devotion to Allah (the Exalted) is charity, for it shows the love of God. That is why Prophet Muhammad (bpuh) went as far as explaining that even lawful sexual intercourse between husband and wife is considered an act of charity that is rewarded by Allah (the Exalted).

This means that sex is not evil in itself. It is a clear proof that sex is part of the human nature implanted by Allah (the Exalted) in human beings, and that its purpose must be good: for procreation and the perpetuation of the human race and for the expression of that kind of love between husband and wife that solidifies their relationship.

{Your wealth and your children are but a trial, and Allah has with Him a great reward. So fear Allah as much as you are able, and listen and obey, and spend [in the way of Allah]; [that] is best for you. Whoever is protected from the stinginess of his soul, it is those who will be successful. If you loan Allah a goodly loan, He will multiply it for you and forgive you, and Allah is Most Appreciative and Forbearing.}

(Qur'an 64: 15-17)

We have also been dissuaded from miserliness, for those who are protected from miserliness and are charitable are indeed the successful ones, according to the preceding verse.

As Muslims, we are continuously urged to be benevolent and charitable. We are reminded always of paradise, hell, death, the Day of Judgment, and eternal life in the hereafter, in order to help us and motivate us to take control of our desires. We are also reminded that if we spend in charity to please Allah, then Allah (the Exalted) will reward us abundantly – by increasing our wealth in this world and by granting us paradise by His mercy in the hereafter.

{O you who have believed, do not let your wealth and your children divert you from the remembrance of Allah. Whoever does that, then those are the losers. Spend [in the way of Allah] from what We have provided you, before death approaches one of you and he says: My Lord, if only You would delay me for a brief term so I could give in charity and be among the righteous. But never will Allah delay a soul when its time has come, and Allah is Well-Acquainted with what you do.} *(Qur'an 63: 9-11)*

{Wealth and children are adornments of the life of this world; but the things that endure [good deeds] are best in the sight of your Lord as rewards and best as [the foundation for] hope.}

(Qur'an 18: 46)

{The likeness of those who spend their wealth in the way of Allah is like a grain [of corn]; it grows seven ears, and each ear has a hundred grains. Allah gives manifold increase to whom He wills, and Allah is All-Sufficient for His creatures' needs, Knower of everything.}

(Qur'an 2: 261)

{...Whatever you spend of anything in Allah's because, He will replace it; and He is the best of providers.}

(Qur'an 34: 39)

When we read such beautiful passages from the Qur'an that are full of promises of great rewards in paradise, and we read the many hadiths from Muhammad (bpuh), such as those quoted above, they act as reminders to inculcate good manners and moral values in our lives as well as in our community. It is this which consequently makes life happier and worth living.

Chapter Fifteen: Cooperation

It was narrated by Nu'mân ibn Basheer (may Allah be pleased with him) that the Prophet (bpuh) said:

«The situation of the person abiding by Allah's orders and limits, in comparison to the one who does wrong and violates Allah's orders and limits, is like the example of people drawing lots for seats in a boat. Some of them get seats in the upper part, while the others get seats in the lower part. Those in the lower part have to pass by those in the upper one to get water, and that troubles the latter.

One of the people (in the lower part) takes an axe and starts making a hole in the bottom of the boat.

The people of the upper part come and ask him: What is wrong with you?

He replies: You have been troubled much by me (coming up to your section), and I have to get water.

Now if the people of the upper part prevent him from doing what he is doing, they will save him and themselves, but if they leave him (to do what he wants), then they will all be destroyed.» (Bukhari)

Commentary on the hadith

In this example of those who are mindful of the limits set by Allah (the Exalted) for His creation and those who are careless about guarding the limits set by Allah (the Exalted) in this world, the Prophet (bpuh) in his most eloquent way has taught us several lessons, including the fact that cooperation in good works is the key to a healthy, vibrant, peaceful, and morally upright society. When the rich and fortunate are mindful of the state of the poor and needy in society, when they do not feel tired or bothered about taking care of the basic necessities of life for the less fortunate, then the poor and needy will respect those who are well-to-do.

The poor will know that their needs are being considered and taken care of and that they will not be left and forgotten, languishing in the doldrums of poverty. Then the poor and needy will work hand-in-hand with the rich because they do not feel that they have been despised or looked down upon by the rich, and the rich will not feel any pride in their hearts since they will all be sharing common facilities.

Thus, when the rich and poor cooperate with each other in good works, the rich taking care of the poor and the poor respecting the rich, within the limits ordained by Allah (the Exalted), there will be minimal crime and immorality. That is why Allah (the Exalted) has expressly directed us to cooperate and help each other in good works and piety but not to help each other in sin, transgression, or enmity:

{...Cooperate with one another on the basis of righteousness and piety; do not cooperate with one another on the basis of sin and enmity. And fear Allah; indeed Allah is severe in punishment.}

(Qur'an 5: 2)

Part of cooperating with each other for mutual good and benefit, as we learn from this hadith, is advising one another against moral corruption both on an individual level and a community level. If those who are intent on corrupting the society through their greed and desires are not prevented from doing so, then the whole society will go into ruin.

This applies to the wealthy in society, who enjoy their riches and luxuries while the needy are starving to death without food, clothing, or shelter. This can lead to the less fortunate resorting to theft and robbery with violence simply in order to keep alive, in which case the society will degenerate into lawlessness. It is for this reason that Allah's Messenger (bpuh) is reported by Abu Dharr (may Allah be pleased with him) to have said:

«If you cook some soup, add extra water and send some to your neighbor.» (A sound hadith recorded by Ibn Mâjah)

In another narration, Ibn 'Umar (may Allah be pleased with both of them) reported that the Messenger of Allah (bpuh) said:

«Angel Gabriel kept on enjoining the good treatment of neighbors until I thought he would order me to include them as heirs.» (Bukhari)

As human beings, we are not all created alike, with all the same capabilities and dispositions. Allah (the Exalted) – in His perfect knowledge, power, and wisdom – has deliberately made some excel in terms of wealth, intelligence, children, knowledge, power, and so on. Some people have been made weak, poor, needy, orphans, widows, and the like, so that we all may realize the need to assist and cooperate with each other in goodness and piety rather than sin and transgression.

{Is it they who portion out the mercy of your Lord? It is We who have portioned out among them their livelihood in the life of this world and have raised some of them above others in degrees [of rank, capabilities, wealth, and so on] that they may make use of one another for service; but the mercy of your Lord is better than all that they amass.}

(Qur'an 43: 32)

This suggests that people are not created all alike in their dispositions and capabilities (neither are countries or nations). If people were all alike in their disposition then they would not need any service or help from each other. God has created people with different physical, spiritual, intellectual and emotional capabilities. And for countries and nations, Allah has given them different natural resources and capabilities, and different languages and cultures.

Therefore, Allah (the Exalted) has deliberately made some superior in some ways and others superior in other ways. He has made all need each other in a unique and natural way. This is thus the social or interconnected life of human beings.

People, communities and nations in the world are therefore naturally in need of one another for their mutual benefit. This is why withdrawal from society is not encouraged in Islam. No one should just disappear into his or her green and luscious valley and forget about others. A community, society or country will suffer if it tries to exist in isolation from other communities, societies or countries.

Since humanity was created in a naturally good state with abilities and a mind to do good or evil, the purpose of the community and society is to promote and work for all that which is good and help humanity enhance its good nature and overcome the inclination to do evil.[51]

The need for such interaction and cooperation is what Allah's Messenger (bpuh) expressed in the beautiful parable that is being discussed in this chapter.

Spouses should cooperate in bringing up a morally upright family; citizens should cooperate with their leaders in developing an upright and vibrant stable society that is free from immorality; and masters should cooperate with their servants in discharging their duties, especially if they have been given a hard or difficult task. Parents should cooperate with their children in order to guide them through their youth to grow up as responsible human beings.

Teachers should cooperate with their students, their fellow teachers, and the administration in order to succeed in imparting to the pupils correct and beneficial knowledge, positive attitudes, and discipline. Politicians should cooperate with the general population, especially those in their constituencies, in order to discharge their duties and spread justice in the land... and the list goes on.

Cooperation is a moral virtue that, if properly understood and internalized, will reform the whole society and improve the wellbeing of everyone in the community.

Chapter Sixteen: Justice

'Amr ibn Aws narrated from a chain leading to Zuhayr that the Messenger of Allah (bpuh) said:

«Those who are fair and just will be near Allah, on thrones or pulpits of light by the right Hand of the Most Merciful (Allah), Glorified and Exalted is He – and both His Hands are right,[52] those who deal justly in their decisions with their families and all that they are in charge of.» (Muslim)

Commentary on the hadith

Justice is one of those moral virtues which every society and culture advocate, yet it is lacking in many societies. In this hadith, Prophet Muhammad (bpuh) has promised those who dispense justice in all their dealings with their families and those under their authority, and who are fair in all their decisions, that they will be rewarded with paradise and will be on thrones or pulpits of light near Allah (the Exalted). This is because justice – at all levels and in all its various forms – is close to piety and righteousness, as Allah (the Exalted) described it in a number of passages in the noble Qur'an:

{O you who believe, stand out firmly for Allah, as witnesses to fair dealing, and let not the hatred of a people make you depart from justice. Be just; that is nearer to piety, and fear Allah. Indeed Allah is Well-Acquainted with what you do.}

(Qur'an 5: 8)

Justice is a spiritual, moral, socio-economic, and political virtue. It is aptly described by Allah (the Exalted) and His Messenger (bpuh) as a means of dealing fairly in all matters in society without allowing our souls to follow our vain desires and to thereby veer away from fair dealing. Justice should be applied with everyone, including oneself and one's family, neighbors, workmates, friends, and enemies. Because Allah (the Exalted) is the wisest and most just in all His dealings with His creation, He therefore described those who dispense justice as His own witnesses who stand up by Him in all their fair dealings. That is why justice is not an easy affair except for those who fear Allah, and it is why its meritorious rewards are immense. Allah, the Exalted, says:

{Verily, Allah enjoins justice and iḥsân [being patient in performing your duties to Allah, totally for Allah's sake and in accordance with the Sunnah of the Prophet (bpuh) in a perfect manner] and giving to relatives[53] [by giving them all the rights that Allah has ordered you to give them, such as wealth, visiting, looking after them, and any other kind of help they need] and forbids all evil deeds [and all that is prohibited by Islamic law] and all kinds of oppression. He admonishes you, that you may take heed.}

(Qur'an 16: 90)

Justice, as spoken of in the hadith under discussion and as implied by the meritorious rewards promised for those who dispense it, is an all-inclusive and all-embracing socio-moral virtue.

Justice in spiritual matters

On a spiritual level, believers have to be just and fair with themselves by not overburdening themselves with respect to devotional acts of worship. On a number of occasions, Allah's Messenger (bpuh) forbade his Companions from overdoing acts of worship to an extent that they would not be able to continue with; he recommended that they be fair and just to themselves with regard to devoting some of their energy and time to worshiping Allah (the Exalted).

«The Prophet (bpuh) established a bond of brotherhood between Salmân (may Allah be pleased with him) and Abu ad-Dardâ' (may Allah be pleased with him).

Salmân paid a visit to Abu ad-Dardâ' and found Umm ad-Dardâ' dressed in shabby clothes and asked her why she was in that state.

She replied: Your brother Abu ad-Dardâ' is not interested in the luxuries of this world.

In the meantime, Abu ad-Dardâ' came (back), prepared a meal for Salmân and said to him: Please eat, for I am fasting.

Salmân said: I am not going to eat unless you eat.

So Abu ad-Dardâ' ate.

When it was night, Abu ad-Dardâ' got up (for the night prayer).

Salmân said to him: Sleep.

So he slept.

Again Abu ad-Dardâ' got up (for the prayer), and Salmân said to him: Sleep.

When it was the last part of the night, Salmân said to him: Get up now (for the prayer).

So both of them offered their prayers, and Salmân said to Abu ad-Dardâ': Your Lord has a right on you; your soul has a right on you; and your family has a right on you; so you should give the rights to all those who have a right on you.

Later on, Abu ad-Dardâ' visited the Prophet (bpuh) and mentioned that to him.

The Prophet (bpuh) said: Salmân has spoken the truth.» (Bukhari and at-Tirmidhi)

«Anas ibn Mâlik (may Allah be pleased with him) narrated that a group of three men came to the houses of the wives of the Prophet asking about how the Prophet (bpuh) worshipped (Allah)

When they were informed about that, they considered their worship insufficient and said: Where are we with respect to the Prophet (bpuh), as his past and future sins have been forgiven?

Then one of them said: I will offer the prayer throughout the night forever.

The other said: I will fast throughout the year and will not break my fast.

The third said: I will keep away from women and will never marry.

Allah's Messenger (bpuh) came to them and said: Are you the same people who said such-and-such? By Allah, I am more fearful of Allah and more conscious of Him than you. Yet, I fast and break my fast; I pray and I sleep; and I also marry women. Therefore, whoever turns away from my way of life is not from me (not one of my followers).» (Bukhari)

«Abu 'Uthmân narrated from Ḥandhalah al-Usaydi (may Allah be pleased with him) – one of the scribes of Allah's Messenger (bpuh) – that Abu Bakr (may Allah be pleased with him) came across him once and found him (Ḥandhalah) weeping.

So Abu Bakr asked him: What is wrong with you, Ḥandhalah?

He replied: Abu Bakr, Ḥandhalah has become a hypocrite! When we are with the Messenger of Allah (bpuh), we remember the fire and paradise as if we are looking at them with the naked eye, but when we return, we busy ourselves with our wives and livelihood and we forget so much.

Abu Bakr said: By Allah! The same thing happens to me. Let us go to the Messenger of Allah (bpuh).

[So they went.]

When the Messenger of Allah (bpuh) saw Ḥandhalah, he asked: What is wrong with you, Ḥandhalah?

He said: O Messenger of Allah, Ḥandhalah has become a hypocrite! When we are with you, we remember the fire and paradise as if we can see them with the naked eye, but when we return we are busy with our wives and livelihood, and we forget so much.

So the Messenger of Allah (bpuh) said: If you were to continually abide in the same state that you are in when you are with me, then the angels would shake hands with you in your gatherings, in your homes, and on the streets!

But, Ḥandhalah, there is time for this and time for that –

and Allah's Messenger repeated that final statement three times.» (Muslim and at-Tirmidhi)

Justice in moral matters

On an individual level, people have to be truthful, honest, sincere, and just, both in their speech and actions, even if the truth goes against themselves or against their parents, relatives or friends, be they rich or poor. This is what ensures fairness and justice to oneself and the society. Allah (the Exalted) says about this kind of honesty, sincerity, and justice with oneself:

{O you who believe, stand out firmly for justice, as witnesses to Allah, even if it be against yourselves, or your parents, or your relatives, and whether it be [against] rich or poor, for Allah can best protect both. Follow not the lusts [of your hearts] lest you swerve [from justice and doing right], and if you distort [justice] or decline to do justice, verily Allah is Well-Acquainted with what you do.}

(Qur'an 4: 135)

Justice in economic affairs

Even in our daily business dealings, we must conduct business in a just and honest manner that does not harm anyone in our society. There should be no exploitation of one another such that the rich become richer and the poor become poorer, thereby widening the gap between rich and poor and encouraging crime and lawlessness in society. Allah (the Exalted) warned those who are not honest in their business deals and those who do not measure their goods equitably; He mentioned those who short-change customers in their business transactions, but who demand full measure when they extract their own due. Allah, the Exalted, says:

{Woe to those who give less [than due],⁵⁴ those who, when they take a measure from people, take in full; but if they give by measure or by weight to them, they cause loss [by giving less than due]. Do they not think that they will be resurrected for a tremendous day – the day when humankind will stand before the Lord of the Universe [and be held accountable]?}

(Qur'an 83: 1-6)

It was also narrated from Ḥakeem ibn Ḥizâm (may Allah be pleased with him) that the Prophet (bpuh) said:

«The two parties to a transaction have the option (of cancelling it) until they part. If they are honest and they disclose any defects, their transaction will be blessed, but if they lie and conceal defects, the blessing will be erased.» (Muslim)

In several passages in the glorious Qur'an, Allah (the Exalted) mentions economic justice in business transactions and payment of debts, saying that we should deal justly and fairly in mutual trade among ourselves and not exploit each other. Allah's Messenger Muhammad (bpuh) also encouraged fair dealing in business, for certainly unfair dealings and exploitation only deprive us of Allah's blessings in our businesses.

{O you who believe, when you contract a debt for a fixed period of time, write it down. Let a scribe write it down between you justly and faithfully. Let not the scribe refuse to write, as Allah has taught him, so let him write. Let him who incurs the liability dictate, but let him fear his Lord Allah, and not diminish anything of what he owes. If the debtor is poor in understanding, or weak, or is unable to dictate for himself, let his guardian dictate faithfully and justly. Get two witnesses, out of your own men, and if there are not two men, then a man and two women, such as you choose for witnesses, so that if one of them errs, the other can remind her. The witnesses should not refuse when they are called on [for evidence]. Do not disdain to write down [your contract] for a future period, whether it is small or big. It is more just in the sight of Allah, more suitable as evidence, and more convenient to prevent doubts among yourselves. If it is a transaction which you carry out on the spot among yourselves, there is no blame on you if you do not write it, but take witnesses whenever you make a commercial contract, and let neither scribe nor witness suffer any harm. If you do [harm them], it would be wickedness in you. So fear Allah; for it is Allah that teaches you, and Allah is Well-Acquainted with all things.}

(Qur'an 2: 282)

{O you who believe, do not consume your property among yourselves unjustly, but only [in lawful] commerce amongst you by mutual consent. Do not kill yourselves [or one another].

Verily Allah has been Most Merciful to you. And whoever commits that through aggression and injustice, We shall cast him into the fire, and that is easy for Allah.}

(Qur'an 4: 29-30)

«It was narrated from Ismâ'eel ibn 'Ubayd ibn Rifâ'ah that his grandfather Rifâ'ah (may Allah be pleased with him) said: We went out with the Messenger of Allah (bpuh), and the people were trading in the early morning.

He called to them: O merchants!

When they looked up and craned their necks (straining to hear him), he said: The merchants will be raised on the Day of Resurrection as immoral people, except for those who fear Allah and act righteously and speak the truth (are honest and just in their business dealings).» (A reliable hadith recorded by Ibn Mâjah)

'Uthmân ibn 'Affân (may Allah be pleased with him) narrated that the Messenger of Allah (bpuh) said:

«Allah will admit to paradise a person who is lenient when buying and selling.» (A sound hadith recorded by Ibn Mâjah)

In yet another passage, Allah (the Exalted) directed us to be just and fair when handling the property of orphans, when dealing with weights and measurements, and when we speak and use persuasive language in selling our items of trade. This is part of the economic justice discussed in this section. Allah, the Exalted, says:

{Do not approach the orphan's property, except to improve it, until he [or she] attains the age of maturity. Give measure and weight with [full] justice. No burden do We place on any soul, except that which it can bear. Whenever you speak, speak justly, even if a near relative is concerned, and fulfil the covenant of Allah. This He commands you that you may remember.}

(Qur'an 6: 152)

It was narrated from Abu Qatâdah (may Allah be pleased with him) that the Messenger of Allah (bpuh) said:

«Beware of swearing oaths when selling, for it may help you to make a sale, but it destroys the blessing.» (A sound hadith recorded by Ibn Mâjah)

Justice in political affairs

Politicians and lawyers, accountants and financial controllers, CEOs and other people who hold influential positions in government and private sectors in society must be honest and just in their work. They must render trusts back to those to whom they are due. Otherwise they will go against the balance of justice, cause corruption in the land, and create turmoil in society. Allah, the Exalted, says:

{Verily, Allah commands that you should render back the trusts to those to whom they are due, and that when you judge between people, judge with justice. How excellent is the teaching which He [Allah] gives you! Truly, Allah is Ever All--Hearing, All--Seeing.}

(Qur'an 4: 58)

Governments and government officials must dispense justice by giving their citizens basic human rights. This includes helping citizens acquire the basic necessities of life, including food, education, housing, medical care, and so on, in an equitable manner without discrimination. This is part of rendering back the trust and covenant which they have taken from Allah (the Exalted) and from those people who elected them to their positions of power and authority. Allah (the Exalted) mentions:

{We did indeed offer the trust to the heavens and the earth and the mountains, but they refused to undertake it, being afraid of it. But humans undertook it, and they were indeed unjust and ignorant. [The result is] that Allah will punish the hypocrites, men and women, and those men and women who associate partners with Allah; and Allah accepts repentance from the believers, men and women. And Allah is Oft-Forgiving, Most Merciful.}

(Qur'an 33: 72-73)

«It was narrated that 'Adiy ibn 'Amirah al-Kindi heard Allah's Messenger (bpuh) say: Whenever we appoint one of you to any task, and he conceals a needle or more (for his own personal benefit), it is (the same as) stolen spoils of war that he will bring (for account) on the Day of Resurrection.

A black man from among the Anṣâr stood up – it is as if I can see him now – and he said: O Allah's Messenger, take back from me your assignment.

He said: Why are you saying that?

He said: I heard you saying such-and-such (and I fear for myself, even if done inadvertently).

The Messenger (bpuh) said: I say it (again) now. If anyone among you is appointed to do any task, let him bring (to account) everything, small or large. If anything is given to him, let him take it; but if anything is forbidden to him, let him refrain (from it).» (Muslim)

«It was narrated that al-Ḥasan said: 'Ubaydullâh ibn Ziyâd visited Ma'qil ibn Yasâr al-Muzani during his final sickness.

Ma'qil said: I am going to tell you of a hadith that I heard from Allah's Messenger (bpuh). If I knew that I was going to live, I would not tell it to you. I heard Allah's Messenger (bpuh) say: Any person whom Allah puts in charge of others and who dies while he has cheated his subjects, Allah will forbid paradise to him.» (Muslim)

It is precisely for this reason that Allah (the Exalted) sent prophets and messengers with revelation and legislation from Him, so that various governments could rule according to Allah's laws and regulations so as to dispense justice and fairness in their governance. Allah, the Exalted, says:

{We have already sent Our messengers with clear evidence and sent down with them the Scripture and the balance [of justice], that the people may maintain [their affairs] in justice...}

(Qur'an 57: 25)

{It is Allah Who has sent down the Book in truth and [also] the balance [of justice]. And what will make you realize that perhaps the Hour is near? Those who do not believe in it [the Hour] are impatient for it, but those who believe are fearful of it and know that it is the truth. Without doubt, those who dispute concerning the Hour are in extreme error. Allah is Subtle [kind and gentle] with His servants. He gives provision to whom He wills, and He is the Powerful, the Exalted in Might. Whoever desires the [good] harvest of the hereafter, We increase for him his harvest [or reward]. And whoever desires the harvest [or benefits] of this world, We give him some of it, but there is not for him in the hereafter any share [of good].}

(Qur'an 42: 17-20)

Justice in social affairs

When we look at the tendencies around the world: increasing crime rates, wars between nations, terrorist acts of extreme violence, insecurity, biting poverty and malnourishment of human beings in many communities, the suffering of ordinary people in every country in the contemporary world, the global economic crisis that leads many societies to crime and violence, misery, bitterness, and a lack of happiness... all are attributable to oppression and lack of justice.

Oppression may be defined as violating the limits of or taking away peoples' God-given rights. Oppression or injustice can oc-cur at different levels. It may begin at the individual level, where-in one oppresses him/herself by overtaxing his/her body or deny-ing his/her human nature. On a state level, oppression can be most abusive, for it can lead to mass destruction and terror.

The world today is full of all forms of oppression and injustice. It is in the international arena of big and powerful nations coerc-ing small and weak ones into political and economic subjugation and enslavement. It is on a national level where corrupt and dicta-torial governments constantly violate human rights in all areas of human life: political, economic, or otherwise. People blackmail or attack each other's character for political mileage, power, wealth, or influence. Indeed, one of the most poisonous habits, inherent in our contemporary society, is oppression and injustice.

Businesspeople oppress each other and as a consequence, they end up exploiting everyone. Most governments in the world today commit all kinds of injustices and oppression against their citi-zens, which translates to bad governance and dictatorship. Mar-ried couples oppress each other in one way or another, sometimes in the form of domestic abuse. Laborers are oppressed at work; they are deprived of their due rights commensurate with their pro-duction output. Hence, we see strikes and demonstrations at gov-ernment and private institutions, and we hear of trade unions cry-ing foul.

Parents at home similarly oppress their children, and the list goes on and on. Little wonder then that there is no true peace and happiness in the world today.[55]

Allah (the Exalted) placed a balance of justice in the universe; that is why we find that at the cosmic level, there is no chaos of any kind. The planets, the sun, the moon, and the earth, as well as other stars, all swim in their fixed orbits according to the predetermined balance that Allah (the Exalted) placed in His creation. In contrast, when we look at human beings, who were given intellect and the responsibility of taking care of themselves and other creatures, we see nothing but chaos. This is because human beings think they are clever; they have gone against the balance placed in this creation, otherwise called the ecosystem, and have followed their whims and desires. Allah, the Exalted, says:

{The Entirely Merciful [Allah] taught the Qur'an, created man, [and] taught him eloquence. The sun and the moon [move] by precise calculation, and the stars and trees prostrate [to Allah].[56] He raised the heaven and imposed the balance so that you do not transgress in the balance, so establish [measuring] the weight [of all matters] in justice, and do not make the balance deficient.}

(Qur'an 55: 1-9)

Chapter Seventeen: Forgiveness

«Abu Is-ḥâq reported that he heard Abu 'Abdullâh al-Jadali narrate: I asked 'Â'ishah about the character of the Messenger of Allah (bpuh).

She said: He was not obscene, or uttering obscenities, or yelling in the markets. He would not return an evil with an evil, but rather he was pardoning and forgiving.» (A sound hadith recorded by at-Tirmidhi)

Commentary on the hadith

This was the excellent character of Allah's Messenger (bpuh), and Allah (the Exalted) directed the Messenger's Companions (may Allah be pleased with all of them) and the Muslims who would come after them to emulate it:

{You have indeed in the Messenger of Allah (bpuh) a beautiful pattern [of conduct] to emulate, for anyone whose hope is in Allah and the Final Day, and who engages much in the remembrance [and praise] of Allah.}

(Qur'an 33: 21)

The Prophet (bpuh) was known for his leniency. He pardoned most of the mistakes of his Companions, and Allah (the Exalted) bore witness to the Prophet's excellent behavior towards his Companions and the whole of humankind. Allah, the Exalted, mentions:

{Verily, there has come to you a Messenger [Muhammad (bpuh)] from amongst yourselves. It grieves him that you should receive any injury or difficulty. He [Muhammad (bpuh)] is ardently anxious about you [to be rightly guided, to repent to Allah, to beg Him to pardon and forgive your sins in order that you may enter paradise and be saved from the punishment of the hellfire]; to the believers, he is full of pity, most kind, and merciful.}

(Qur'an 9: 128)

{So by the mercy of Allah, you [Muhammad (bpuh)] dealt gently with them. Had you been severe and harsh-hearted, they would have broken away from about you. So pass over [their faults], and ask for [Allah's] forgiveness for them, and consult with them in the matter. Then when you have made a decision, put your trust in Allah. Certainly Allah loves those who put their trust [in Him].}

(Qur'an 3: 159)

No human being is perfect. All children of Adam are prone to make mistakes and to offend each other in one way or another. We are emotional creatures who become angry and falter in our interaction with each other. As such, we are bound to wrong and offend each other, for the Prophet (bpuh) said:

«All of Adam's descendants are prone to error, and the best of the error-prone are those who are often repentant.» (A reliable hadith recorded by Ibn Mâjah)

The strong ones are those who pardon and forgive their fellow human beings. Overlooking and pardoning those who have wronged and offended us is not a point of weakness, as wrongly construed by many. In reality, forgiving peoples' mistakes is a great moral virtue, as can be seen from the lives of the prophets and messengers of God.

Prophet Joseph (pbuh) forgave his brothers, who had first plotted to kill him but later decided to leave him to be sold as a slave. Allah, the Exalted, says:

{Verily in Joseph and his brothers are signs [lessons, proofs, evidence, and symbols] for seekers [of truth]. [Remember] when they [Joseph's brothers] said: Truly, Joseph and his brother [Benjamin] are dearer to our father than we, while we are a stronger group. Really, our father is in plain error. Kill Joseph or cast him out to some [other] land, so that the favor of your father may be for all of you only, and after that you will be a righteous folk [by intending repentance before committing the sin]. One of them said: Do not kill Joseph. If you must do something, then throw him down to the bottom of a well; he will be picked up by some caravan of travelers. They said: O our father, why do you not trust us with Joseph when we are indeed his well-wishers? Send him with us tomorrow to enjoy himself and play, and we will take care of him. He [Jacob] said: Truly, it saddens me that you should take him away. I fear that a wolf might devour him while you are careless about him. They replied: If a wolf devours him while we are such a strong group [to guard him], then surely we are the losers. So when they took him away and they all agreed to throw him down to the bottom of the well [and they did so]. We revealed to him [Joseph]: Indeed, you shall [one day] inform them of this their affair, when they do not know you. And they came weeping to their father in the early part of the night.} (Qur'an 12: 7-16)

{They said: O our father! We went racing with one other, and left Joseph by our belongings, and a wolf devoured him, but you will never believe us even when we speak the truth. They brought his shirt stained with false blood. He said: No, but you have made up a tale. So [for me] beautiful patience is most fitting, and it is Allah [alone] Whose help can be sought against that [lie] which you describe. There came a caravan of travelers, and they sent their water-drawer, and he let down his bucket [into the well]. He said: What good news! Here is a boy. So they hid him as merchandise [to sell as a slave]. Allah was All-Knower of what they did. They sold him for a low price, for a few dirhams [silver coins], and they were of those who regarded him as insignificant.}

(Qur'an 12: 17-20)

{Then [years later] when [the brothers] met [with Joseph], they said: O ruler of the land! A hard time has hit us and our family. We have brought but poor capital, so pay us full measure and be charitable to us. Truly, Allah does reward the charitable. He asked: Do you know what you did to Joseph and his [other] brother [Benjamin, whom they also wronged because he was so beloved by his father], when you were ignorant? They asked: Are you indeed Joseph? He replied: I am Joseph, and this is my brother [Benjamin]. Allah has indeed been gracious to us [and blessed us far above you]. Verily, he who fears Allah with obedience to Him and is patient, then surely, Allah does not let the reward of the good-doers to be lost. They said: By Allah! Indeed Allah has preferred you over us, and we certainly have been sinners. He said: No reproach for you this day; may Allah forgive you, and He is the Most Merciful of those who show mercy!}

(Qur'an 12: 88-92)

In other examples of forgiveness from the prophets, Prophet Muhammad (bpuh) forgave the people of Taif who threw stones at him when he went to preach to them the message of accepting the belief in one God and shunning the worship of their idols. He also forgave the idolaters of Makkah, who persecuted him for thirteen long years, plotted to assassinate him and eventually drove him out of his homeland, Makkah.

«Abu Hurayrah (may Allah be pleased with him) reported: It was said to Allah's Messenger (bpuh): O Messenger of Allah, pray against the idolaters.

He said: I was not sent as an invoker of curses; I was sent as a mercy (to guide people).» (Muslim)

Why should we not forgive each other if this is the way of the prophets of God, who were wronged in various ways but were humble enough to overlook and pardon those who wronged and persecuted them? Furthermore, Allah (the Exalted) says that good words and forgiveness of each other's faults are better than charity given as a way of showing off:

{Kind words and forgiving of faults are better than charity followed by injury. Allah is Rich [Free of all wants], and He is Most-Forbearing.}

(Qur'an 2: 263)

If we truly want Allah (the Exalted) to forgive us our daily sins and shortcomings, then we must be ready to pardon and forgive those who have wronged us. We should not hold grudges against people for many months and years, not wanting to let go and reconcile with them. Indeed, if Allah were to hold us responsible for all that we do against our fellow human beings, and even the wrongs we do to ourselves, He would not let any creature live on the face of the earth.

{If Allah were to punish the people for their wrongdoing, He would not leave on it [the earth] a single living creature; but He gives them respite for a stated term. When their term expires, neither can they delay nor can they advance it an hour [or a moment].}

(Qur'an 16: 61)

{If Allah were to punish the people according to what they deserve, He would not leave on the surface of the [earth] a single living creature, but He gives them respite for a stated term. When their term expires, verily [they will know that] Allah is Seeing of all [that concerns] His servants.}

(Qur'an 35: 45)

If we truly want to be pardoned for our own many mistakes and shortcomings, we must learn how to swallow our pride; conquer our egos; and forgive, overlook, and pardon our fellow human beings – however much they may have wronged us – as Allah (the Exalted) and His Messenger Muhammad (bpuh) have directed us. Allah, the Exalted, says:

{Whatever you have been given [here on Earth] is [but] a convenience of this life, but that which is with Allah is better and more lasting. [It is] for those who believe and put their trust in their Lord, those who avoid the greater crimes and shameful deeds, and, when they are angry, even then forgive.}

(Qur'an 42: 36-37)

Allah (the Exalted) praised and promised great rewards for those who, when they become angry, pardon and forgive their fellow human beings. Forgiveness is an indication of strength and not weakness, as we have already pointed out. Allah, the Exalted, says:

{...And those who restrain anger and pardon [other] people; for Allah loves the good-doers.}

(Qur'an 3: 134)

It was narrated by Abu Hurayrah (may Allah be pleased with him) that Allah's Messenger (bpuh) said:

«Charity does not decrease wealth. If anyone forgives, Allah increases his honor, and no one humbles himself for the sake of Allah except that Allah raises him in status.» (Muslim and at-Tirmidhi)

Chapter Eighteen: Love

Abu Hurayrah (may Allah be pleased with him) narrated that the Messenger of Allah (bpuh) said:

«Allah will say on the Day of Resurrection: Where are the two who loved one another for my sake? Today I will shade them with My shade, on a day when there will be no shade but My shade.» (Muslim)

Commentary on the hadith

True love of one human being by another is a manifestation of Allah's attribute of perfect love for His creation. Thus, any kind of love that does not emanate from our belief in God is false love. Allah (the Exalted) apportioned some part of His perfect attribute of love in the hearts of humans, and this manifests itself as emotions of love. That is why, in the above hadith, Allah's Messenger (bpuh) has expressly said that those who truly love each other based on belief in Allah – meaning that their love for each other is not for worldly gain, fortune, or any other worldly reason, but only in order to please Allah and gain his pleasure – will be saved on the terrifying Day of Judgment.

{O humankind, fear your Lord. Indeed, the convulsion of the [final] Hour is a terrible thing. On that day when you behold it, every nursing mother will forget that [child] she was nursing, every pregnant woman will spontaneously abort her pregnancy, and you will see the people [appearing] intoxicated while they are not intoxicated; oh, but the punishment of Allah will be severe!}

(Qur'an 22: 1-2)

It is a day when the surface of the earth will be turned into metal, the sun will be close over our heads, and people will be drowning in their sweat according to their sins. People will act as if they are drunk, yet they will not be drunk. Rather, the day and its terror will be too heavy to handle, as Allah (the Exalted) described in the preceding verse. Allah's Messenger (bpuh) also described that day to us:

«Al-Miqdâd ibn al-Aswad (may Allah be pleased with him) narrated that he heard the Messenger of Allah (bpuh) say: The sun will be brought near to the people on the Day of Resurrection, until it is one *mil'* away from them.

– Sulaym ibn 'Âmir said: By Allah, I do not know what he meant by the word *mil'*: was it a measure of distance (like a mile) or the stick which is used to apply kohl to the eyes? –

And the people will be submerged in sweat according to their deeds. For some it will come up to their ankles, for some it will come up to their knees, and for some it will come up to their mouths.

And the Messenger of Allah (bpuh) pointed with his hand to his mouth.» (Muslim)

Another statement from Allah's Messenger (bpuh) explains that on this dreadful day, seven categories of people will be under the shade of Allah (the Exalted) on a day in which there will be no shade except the shade of His throne. One of the categories mentioned is two people who loved each other only for the sake of Allah (the Exalted), always meeting and departing from each for the sake of Allah.

«Abu Hurayrah (may Allah be pleased with him) narrated that the Prophet (bpuh) said: There are seven whom Allah will shade with His shade on the day when there will be no shade but His: a just ruler; a young person who grows up worshipping Allah; a man whose heart is attached to the mosques; two people who love one another for the sake of Allah, who meet and part on that basis; a man who is called (to sin) by a woman of status and beauty, but he (abstains and) says: I fear Allah; a person who gives charity so secretly that his left hand does not know what his right hand is giving; and a person who remembers Allah when he is alone and his eyes fill with tears.» (Bukhari and Muslim)

This is how great the concept of genuinely 'loving one another for the sake of Allah' is in the sight of Allah (the Exalted). People who truly love each other are compassionate and merciful to each other. They respect each other and do not hurt each other's feelings. They care about each other in a special way and fulfil each other's needs to the best of their abilities, within the boundaries of Allah's laws. They are kind, considerate, and sympathetic to each other in all circumstances. In short, they please each other as long as it does not go against the Sharia of Allah (the Exalted). They love for one another what they love for themselves, as Allah's Messenger (bpuh) said:

«None of you is a believer until he loves for his brother what he loves for himself.» (Bukhari and Muslim)

Anyone who does not feel such love must question and evaluate his or her own faith. Nevertheless, one should not think that he or she is not a believer. Sincere love for the sake of Allah (the Exalted) is not easy to achieve, except for one who is pure of heart, who has attained a high spiritual level, and who knows that this world is insignificant compared to the pleasure of Allah (the Exalted). Hence, people's rewards will be commensurate with the spiritual level that they attained in this world. Mu'âdh ibn Jabal (may Allah be pleased with him) narrated that Allah's Messenger (bpuh) said:

«Allah, the Mighty and Sublime, said: Those who love each other for the sake of My Majesty shall be upon podiums (or thrones) of light, and they will be admired by the prophets and the martyrs.» (A sound hadith recorded by at-Tirmidhi)

The English translator of *Jâmi' at-Tirmidhi* made a good comment about the above hadith:

To love someone for no other reason than for the sake of Allah's might and majesty – a distinct mark of a true believer – is an act that wins the approval and appreciation of Allah and endears the concerned individuals to Him, so that they will be placed on podiums of light, whose enchanting beauty shall even draw the admiration and envy of the prophets and martyrs, although their own ranks would be much higher and superior to those individuals.[57]

Furthermore, we should never undervalue the importance of loving each other for the sake of Allah (the Exalted), since it is this true love that brings closeness and friendship among the believers. That feeling of closeness manifests itself in how we care for each other, which consequently earns Allah's pleasure and love and entry into paradise. Abu Hurayrah (may Allah be pleased with him) narrated that Allah's Messenger (bpuh) said:

«When Allah loves a person, He calls Gabriel (pbuh) and says: I love So-and-so, so love him.

So Gabriel loves him, and then he calls out to the people of the heaven: Allah loves So-and-so, so love him.

So the people of the heaven love him, and he (also) finds acceptance on earth.

If Allah hates someone, He calls Gabriel and says: I hate so-and so, so hate him.

So Gabriel hates him, and then he calls out to the people of the heaven: Allah hates So-and-so, so hate him.

So they hate him, and he is hated on Earth.» (Bukhari and Muslim)

It was also narrated from Abu Hurayrah (may Allah be pleased with him) from the Prophet (bpuh):

«A man visited a brother of his in another town, and Allah sent an angel to wait for him on the road. When the man came to him, the angel asked: Where are you headed?

He said: I am headed to my brother in this town.

The angel asked: Have you done him any favor for which you hope to be recompensed?

He said: No, but I love him for the sake of Allah.

The angel said: I am a messenger from Allah to you, to tell you that Allah loves you as you love this person for His sake.» (Muslim)

Amira Ayad, in her health science guidebook, *Healing Body & Soul*, mentions a unique incident related to true love among Muslim brothers and sisters, which is worth mentioning here. She says:

To love [in the true Islamic meaning] is to relate everything we love to Allah and avoid associating worldly partners and idols with Him. This higher meaning of love takes it beyond mere human relations into a more sacred and spiritual level. I have heard the expression 'to love for the sake of Allah' many times before, but I did not truly understand its meaning until recently. I met a group of enthusiastic young women who were preparing for a conference about true Islamic relationships and morality. The organizers lived in different countries and communicated through e-mail; they had never met before, but they were all so dedicated and believed so much in the Islamic values they were teaching, that they had experienced an incredibly strong bonding, connecting their souls. They met each other for the first time at the conference and lived together for only one week; a week of hard work and extreme dedication. At the end of the conference, I saw them crying because they were soon to be separated. I felt true love, a divine affection that bonded their hearts and freed it from all worldly greed and personal interests; a love that generated an immense energy revealed in their beautiful work and a successful conference. They found their happiness in each other's success, in self-denial and in the Divine love that filled their hearts and overflowed, as if bathing everything and everybody around them in a sacred divine blessing. I then remembered these words by Ghazâli, "Love for Allah envelopes the heart; it rules the heart and it even spreads over everything."[58]

This kind of love for the sake of Allah (the Exalted) emanates from our true belief in God, and that is why Prophet Muhammad (bpuh) said that such love deserves paradise.

However, to put love in the correct perspective according to the teaching of the traditions of Prophet Muhammad (bpuh), we should know that love is not blind. We cannot love our fellow human beings, or any other creature, to the same extent that we should love Allah (the Exalted), because this will lead to the serious sin of associating partners with Allah (the Exalted). In this respect, Allah, the Exalted, says:

{There are people who take [for worship] others besides Allah, as equal [with Allah]. They love them as they should love Allah, but those of true faith are overflowing in their love for Allah. If only the unrighteous could see, behold, they would see the punishment [that awaits them for loving other people with the love that should be exclusively for Allah]. To Allah belongs all power, and Allah will strongly enforce His punishment. Then would those who were followed clear themselves of those who followed [them]. They would see the penalty [that awaits them], and all relations between them would be cut off. Those who followed would say: If only we had one more chance, we would clear ourselves of them, as they have cleared themselves of us. Thus will Allah show them [the fruits of] their deeds as [nothing but] regrets, nor will there be a way for them out of the fire.}

(Qur'an 2: 165-167)

Thus, the first and most important aspect of love is to love Allah (the Exalted) sincerely from the bottom of our hearts. This absolute love of Allah (the Exalted), which surpasses all other forms of love, does not come about until we know who Allah (the Exalted) is and we try to understand His perfect names and attributes, such as His majesty, greatness, supremacy, wisdom, sovereignty, purity, beneficence, might, extreme leniency, extreme gentleness, extreme patience, extreme grace, extreme justice, extreme kindness, extreme benevolence, extreme generosity, intense and continuous mercy, as well as his perfect and extreme love over His creation and control over all things in the universe.

From our true and sincere love of Allah (the Exalted) proceeds the love of His divine revelation, His prophets and messengers including the angels, and love of fellow human beings as well as all other creatures who obey Allah (the Exalted). Allah, the Exalted, says:

{Say: If you truly love Allah, then follow me [Muhammad (bpuh)]. Allah will love you and forgive you your sins; for Allah is Oft-Forgiving, Most Merciful. Say: Obey Allah and His Messenger. But if they turn back, Allah does not love those who reject faith.}

(Qur'an 3: 31-32)

It is for this same reason that the Prophet (bpuh) said, as we saw in Chapter 10 about moderation, that we should love and hate in moderation. The Messenger of Allah (bpuh) made it clear that whoever has the following three qualities has tasted the 'sweetness' of faith and belief in Allah. It was narrated from Anas (may Allah be pleased with him) that the Prophet (bpuh) said:

«There are three characteristics, and whoever attains them has found the sweetness of faith: Allah and His Messenger are dearer to him than all others, he loves a person only for the sake of Allah, and he hates to return to disbelief after Allah has saved him from it, as he hates to be thrown into the fire.» (Muslim)

We can supplicate for Allah's love to come into our lives as Prophet David (pbuh) used to supplicate. Abu ad-Dardâ' (may Allah be pleased with him) narrated:

«Allah's Messenger (bpuh) said: David used to supplicate thus:

O Allah, indeed, I ask You for Your love and the love of those who love You, and for the actions that will cause me to attain Your love. O Allah, make Your love more beloved to me than myself, my family, and cool water. (*Allâhumma inni as'aluka ḥubbaka wa ḥubba man yuḥibbuk wal-'amal alladhi yuballighuni ḥubbak. Allâhumma aj'al ḥubbak aḥabba 'ilaya min nafsi, wa ahli, wa min al-mâ' il-bârid.*)

When the Prophet (bpuh) mentioned David (pbuh), he would say about him: He was the best in worship out of all men.» (A reliable hadith recorded by at-Tirmidhi)

Chapter Nineteen:
Patient perseverance

«It was narrated from Abu Sa'eed al-Khudri (may Allah be pleased with him) that some people from among the Anṣâr asked Allah's Messenger (bpuh) (for some material assistance) and he gave it to them. They asked him (again), and he gave it to them. Then they again asked him (a third time), and he gave it to them until what he had was exhausted.

He said: Whatever I have of good, I would never withhold from you; but whoever refrains from asking, Allah will make him content; whoever seeks to be independent of means, Allah will make him independent; and whoever patiently perseveres, Allah will bestow patience and perseverance upon him. No one is ever given anything better and more generous (and all-encompassing) than patient perseverance.» (Bukhari, Muslim, at-Tirmidhi, and Abu Dâwood)

Commentary on the hadith

Patience, according to this hadith from Allah's Messenger (bpuh), is a moral virtue that encompasses all other virtues. It is a great blessing from Allah (the Exalted) for a person to be bestowed with patience. Life without patience becomes unbearable in every aspect.

The Arabic word *ṣabr* is most often translated as patience; however, it literally means patience, perseverance and endurance, all together. The full linguistic definition of ṣabr also includes restraint and forbearance – restraining the soul from panic, anger, fear, greed, and so on; restraining the tongue from complaining; and restraining the limbs from improper actions.[59]

Patient perseverance is a quality needed by every human. Some aspects of patience and perseverance are inborn, while others are learned as we grow. Without patient perseverance, life with all its mishaps and challenges becomes almost impossible. Some of those who cannot endure the challenges of life, because they lack patience and perseverance, take the seemingly easy way out: suicide has become common in most secularist societies.

Among the best of the moral virtues taught by Prophet Muhammad (bpuh) both from the noble Qur'an and the Hadith is ṣabr, meaning patience and bearing affliction for the sake of Allah (the Exalted). Patient perseverance involves restraining oneself from what is harmful and enduring what one dislikes, with a sense of acceptance and submission.

The importance and significance of patient perseverance is further emphasized in many verses of the glorious Qur'an. In fact, in over ninety passages of the Qur'an, Allah (the Exalted) recommends patience. Prophet Muhammad (bpuh) also verbally recommended patience and set an example of patient perseverance through his chosen lifestyle. Thus, every Muslim is required to practice patient perseverance and uphold the truth as an essential moral precept of success in our earthly trials. Allah, the Exalted, says:

{By [the token of] time [throughout the ages], verily humankind is in a perpetual state of loss, except for those who believe and do righteous deeds, join together in the mutual teaching of truth, and exhort one another to patience and perseverance.}

(Qur'an 103: 1-3)

In another hadith, the Prophet (bpuh) described as amazing the affairs of Muslims who practice patient perseverance, for there is good in all their affairs. When something pleasing happens to them, they are grateful to Allah, and that is good for them. If something displeasing happens to them, they exercise patience and forbearance, and that is good for them too. 'Abdur-Raḥmân ibn Abu Laylah narrated from Ṣuhayb that Allah's Messenger (bpuh) said:

«Wonderful are the ways of a believer, for there is good in every affair of his; this is not the case with anyone else, only in the case of a believer. If he has an occasion to feel delight, he thanks (God). Thus, there is a good for him in it. If he gets into trouble and shows resignation (and endures it patiently), there is also good for him in it.» (Muslim)

This teaching trains us to respond positively to the many challenging aspects of our daily lives in such a way that each moment brings more of Allah's blessings. When things go right, Muslims who are truly faithful will respond with sincere gratitude – to Allah first and then to their fellow human beings. When things seem to go wrong, they respond with ṣabr so that they consistently please their Lord with their faithfulness.

The Prophet's practice of *ṣabr*

Among the many important lessons that we learn from the biography of Prophet Muḥammad (bpuh) is his practice of ṣabr. The Prophet's patience and endurance were severely tested throughout his life. He was orphaned at a very early age with the death of his father 'Abdullâh before his birth, the death of his mother Âminah when he was only six years old, and the death of his grandfather, who had taken charge of him, when he was a boy of eight.

The Prophet's life was full of hardships: persecution by the idol-worshippers and betrayal by the hypocrites. He faced the world almost all alone when his call to prophethood began at the age of forty. At that time, almost the whole of the Arabian Peninsula was full of idolatry, and it was hard to imagine how one man could – in only 23 years – transform a land full of idolatry and socio-moral and political malaise into a land of pure monotheism and morality.

The occasion when he was stoned and driven out of the city of Taif illustrates his patience, extreme endurance, and forbearance. After losing his most beloved wife Khadeejah (may Allah be pleased with her) and his uncle Abu Ṭâlib, he decided to go out of Makkah to a place called Taif (about 60 kilometers away) to call its inhabitants to Islam. The leaders of Taif commanded the children and the insensible people to jeer at, laugh at, scoff at, and scold him. When he insisted on preaching to them, the people drove him out of the city and pelted his legs with stones, until both his shoes were full of blood. At this juncture, the Prophet (bpuh) called out to Allah (the Exalted):

> O Allah (the Exalted) to You I complain of the weakness of my strength, the meagerness of my strategy and my insignificance to people. You are the Most Merciful of those who show mercy; You are the Lord of the oppressed and You are my Lord. Into whose hands would you deliver me? To a distant person who will despise me, or to an enemy to whom You have granted power over me? If You are not angry with me then I do not care. However, Your pardon is best for me. I seek refuge in the light of Your Countenance, for which darkness has become illuminated and upon which the prosperity of this world and the hereafter stands, from Your anger befalling me, or Your displeasure afflicting me. It is Your right to scold until You are pleased, and there is no strength nor power save in You.[60]

Allah (the Exalted) heard his supplication and his expression of sorrow, so He sent the angels who take care of mountains to come to his aid. When these angels offered to destroy those people who had abused him, he replied:

«I have not been sent to destroy or to curse people but as a mercy to the entire humankind. O Lord, guide my people, for they do not know what they are doing. Perhaps from their progeny a people will rise up who will worship You and sacrifice for Your sake, O Allah.» (Bukhari and Muslim)

Even after the emigration to Madinah, there followed ten years of constant struggle and warfare in self-defense against the hypocrites, Jews, and pagans of Makkah. After he started receiving the revelation, his life was one of struggle for twenty-three years in Makkah and Madinah. Together with his Companions, he experienced abuse, humiliation, ostracism, boycott, intrigue, and even attempted murder – in Makkah at the hands of Quraysh, and in Madinah by the Jews, who poisoned him.

Patience and perseverance are not limited to the major struggles in one's life. They are also needed to deal with the small bothersome things that are a part of everyday life. Another example of ṣabr in the life of Prophet Muhammad (bpuh) is narrated by Anas ibn Mâlik (may Allah be pleased with him), who said:

«I served the Messenger of Allah (bpuh) for ten years, and by Allah, he never spoke any word of contempt to me. He never said to me for any reason: Why did you do this? Or: Why did you not do that?» (Muslim)

Prophet Muhammad (bpuh) was, in a nutshell, the perfect exemplar of the moral value of ṣabr as mentioned by Allah (the Exalted) in the glorious Qur'an.

{Patiently persevere, for your forbearance is only from Allah. Do not grieve over them, and do not distress yourself because of their plots. For Allah is with those who restrain themselves and those who do good.}

(Qur'an 16: 127-128)

Categories of patience

Muslim scholars past and present have classified patience into three important categories:

1. Patient perseverance in obeying Allah's orders

Patient perseverance in obedience is required, since the human soul always seeks comfort and ease, is reluctant to give those things up, and by nature dislikes submission to another's commands. Prophet Joseph (pbuh) said:

{Nor do I absolve my own self [of part of the blame]. The [human] soul is certainly prone to evil, unless my Lord bestows His mercy [on it], and surely my Lord is Oft-Forgiving, Most Merciful.}
(Qur'an 12: 53)

Laziness and love of possessions must be overcome by patient perseverance in duties and obligations like prescribed prayers, zakâh, and jihad. Faḍâlah ibn 'Ubayd (may Allah be pleased with him) reported that Allah's Messenger (bpuh) said:

«Shall I not tell you who the (true) believer is? It is the person from whom the people are safe and secure with regard to their wealth and lives. While a Muslim is one from whom people are safe and secure from his tongue and his hand, a *mujâhid* is one who struggles and strives with his own self in the obedience of Allah, and a *muhâjir*[61] is one who stays away from evil deeds and sins.» (Recorded by Aḥmad with a sound chain of narration)

«Faḍâlah ibn 'Ubayd (also) narrated that he heard the Messenger of Allah (bpuh) say: The deeds of everyone who dies are sealed, except for the person who dies guarding the frontier from the enemy, in the cause of Allah. For indeed, his (good) actions are increased for him until the Day of Judgment, and he is secure from the tribulation of the grave.

The Messenger of Allah (bpuh) also said: The mujâhid is the one who strives against (the evil inclinations of) his own soul.» (A sound hadith recorded by at-Tirmidhi)

If a good deed is to be accepted by Allah, we must be patient before beginning the deed by perfecting our intentions so that we are doing it sincerely for Allah's pleasure, opposing the urge to show off. We must continue with patient perseverance during the deed itself, not forgetting that Allah (the Exalted) is watching and is well-acquainted with all that we do, and that His angels who are in charge of recording all our deeds are busy doing their work. Remembering this, we perform the deed as well and as completely as possible. Finally, we must show restraint and be patient after completing the good deed to ensure that we do not show pride, boast, or expect praise and gratitude from our fellow human beings.

{Keep yourself patiently with those who call on their Lord morning and evening, seeking His Face; and let not your eyes pass beyond them, seeking the pomp and glitter of this life; nor obey any whose heart We have permitted to neglect the remembrance of Us, one who follows his own desires, whose case has gone beyond all bounds.}

(Qur'an 18: 28)

2. Patient forbearance to refrain from disobedience

Allah's Messenger (bpuh) is reported to have said:

«This world is a prison for the believer and a paradise for the non-believer.» (A sound hadith recorded by at-Tirmidhi)

This means that the true believers conduct their lives such that they struggle to restrain themselves from all forms of disobedience and to stay within the limits of Islamic law. They are not free to do whatever they like; instead, they submit themselves to the laws of Allah. This, coupled with the hurt and evil present in this life, makes the world like a prison for the believers, especially in comparison with what awaits them in the hereafter.

On the other hand, the non-believers follow their own vain desires, succumbing to their passions and disregarding Allah's laws. They feel that they can lead their lives as they please. They wrongly think that they have total freedom to do anything they want, so this world is like a paradise for them, especially in comparison with what awaits them in the hereafter.[62]

For those who have been accustomed to living a lifestyle far from the straight path that pleases Allah (the Exalted), patience is required after repentance in order to keep our evil desires and Satan at bay. Indeed each new temptation requires a vigorous struggle to resist. The most difficult sins to avoid are those that are looked at as minor sins, such as backbiting or looking at sordid pictures and videos; other common bad habits[63] that are taken lightly, committed easily and not always deplored by others; and sins that are committed secretly.

Al-Ḥârith ibn Suwayd reported that 'Abdullâh ibn Mas'ood related two narrations, one a saying of 'Abdullâh's and the other a saying of the Prophet's:

'Abdullâh ibn Mas'ood (may Allah be pleased with him) said: A believer sees his sins as if he were sitting under a mountain which he is afraid may fall on him; whereas the wicked person considers his sins as flies passing over his nose, and he just swats them away. (Bukhari)[64]

«It was narrated from 'Â'ishah (may Allah be pleased with her) that the Messenger of Allah (bpuh) said to her: O 'Â'ishah, beware of (evil) deeds that are regarded as insignificant, for they have a pursuer from Allah (and a person will be held accountable for them).» (A sound hadith recorded by Ibn Mâjah)

3. Patient perseverance in the face of trials and afflictions

This category includes all that happens to us against our own will, such as the loss of property, the death of loved ones, illness, or harm done to us by others (which is perhaps the most difficult of all to bear gracefully). Allah (the Exalted) tells us about this aspect of patience and the rewards we can expect from it:

{Be sure We shall test you with something of fear and hunger, some loss in goods or lives or the fruits [of your toil], but give glad tidings to those who patiently persevere, who say when afflicted with calamity: To Allah we belong, and to Him is our return. They are those on whom [descend] blessings from their Lord and mercy, and they are the ones that receive guidance.}

(Qur'an 2: 155-157)

Such trials from Allah (the Exalted) and our fellow human beings, however distasteful they may be, are in reality opportunities for our own purification, as reported in a number of statements from Prophet Muhammad (bpuh).

It was narrated from Ibn 'Umar (may Allah be pleased with both of them) that the Messenger of Allah (bpuh) said:

«The believer who mixes with people and bears their annoyance with patience will have a greater reward than the believer who does not mix with people and does not put up with their annoyance.» (A reliable hadith recorded by Ibn Mâjah)

Yahyâ ibn Wath-thâb related that a scholar from among the Companions narrated that the Prophet (bpuh) said:

«Indeed when the Muslim mixes with the people and he puts up with their harm, he is better than the Muslim who does not mix with the people and does not put up with their harm.» (A sound hadith recorded by at-Tirmidhi)

«Anas (may Allah be pleased with him) narrated that the Messenger of Allah (bpuh) said: When Allah wants good for his slave, He hastens his punishment in the world; when He wants bad for His slave, He withholds his sins from him until he appears before Him on the Day of Judgment.

With this same chain of narrators, (it was also reported that) the Prophet (bpuh) said: Indeed the greater reward comes with the greater trial. When Allah loves a people, He tries them. So whoever is pleased (with what Allah gives or takes from him), then for him is pleasure; whoever is angry, then for him is wrath.» (A reliable hadith recorded by at-Tirmidhi)

Abu Hurayrah (may Allah be pleased with him) narrated that the Messenger of Allah (bpuh) said:

«Trials will not cease afflicting the believing man and the believing woman in regard to themselves, their children, and their property, until they meet Allah without having any sins (left).» (A reliable hadith recorded by at-Tirmidhi)

It was narrated by both Abu Sa'eed al-Khudri and Abu Hurayrah (may Allah be pleased with both of them) that the Prophet (bpuh) said:

«Every fatigue, illness, distress, worry, grief, or harm that befalls the Muslim, including **the prick of a thorn**, will be accepted by Allah as expiation for some of his or her sins.» (Bukhari and Muslim)

«'Abdullâh (may Allah be pleased with him) narrated: I visited the Prophet (bpuh) during his illness, and he was suffering from a high fever.

I said: You have a high fever. Is it because you will have double reward for it?

He said: Yes, for no Muslim is afflicted with any harm (and he bears it patiently) except that Allah will remove his sins, like the leaves falling off a tree.» (Bukhari)

Patient perseverance in the face of hardships and mishaps, as well as acceptance of Allah's decree in His will and wisdom in such matters, are indeed proof of our faith in Allah (the Exalted). This is not to say that it is wrong to dislike or feel sadness for the afflictions that have occurred; indeed, feelings of loss, frustration, and pain are only a normal part of human life, as long as they do not go beyond the limits of the Sharia ordained by Allah (the Exalted). Patient perseverance illuminates such feelings so that we are able to endure difficulties without panic and without disobeying Allah.

This is why some wise people say that anxiety over what has been lost is a calamity, and impatience over what is expected is foolishness. This implies that it is futile to be annoyed with the decree of Allah. We would do well to remember that Allah (the Exalted) says:

{...It may be that you dislike a thing which is good for you, and that you love a thing which is bad for you. And Allah knows, but you do not know.}

(Qur'an 2: 216)

True believers have no way out of the difficulties and challenges of these worldly affairs except to uphold patient perseverance and trust in Allah, as He has commanded of all believers. This patient perseverance and trust merits immense rewards.

{O you who believe! Persevere in patience and constancy; vie [with one another] in such perseverance; strengthen each other; and fear Allah, that you may be successful.}

(Qur'an 3: 200)

{...Only those who are patient will receive their reward in full without reckoning.}

(Qur'an 39: 10)

This reward of patient perseverance without reckoning, as promised by Allah (the Exalted) Who never fails in His promises, is none other than paradise.

{[Allah] will reward them for what they patiently endured with a garden [in paradise] and silk [garments]. [They will be] reclining therein on adorned couches. They will not see in it any [burning] sun or [freezing] cold. Near above them are the shade [of the garden], and its [fruits] to be picked will be lowered [to them] in compliance. Among them will be circulated vessels of silver and cups having been [created] clear [as glass], [crystal] clear glasses [made] from silver of which they will determine the measure [according to their wishes]. They will be given to drink from a cup [of wine] whose mixture is of ginger [from] a fountain within [paradise] named Salsabeel. There will circulate among them boys of everlasting youth. When you see them, you will think them [as beautiful as] scattered pearls, and when you look there [in paradise], you will see pleasure and a great dominion. Upon them [the inhabitants of paradise] will be green garments of fine silk and brocade, and they will be adorned with bracelets of silver. Their Lord will give them a purifying drink. [It will be said]: Indeed, this is for you a reward, and your effort has been appreciated.}

(Qur'an 76. 12-22)

{Those will be awarded the chamber [the most elevated portion of paradise] for what they patiently endured. They will be received therein with greetings and [words of] peace, abiding there eternally. What an excellent place of settlement and residence!}

(Qur'an 25. 75-76)

Chapter Twenty: Benevolence

Jâbir ibn 'Abdullâh (may Allah be pleased with both of them) narrated that Allah's Messenger (bpuh) said:

«May Allah have mercy on a man who is lenient (easy and benevolent) when he sells and when he buys and when he asks for payment.» (Bukhari, Ibn Mâjah, and Aḥmad)

Commentary on the hadith

Another moral value of utmost importance in a world full of materialism and secularism is benevolence. In this hadith, Allah's Messenger (bpuh) made a very important invocation for Allah to shower His grace and mercy on those who are benevolent in their business transactions, when they buy and sell and when they ask their debtors to pay up their dues. It is known that the supplications of prophets are always answered, since Allah (the Exalted) protected them from deliberate sins.

Furthermore, Prophet Muhammad (bpuh) did not do anything out of his own desires, but spoke or acted as Allah (the Exalted) instructed him to, as Allah (the Exalted) says in the glorious Qur'an:

{He [Muhammad (bpuh)] does not say [anything] of [his own] desire. It is no less than a revelation sent down to him.}

(Qur'an 53: 3-4)

This supplication of Prophet Muhammad (bpuh) is important because no one will enter paradise solely as a result of their righteous deeds. Rather, people will go to paradise through the grace and mercy of Allah (the Exalted). Every one of us needs to gain Allah's grace and mercy so that we can be forgiven the sins that we commit on an almost daily basis and be granted entry into paradise. In this respect, Prophet Muhammad's statement is clear:

«It was narrated by 'Â'ishah, the wife of the Prophet (may Allah be pleased with her), that Allah's Messenger (bpuh) said: Aim to do good and be moderate, and be of good cheer, for none of you will be admitted to paradise by virtue of his deeds (only).

They (his Companions) asked: Not even you, O Messenger of Allah?

He said: Not even me, unless Allah encompasses me with His mercy. And remember that the deed most beloved to Allah is that which is done regularly, even if it is small.» (Muslim)

Many people today have been strongly affected by the materialistic and secularist culture, so much so that many who do business do not care how they earn their money as long as they can make money as quickly as possible. They are ready to swindle people out of their money by selling commodities that are not genuine. They are ready to cheat in business, willing to sell anything, even harmful products, as long as they make quick money. They may even make unreasonable profits up to 400 times (or even more) their cost price, without any shame or mercy. There seems to be no leniency or benevolence in selling and buying.

If the items are bought with loans or mortgages involving usury or compounded interest, and the owners are unable to pay their instalments in time, the situation becomes even worse. People end up losing their homes or cars, as well as all the payments paid over the years of their tireless work and sweat.

Benevolence is defined as an act that benefits persons other than those from whom the act proceeds, without any obligation.[65] Benevolence means being easy and flexible with our fellow human beings. With respect to business transactions, it means giving a debtor appropriate concessions in price and respite. If a buyer asks for an unreasonable concession, then the seller should speak and behave nicely, not by arguing with the client or swearing falsely to sell the items, but by excusing himself or herself without hurting anyone's feelings and without unleashing a hail of abuse upon the person.

If the buyer wants to return the commodity due to obvious damage or a defect in the commodity, then the seller must be benevolent enough to take it back without undue complaints and misbehavior. That is more appropriate to earn Allah's grace and mercy, as Allah's Messenger (bpuh) supplicated.

At the same time, benevolence in buying means that the buyer should not ask for an unreasonable reduction in the price of the items, considering that the seller makes a great deal of effort to make the commodities available without hoarding them.

Moreover, if there exists a minor fault in the commodity that was detected before or after buying the item, then it should be graciously overlooked. If possible, the buyer should try his or her best to pay the price immediately. If the seller misbehaves and shows roughness in selling, the buyer should politely excuse himself or herself without too much commotion, foul speech or unnecessary argument, since those would only cause pain and hatred. This is what Allah (the Exalted) directs us to do, as we saw in Chapter 16 about justice:

{O you who believe! Do not consume your property among yourselves unjustly, but let there be commerce and trade among you by mutual consent and good will; and do not kill [or destroy] yourselves. Verily, Allah has been Most Merciful to you! If anyone commits these wrongs through aggression and injustice, We shall cast him into the fire, and that is easy for Allah.}

(Qur'an 4: 29-30)

{To the Madyan people We sent Shu'ayb, one of their own brethren. He said: O my people, worship Allah; you have no other god but Him. Now has come unto you a clear sign from your Lord! Give just measure and weight, do not withhold from people the things that are their due, and do no mischief on the earth after it has been set in order. That will be best for you, if you have faith.}

(Qur'an 7: 85)

According to Imam al-Ghazzâli, as quoted by Umar-ud-Din Muhammad in his book, *The Ethical Philosophy of al-Ghazzali,* there are six kinds of benevolence:

a.
 If a person needs something, one should give it to him or her, making as little profit as possible. If the giver forgoes the profit, it will be better.

b.
 If a person purchases anything from a poor person, it will be more graceful to suffer a little loss by paying the poor person more than what is considered the right price. Such an act must produce an ennobling effect, and a contrary act is likely to have the reverse effect. It is not praiseworthy to pay a rich person more than what is due when the rich person is notorious for extracting high rates of profit.

c.
 In realizing one's dues and loans, one must act benevolently by giving debtors more time to pay than was originally stipulated; if necessary, one should make reductions in loans to provide relief to the debtors.

d.

It is only proper that people who want to return the goods they have purchased should be permitted to do so as a matter of benevolence.

e.

It is a graceful act on the part of a debtor to pay one's debts without being asked to do so, if possible long before they are due.

f.

After selling items on credit, one should be generous enough not to press for payment when people are not able to pay on the stipulated terms.

Furthermore, benevolence applies not only in trade and business transactions; it is applicable in all aspects of our lives in the way we deal with and interact with other people on a daily basis. We should be polite, amicable, and easygoing. We should not make things unnecessarily complicated, nor should we always be stubborn trying to make people's lives difficult and unbearable for no good reason.

The Prophet (bpuh) himself was always easy and flexible. In addition, he always advised his Companions, especially whenever he sent them out for any mission anywhere, to be easygoing and welcoming. It was narrated that Â'ishah (may Allah be pleased with her), the wife of the Prophet (bpuh), said:

«Whenever Allah's Messenger was given a choice between two things, he would choose the easier of the two, as long as it was not a sin. If it was a sin, he would be the furthest of people from it. Allah's Messenger (bpuh) never took revenge for his own sake, but only if the sacred limits of Allah were transgressed.» (Muslim)

The Prophet (bpuh) also ordered his callers to Islam to exhibit ease and to facilitate things for the people. He said to two of his Companions, Mu'âdh ibn Jabal and Abu Moosâ (may Allah be pleased with both of them), when he was sending them as his emissaries to Yemen:

«Be easygoing with the people and do not be harsh. Give glad tidings and do not put people off, and cooperate (with them) and do not be divided.» (Muslim)

Chapter Twenty-One: Mercifulness

Jareer ibn 'Abdullâh (may Allah be pleased with him) narrated that Allah's Messenger (bpuh) said:

«Allah will not be merciful to those who are not merciful to people.» (Bukhari)

'Abdullâh ibn 'Amr (may Allah be pleased with both of them) narrated that Allah's Messenger (bpuh) said:

«The merciful are shown mercy by the Most Merciful (Allah). Be merciful to those on earth, and you will be shown mercy by the One above the heavens. The womb (*ar-raḥm*) is named after the Most Merciful (*ar-Raḥmân*). So whoever connects to it, Allah connects to him, and whoever severs (him or herself from) it, Allah severs (Himself from) him.» (A reliable hadith recorded by at-Tirmidhi)

Commentary on the hadiths

Mercifulness, like love, is one of the perfect attributes of Allah (the Exalted), and He has bestowed a bit of it on His creation, especially to human beings, so that we can show mercy to each other. Thus it is by Allah's mercy that we are merciful to each other. Salmân (may Allah be pleased with him) narrated that Allah's Messenger (bpuh) said:

«Verily, on the day that Allah created the heavens and the earth, he created one hundred parts of mercy, each of which is as great as the distance between the heavens and the earth, and He put one part (one-hundredth) of that mercy on the earth. It is by this one part of mercy that a parent feels pity (and compassion) for her child, and animals and birds show mercy to one another. Allah has reserved ninety-nine parts of mercy, with which He will treat His servants on the Day of Resurrection.» (Muslim)

Therefore, according to the hadith under discussion, those who show mercy to others will be among those on whom Allah (the Exalted) will bestow His special grace and mercy, both in this world and the hereafter. We are all in need of Allah's mercy for our success in this world and salvation in the hereafter. Hence, we should be merciful and kind to each other and to all other creatures of God.

{Then he became one of those who believed and exhorted one another to perseverance and patience and exhorted one another to pity and compassion.}

(Qur'an 90: 17)

{The believing men and believing women are allies of one another. They enjoin what is right, forbid what is wrong, establish prayer, give zakâh and obey Allah and His Messenger. Those are the ones upon whom Allah will shower His mercy. Indeed, Allah is Exalted in Might and Wise.}

(Qur'an 9: 71)

«Usâmah ibn Zayd (may Allah be pleased with both of them) narrated: We were with the Prophet (bpuh) when suddenly there came to him a messenger from one of his daughters, who was asking him to come and see her (young) son, who was dying.

The Prophet (bpuh) said (to the messenger): Go back and tell her that whatever Allah takes is for Him, and whatever He gives is for Him, and everything with Him has a limited fixed term (in this world). So order her to be patient and hope for Allah's reward.

But she sent the messenger to the Prophet (bpuh) again, swearing that he should come to her.

So the Prophet (bpuh) got up, and so did Sa'd ibn 'Ubâdah and Mu'âdh ibn Jabal (and they all went to her).

When the child was brought to the Prophet (bpuh), the child's breath was disturbed in his chest as if it were in a water skin. On seeing that, the eyes of the Prophet (bpuh) became flooded with tears.

Sa'd asked him: O Allah's Messenger, what is this?

The Prophet (bpuh) said: This is mercy, which Allah has lodged in the heart of His slaves, and Allah is Merciful only to those of His slaves who are merciful (to others).» (Bukhari)

How to be merciful to one another[66]

Some ways of being merciful to each other have already been discussed in other chapters of this work. There are many things that the believers should do to show their mercy for each other:

- Forgive each other's faults

- Feel sympathy for each other's suffering

- Love each other for Allah's sake

- Visit each other in times of sickness

- Help each other financially or otherwise

- Not oppress or do any form of injustice to each other

- Not spy, backbite, slander, despise, or lie to each other

- Not hate or quarrel with each other when there is no legitimate reason to do so

Being merciful to our families and relatives

To gain Allah's gracious mercy we also have to be kind, compassionate, forgiving, and continuously merciful to our spouses and children, as Allah (the Exalted) says in the following beautiful words:

{Of His signs is that He created for you mates from among yourselves that you may find tranquility [peace of mind, joy, and happiness] in them, and He placed between you compassionate love and mercy. Indeed in that are signs for a people who reflect.}

(Qur'an 30: 21)

{O you who believe! Truly, among your wives and your children are [some that are] enemies for you. So beware of them! But if you forgive and overlook, and cover up [their faults], verily Allah is Oft-Forgiving, Most Merciful.}

(Qur'an 64: 14)

«Hakeem ibn Mu'âwiyah al-Qushayri reported that his father asked: O Messenger of Allah, what are the rights that our wives have and are due from us?

He replied: That you feed her when you eat, that you clothe her with what you wear, that you avoid hitting her in the face or humiliating her (by using insulting or nasty language with her), and that you avoid abandoning her, except within the home.» (A sound hadith recorded by Abu Dâwood)

According to one hadith, some women went to the wives of the Prophet (bpuh) and complained about the way their husbands treated them. The Prophet (bpuh) announced to the men of the community:

«Many women have visited the family of Muhammad, complaining about their husbands. Indeed, those are not the best among you.» (Recorded by Abu Dâwood, an-Nasâ'i and Ibn Mâjah; authenticated by Ibn Hajar)

The Prophet (bpuh) is reported to have spoken on a number of occasions about benevolent treatment of children, especially in respect to daughters:

«Whoever has three daughters, or three sisters, or two daughters or two sisters, and is very kind to them and takes good care of them and fears Allah in their treatment, will enter paradise (as a result of his good actions to these females).» (A reliable hadith recorded by at-Tirmidhi and Abu Dâwood)

«Whoever takes care of three girls and educates them, sees to it that they marry, and treats them kindly, paradise will be his.» (A reliable hadith recorded by Abu Dâwood)

Being merciful to fellow human beings

A fact that is rarely talked about, and is distorted in many instances, is that one way of gaining the gracious mercy of our Lord is fair treatment of our fellow human beings. In fact, fair treatment is the right of other Muslims and non-Muslims, as long as they do not show any hostility towards Muslims and Islam and do not assist the enemies of Islam in driving innocent Muslims out of their lands and homes.

{Allah does not forbid you from being righteous and acting justly toward those who do not fight you because of religion and do not expel you from your homes. Indeed, Allah loves those who act justly. Allah only forbids that you make allies of those who fight you because of religion and expel you from your homes and aid in your expulsion; whoever makes allies of them, it is those who are the wrongdoers.}

(Qur'an 60: 8-9)

Being merciful to all other creatures and the environment

Causing wanton destruction to our physical environment just because Allah (the Exalted) subjected everything in this world to our service is not the way to gain Allah's gracious mercy; rather it is the way to deny oneself Allah's benevolence and mercy. Allah, the Exalted, says:

{Corruption [and mischief] has appeared on the land and the sea because of what the hands of people have earned, that [Allah] may make them taste part of that which they have done, in order that they may turn back [from evil].}

(Qur'an 30: 41)

{The heaven He has raised high, and He has set up the balance in order that you may not transgress [due] balance. So establish weight with justice and fall not short in the balance.}

(Qur'an 55: 7-9)

This means that we should not cut down trees unnecessarily, kill animals simply for games or sport, or dispose of our waste in a reckless manner, without caring about the consequences of the toxic and other harmful hazards we create. We must show mercy to the environment we live in so that the environment will in turn serve us, and above all so that Allah (the Exalted) will shower us with His mercy and blessings.

The teachings of Allah's Messenger Muhammad (bpuh) with regard to this topic are clear and numerous. On a number of occasions, Allah's Messenger advised His Companions to show mercy to the environment and the creatures that live in it.

«Abu Hurayrah (may Allah be pleased with him) narrated that the Prophet (bpuh) said: While a man was walking, he became intensely thirsty. He found a well, descended into it, and drank from its water. When he climbed out, he found a dog lolling out its tongue on account of (extreme) thirst, eating the moistened earth.

He said: This dog is experiencing thirst like I have just experienced it. So he climbed back down into the well, filled his shoe with water, held it in his mouth, climbed back up and let the dog drink. Allah appreciated this (action) and forgave him (all his sins).

The Companions asked: O Messenger of Allah, are we rewarded for kindness to animals?

He responded: There is a reward in (doing good to) every living animal.» (Muslim)

It was narrated from 'Abdullâh (may Allah be pleased with him) that Allah's Messenger (bpuh) said:

«A woman was punished because of a cat which she imprisoned until it died, and she was condemned to hell because of that. She did not feed it, and she did not let it (go free to) eat from the vermin of the earth.» (Muslim)

«It was narrated that Shaddâd ibn Aws (may Allah be pleased with him) said: There are two things that I memorized from Allah's Messenger (bpuh).

He said: Allah has prescribed goodness (iḥsân), proficiency, and kindness in all things. So if you kill, kill well; and if you slaughter, slaughter well. Sharpen your blade, and spare the animal you slaughter from suffering.» (Muslim)

«It was narrated that Sa'eed ibn Jubayr said: Ibn 'Umar came across some young men of Quraysh who were using a bird as a target to shoot at. They had agreed to give the owner of the bird every arrow that missed its mark, but when they saw Ibn 'Umar, they scattered.

Ibn 'Umar said: Who did this? May Allah curse the one who did this! Allah's Messenger (bpuh) cursed the one who uses any living being as a target.» (Muslim)

«Jâbir ibn 'Abdullâh said: Allah's Messenger (bpuh) forbade capturing any animal for the purpose of killing (it for sport).» (Muslim)

It was also narrated by Jâbir that Allah's Messenger (bpuh) said:

«If a Muslim plants a plant, whatever is eaten of it is (counted as) charity for him, whatever is stolen from it is charity for him, whatever the wild animals eat from it is charity for him, and whatever the birds eat from it is charity for him. Anything taken from it will be charity for him.» (Muslim)

All that exists in the whole universe – including the human species – exists and continues to do so by Allah's mercy. We will ultimately need Allah's mercy on the day that our property and children will avail us nothing, and mercy will be shown only to the person who comes before Allah with a merciful soul. In other words, being merciful on this earth will qualify us for Allah's mercy on that dreadful day.

«It was narrated by 'Â'ishah, the wife of the Prophet (may Allah be pleased with her), that Allah's Messenger (bpuh) said: Aim to do good and be moderate, and be of good cheer, for none of you will be admitted to paradise by virtue of his deeds (only).

They (his Companions) asked: Not even you, O Messenger of Allah?

He said: Not even me, unless Allah encompasses me with His mercy. And remember that the deed most beloved to Allah is that which is done regularly, even if it is small.» (Muslim)

To help us be among the most merciful creatures, we should remember that in our daily prayers we repeat a minimum of seventeen times a day the beautiful formula *Bismillâh ir-Rahmân ir-Raheem* (In the name of Allah, the Most Gracious, the Most Merciful).

{...Surely, the mercy of Allah is [always] near to the good-doers.}

(Qur'an 7: 56)

May Allah (the Exalted) soften our hearts and fill them with sympathy so that we may be merciful to all of Allah's creation. Âmeen.

Chapter Twenty-Two: Respect

«Zarbi narrated that he heard Anas ibn Mâlik (may Allah be pleased with him) say: An old man came to talk to the Prophet (bpuh), and the people were hesitant to make room for him.

The Prophet (bpuh) said: Anyone who does not have mercy on our young and does not respect our elders is not one of us.» (Recorded by at-Tirmidhi, Abu Dâwood, and Ahmad)[67]

«'Amr ibn Shu'ayb narrated from his father, from his grandfather, that the Messenger of Allah (bpuh) said: Anyone who does not have mercy upon our young or does not know the honor of our elders is not one of us.

(Another chain has a similar meaning except that he (bpuh) said in it: know the rights of our elders.)» (A reliable hadith recorded by at-Tirmidhi, Abu Dâwood, and Ahmad)

Commentary on the hadiths

Respect for our elders is yet another moral virtue that is not only taught by Islam but is generally accepted universally in all cultures and religions. In these two narrations, Allah's Messenger Muhammad (bpuh) used strong words, emphatically stating that those who show no mercy to the young (since they cannot help themselves in many cases) and show no honor or respect to the elderly are not his true followers. This does not mean that they are not believers in Allah and His Messenger (bpuh); it means they are not true practitioners of the noble moral virtues that the Prophet (bpuh) brought for the guidance of humanity.

Prophet Muhammad (bpuh), as well as all those prophets and messengers who came before him, taught this very important moral virtue. Therefore, those who claim to believe in the prophets of God – including the last and final Prophet, Muhammad (bpuh) – and yet do not respect the elderly are only paying lip service to their belief and love of Muhammad (bpuh), while in reality they are not true followers. If they were, then they would have obeyed him and followed his teachings, as Allah, the Exalted, says:

{Obey Allah and the Messenger so that you may obtain mercy.}

(Qur'an 3: 132)

{...Whatever the Messenger gives you, take it; whatever he forbids for you, abstain [from it]...}

(Qur'an 59: 7)

In yet another of his statements with respect to this moral virtue of respecting and honouring elders, regardless of whether or not they are close relatives, 'Abdullâh ibn 'Umar (may Allah be pleased with both of them) narrated that the Messenger of Allah (bpuh) said:

«The best kind of piety is that a man should keep in touch with and respect his father's friend even after his father has passed away.» (Muslim)

This moral teaching of showing respect and kindness to elderly people, regardless of whether they are relatives or strangers, is culturally accepted in every society. However, in Islam it is given another dimension. In Islam, those who do not honor those who are older than they are, nor give the elders their due right of respect, minding how they respond to them, talk to them, and behave towards them – such people are not true believers.

The wise people say that showing respect to one's elders or to one's equals is not servility; on the contrary, it is a high moral virtue that opens the doors of goodness. It is also said that one who does not listen to, respect, and obey the elderly (as long as they do not order the person to disobey Allah) will not succeed in his or her endeavors.

Prophet Moses (pbuh) was absent from his people for forty days (during which time he received the Torah from Allah). When he returned, he found that had disobeyed him and were worshipping an idol in the form of a golden calf. Moses was annoyed with his younger brother Aaron (pbuh), whom he had left in charge, so he started pulling him by his beard. Aaron excused himself, as recorded in the glorious Qur'an.

{[Aaron] replied: O son of my mother! Do not seize me by my beard, nor by [the hair on] my head! Truly I feared that [if I tried to stop them] you would say: You have caused a division among the children of Israel, and you did not respect my word!}

(Qur'an 20: 94)

Prophet Aaron respected his elder brother. Even though he was not in the wrong, he accepted responsibility but explained the situation by saying that he feared that Prophet Moses (pbuh) would come and find the children of Israel divided and scattered, and that this would demonstrate disrespect for Moses' command to take care of the children of Israel.

Therefore, preference is always given to one's elders with regard to respect, due to their age and, in most circumstances, their more extensive experience. In greeting, the younger person is required to greet the older one first. If there is only one seat left and there are two people, the older one should be given the seat. If an older person comes to a place where there are no seats left, the younger ones should stand up and leave their seats for the elders. Even in the mosques, the elderly always occupy the first rows unless there are no elderly persons. In this regard, 'Abdullâh ibn 'Umar (may Allah be pleased with both of them) reported that Allah's Messenger Muhammad (bpuh) said:

«I saw myself in a dream, using a *siwâk* (small twig used as a natural toothbrush), and two people were competing to take it, one of whom was older than the other. I gave the siwâk to the younger one, and it was said to me: Give it to the older one. So I gave it to the older one.» (Muslim)

It was narrated by Abu Hurayrah (may Allah be pleased with him) that Allah's Messenger (bpuh) said:

«The younger should greet the older, the one who is passing should greet the one who is sitting, and the smaller group should greet the larger.» (Bukhari and Abu Dâwood)

Nevertheless, respect is a 'two-way street'. The young have to respect the elderly, but the elderly also have to be polite and care for the young by showing kindness and mercy to them and by helping them to grow up with beneficial guidance. As the saying goes, "Respect me, and I will respect you, too."

This is why the Prophet (bpuh) was always kind and caring towards the young. He started by greeting them, sat and spoke to them, and even ate and played with them.

«It was narrated from Anas ibn Mâlik (may Allah be pleased with him) that the Messenger of Allah (bpuh) passed by some children and greeted them (with the greeting of salâm).» (Muslim)

«It was narrated from 'Umar ibn Abi Salamah (may Allah be pleased with him): I was under the care of the Messenger of Allah (bpuh), and (when we were eating) my hand used to wander all over the (communal) dish.

Allah's Messenger said to me: Son, mention the name of Allah (when you start to eat), eat with your right hand, and eat from what is nearest to you.» (Muslim)

The moral virtue of behaving respectfully towards each other is something that should flow across the board. The young must respect the old, just as the old must care for and guide the young. The rich and wealthy must take care of (and respect) the poor and needy, just as the needy must respect and honor the rich. Employees must respect the employers, just as the employers must fulfil their part of the bargain by looking after the welfare of their employees without any form of injustice. Wives must obey, respect, and honor their husbands, just as husbands must respect their wives by giving them tender care, being compassionate and loving to them without hurting their feelings, and consulting with them in their affairs. Children must obey and give utmost respect to their parents, just as parents must respect their children by showing a good example in the home with respect to everything that happens between them.

> A man once came to 'Umar ibn al-Khaṭṭâb, the second caliph of Islam, complaining of his son's disobedience to him. 'Umar summoned the boy and lectured him about his disobedience to his father and how he was neglecting his rights.
>
> The boy replied: O *Ameer al-Mu'mineen* (Commander of the Believers)! Does a child not have rights due him from his father?
>
> 'Umar replied: Certainly.
>
> The boy asked: What are they, Ameer al-Mu'mineen?
>
> He answered: That he should choose for him a [good] mother, give him a good name, and teach him the Book [the Qur'an].
>
> The boy said: O Ameer al-Mu'mineen, my father did none of this. My mother was a Magian [a fire-worshipper]. He gave me the name of Ju'alân [meaning dung beetle or scarab], and he did not teach me a single letter of the Qur'an.
>
> Turning to the father, 'Umar said: You have come to me to complain about the disobedience of your son. You have failed in your duty to him before he has failed in his duty to you; you have done wrong to him before he has wronged you.[68]

Allah (the Exalted) has entrusted humanity with the great trust of being His delegates on this earth. This huge trust requires that we respect and fulfil the needs of our bodies, minds, and souls, as well as the rights and needs of all other creatures: human beings, animals, and the environment as a whole. In a real sense, this involves living in total harmony with Allah's laws and regulations as given to the last Prophet and Messenger Muhammad (bpuh):

{We did indeed offer the trust to the heavens and the earth and the mountains; but they refused to undertake it, being afraid of it. But humans undertook it, and they were indeed unjust and foolish. [The result is] that Allah will punish the hypocrites, men and women, and the disbelievers, men and women; and Allah will turn in mercy to the believers, men and women; for Allah is Oft-Forgiving, Most Merciful.}

(Qur'an 33. 72-73)

Chapter Twenty-Three: Generosity

«Anas (may Allah be pleased with him) said: When the Messenger of Allah (bpuh) arrived in Madinah, the Muhâjireen came to him and said: O Messenger of Allah, we have not seen a people more willing to sacrifice when having a lot, nor more patient when having a little, than the people among whom we are staying (the Anṣâr). Our provisions are so sufficient, and we share with them in their produce such that we fear that all of our reward is gone.

So the Prophet (bpuh) said: No (it is not gone), as long as you supplicate to Allah for them, thank Him and show gratitude to them (for it).» (A sound hadith recorded by at-Tirmidhī)

Commentary on the hadith

Generosity is yet another moral virtue valued by most societies. In an Islamic context, generosity can be defined as extreme kindness and compassion coupled with great sacrifice made by one human being towards another for Allah's sake and Allah's pleasure.

This is exactly the way the Anṣâr of Madinah acted towards the Muslim emigrants, the Muhâjireen from Makkah (may Allah be pleased with both groups). The Muhâjireen had migrated for the sake of Allah (the Exalted), to be with the Prophet (bpuh) and the other believers in Madinah and support the cause of Islam.

The believers in Madinah were so generous in offering their wealth, property, homes and even their own families for their fellow Muslim brothers and sisters that they became known by the title Anṣâr, or literally 'helpers'. Their generosity was an impeccably manifested example of their true belief and good behavior. They wholeheartedly came to the aid of their fellow believers, the Muhâjireen, who had migrated to Madinah empty-handed, with nothing to live on or to support themselves with. The Muhâjireen had left everything they owned – their wealth, families, relatives, homes, and businesses.

Allah (the Exalted) graciously acknowledged and appreciated the generosity of the Anṣâr to the Muhâjireen, as well as the extreme sacrifices made by the Muhâjireen when they left behind all that they loved and owned, migrating for the sake of Allah (the Exalted) and His Messenger (bpuh) to support His religion. Allah praised them in a number of passages in the noble Qur'an:

{So the first to embrace Islam of the Muhâjireen and the Anṣâr, and also those who would follow them exactly [in faith], Allah is well-pleased with them as they are well-pleased with Him. He has prepared for them gardens [in paradise] beneath which rivers flow, to dwell therein forever. That is the supreme success.}

(Qur'an 9: 100)

One specific example of generosity was reported by 'Abdur-Raḥmân ibn 'Awf, an emigrant from Makkah, who was paired and joined into brotherhood with Sa'd ibn ar-Rabee', the richest of the Anṣâr of Madinah. Sa'd (may Allah be pleased with him) offered to split his wealth into two equal parts and give one share to 'Abdur-Raḥmân ibn 'Awf (may Allah be pleased with him); he even offered to divorce one of his two wives so that his brother 'Abdur-Raḥmân could marry her. Anas ibn Mâlik (may Allah be pleased with him) reported the incident:

«When 'Abdur-Raḥmân ibn 'Awf arrived in Madinah, Allah's Messenger (bpuh) established a bond of brotherhood between him and Sa'd ibn ar-Rabee'.

Sa'd said to him: Come here; I will divide my wealth and give you half. I have two wives. I will divorce one of them, and when she completes her waiting period (from the divorce), you can marry her.

'Abdur-Raḥmân said: May Allah bless you in your family and your wealth. Show me where the market is.

So they showed him where the market was, and he did not return that day until he had some cottage cheese and cooking fat that he had earned as profit.

Allah's Messenger (bpuh) saw him after that, and he had traces of yellow on him. He asked him: What is this?

'Abdur-Raḥmân said: I married a woman from the Anṣâr.

He said: What dowry did you give her?

He said: A date stone (weight in gold) – Ḥumayd, one of the narrators, reported that he said: Gold equal to the weight of a date stone.

So Allah's Messenger (bpuh) said: Prepare a banquet (to celebrate the wedding), even if it is with only one sheep.» (Bukhari and at-Tirmidhi)

This was the characteristic of the Muslim society in the time of Prophet Muhammad (bpuh). Their sacrifice and generosity were unparalleled in human history. They were charitable in helping their fellow Muslims in difficulty. Allah (the Exalted) described to us their generosity, which spread humane compassion in their society, opened closed hearts, and spread the spirit of love and goodwill.

{Those who, before them, had homes [in Madinah] and had adopted the faith, love those who emigrate to them, and have no jealousy in their breasts for that which they have been given [from the booty of Banu an-Nadeer], and give them [the emigrants] preference over themselves, even though they were in need of that. Whosoever is saved from their own covetousness, it is they who will be the successful.}

(Qur'an 59: 9)

The reason for the revelation of this verse of the Qur'an is an incident that took place during the lifetime of Allah's Messenger (bpuh). The following was reported by Abu Hurayrah (may Allah be pleased with him):

«A man came to Allah's Messenger (bpuh) and said: O Messenger of Allah, I am suffering from fatigue and hunger.

The Prophet (bpuh) sent (someone) to his wives (to get something for the man), but the messenger found nothing with them.

Then Allah's Messenger (bpuh) said (to his Companions): Is there nobody who can entertain this man tonight so that Allah may be merciful to him?

An Ansâri man got up and said: I (will entertain him), Messenger of Allah!

He went to his wife and said to her: This is the guest of Allah's Messenger, so do not keep anything away from him.

She said: By Allah, I have nothing but the children's food.

He said: When the children ask for their dinner, put them to bed and put out the light. We shall not take our meals tonight (but we will pretend to be eating with him as he eats).

She did so.

In the morning, the Anṣâri man went to Allah's Messenger (bpuh), who said: Allah was pleased with (or He bestowed His mercy) on So-and-so and his wife (because of their good deed).

Then Allah revealed:

{...But [they] give them preference over themselves even though they were in need of that...}
(Qur'an 59: 9)» (Bukhari)

Generosity requires that we seek out the poorer people in the community and alleviate their poverty and help them out of the difficulties that they are suffering, including paying their debts. We must do so only for the sake of Allah, seeking through our actions only to earn the great rewards that Allah (the Exalted) has promised. Abu Hurayrah (may Allah be pleased with him) narrated that Allah's Messenger (bpuh) said:

«If anyone relieves a believer's burden and distress in this world, Allah will rescue him from difficulty in the hereafter. If anyone alleviates (the situation of) one in dire straits who cannot pay his debt, Allah will alleviate his lot in both this world and the hereafter. If anyone conceals (the faults of) a Muslim, Allah will conceal (his faults) in this life and the hereafter. Allah continuously helps His servant as long as the servant is helping his (Muslim) brother...» (Muslim)

As for those who have received the generosity of their fellow human beings, they have an obligation to be thankful, to show gratitude and to supplicate for Allah to bless those who were generous with them. Prophet Muhammad (bpuh) said:

«Whoever is not grateful to people is not grateful to Allah.» (A sound hadith recorded by at-Tirmidhi)

Usâmah ibn Zayd (may Allah be pleased with both of them) narrated that the Messenger of Allah (bpuh) said:

«Whenever some good is done to a person and he says: May Allah reward you in goodness (*Jazâk Allâh khayr*), then he has done the most that he can to praise (and appreciate the other person's generosity).» (A reliable hadith recorded by at-Tirmidhi)

Chapter Twenty-Four: Amicability

Allah's Messenger (bpuh) said:

«The most virtuous of virtues is to connect (and have good relations) with those who cut you off, to give to those who deny you, and to overlook and pardon those who revile (or falsely accuse) you.» (Recorded by Aḥmad; graded weak by al-Albâni)

Commentary on the hadith

This hadith from Allah's Messenger (bpuh) describes some of the loftiest moral virtues needed for every family, community, and society to lead lives of harmony and peace. These virtues are among many that Prophet Muhammad (bpuh) taught, inculcated, and nurtured in his Companions (may Allah be pleased with all of them). This made them the best of all generations[69] to be emulated, unparalleled in human history.

If we take the harsh, rough approach of cutting off relations with those who turn away from us, and we withhold our goodness from those who deny us, and we take revenge upon all those who wrong us, then what kind of lives are we going to lead? They will be lives of misery, complaints, anxiety, worry, guilt, hatred, anger, and enmity. That is why the Messenger of Allah (bpuh) said that it is virtuous to refrain from reciprocating these hurtful actions.

«One of the Companions of Prophet Muhammad (bpuh) came and said to him: O Messenger of Allah! I stayed with a man who did not entertain me or show me any hospitality. Now he has come to stay with me. Should I treat him the same?

The Prophet (bpuh) said: No, entertain him.» (A reliable hadith recorded by at-Tirmidhi)

«Anas (may Allah be pleased with him) narrated that Allah's Messenger (bpuh) said: Do not cut off relations with one another, desert one another, hate one another, or envy one another. Instead, you worshippers of Allah should be like brothers. It is not lawful for the Muslim to shun his brother Muslim for more than three days.» (A sound hadith recorded by at-Tirmidhi)

These lofty moral teachings, taught in the Qur'an, bind the community together. They teach us to nurture good relations, even with those who have wronged us, by pardoning their shortcomings and mending relations with them. In several passages of the glorious Qur'an, Allah (the Exalted) advises us to take this moral high ground:

{Pardon, [show forgiveness,] enjoin what is good, and turn away from the foolish [without punishing them].}

(Qur'an 7: 199)

{Allah does not like public mention of evil except by one who has been wronged, and Allah is ever All-Hearer, All-Knower. Whether you disclose [by words of thanks] a good deed [done to you in the form of a favor by someone], or conceal it, or pardon an evil, verily, Allah is Ever Oft-Forgiving, All-Powerful.}

(Qur'an 4: 148-149)

{The recompense for an injury is an injury equal to it, but if a person forgives and makes reconciliation, his reward is due from Allah. Verily, He [Allah] does not love those who do wrong.}

(Qur'an 42: 40)

«Al-Barâ' ibn 'Âzib (may Allah be pleased with him) said: Allah's Messenger (bpuh) ordered us to do seven things and forbade us from seven things. He ordered us to visit the sick; to follow funeral processions; (to say) to a person who sneezes: May Allah bestow His mercy on you (*Yarḥamak Allâh*), if he says (after sneezing): All praise is for Allah (*Alḥamdulillâh*); to accept invitations; to propagate the greeting of peace; to help the oppressed; and to help others fulfil their oaths...» (Bukhari)

Once, the Prophet's wife 'Â'ishah (may Allah be pleased with her), the daughter of his close Companion Abu Bakr (may Allah be pleased with him), was falsely rumored to have committed adultery. The accusation was made by the hypocrites, whose aim and objective was to discredit the Prophet's status in Madinah, and the rumor was spread by one of Abu Bakr's own relatives. As a result, Abu Bakr swore that he would cut off relations with the relatives who were involved, no longer helping them or giving them charity.

Abu Bakr (may Allah be pleased with him) was a kind-hearted and generous man, but when he confirmed that the rumor was being spread by one of his relatives, this hurt him deeply and made him swear to cut off the charity and acts of kindness that he used to extend to them. When Abu Bakr made that oath, Allah (the Exalted) revealed verses of the Qur'an advising him, and those who would have such feelings in the future, to overlook and pardon:

{Let not those among you who are endued with grace and amplitude of means resolve by oath against helping their relatives, those in want, and those who have left their homes in Allah's cause. Instead, let them forgive and overlook. Do you not wish that Allah should forgive you? For Allah is Oft-Forgiving, Most Merciful.}

(Qur'an 24: 22)

As we have repeatedly said, pardoning people who have wronged us is not an indication of weakness on our part; on the contrary, it demonstrates strength of character and personality. The weak cannot forgive. Forgiveness is only an attribute of the strong. Abu Bakr aṣ-Ṣiddeeq, the close and beloved Companion of Prophet Muhammad (bpuh), was at the highest levels of faith. Thus, Allah (the Exalted) reprimanded him with such sublime words as quoted in the previous verse. Another incident that happened to Abu Bakr aṣ-Ṣiddeeq in the presence of Allah's Messenger (bpuh) shows us the strength of Abu Bakr's character and personality with respect to amicability:

«It was narrated that Saʿeed ibn al-Musayyib (may Allah be pleased with him) said: While the Messenger of Allah (bpuh) was sitting and his Companions were with him, a man reviled Abu Bakr (may Allah be pleased with him) and offended him, and Abu Bakr remained silent.

He offended him again, and Abu Bakr remained silent.

Then he offended him a third time, and Abu Bakr retaliated.

The Messenger of Allah (bpuh) stood up when Abu Bakr retaliated, and Abu Bakr asked: Are you angry with me, Messenger of Allah?

The Messenger of Allah (bpuh) said: An angel came down from heaven and refuted what he said to you, but when you retaliated, Satan joined in. I do not want to sit where Satan has joined in.» (A reliable hadith recorded by Abu Dâwood)

This is the same Abu Bakr aṣ-Ṣiddeeq, the beloved Companion of Prophet Muhammad (bpuh), whom Abu Hurayrah reported had the following conversation with the Prophet (bpuh) one day while in the presence of the Companions:

«Allah's Messenger (bpuh) asked: Who among you fasted today?

Abu Bakr (may Allah be pleased with him) said: I did.

He asked: Who among you attended a funeral prayer today?

Abu Bakr said: I did.

He asked: Who among you fed a poor person today?

Abu Bakr said: I did.

He asked: Who among you visited a sick person today?

Abu Bakr said: I did.

The Messenger of Allah (bpuh) said: These qualities are not combined in a man except that he will enter paradise.» (Muslim)

To maintain amicable relations with those who wrong us, cut us off, and even deny us our rights is a great moral virtue that requires a strong personality, belief in Allah's help, and belief that He is always with those who patiently persevere with endurance despite all the harm done to them. Prophet Muhammad (bpuh) persevered through all the harm and plotting done by his own tribe and clansmen, and Allah (the Exalted) revealed these verses to reassure and comfort him and those with him who were facing the same persecution and harm:

{If you punish [your enemy], then punish them with the like of that with which you were afflicted; but if you endure patiently, verily, it is better for those who are patient. So endure patiently. Your patience is not but from Allah. Do not grieve over them [polytheists and pagans], and do not be distressed because of what they plot. Truly, Allah is with those who fear Him [and keep their duty to Him], and those who are good-doers.}

(Qur'an 16: 126-128)

Chapter Twenty-Five: Upholding ties of kinship

Abu Hurayrah (may Allah be pleased with him) narrated that the Prophet (bpuh) said:

«Learn enough about your lineage to facilitate keeping good ties of kinship, for indeed, keeping ties of kinship encourages affection among relatives, increases the wealth, and increases the lifespan.» (A reliable hadith recorded by at-Tirmidhi)

«It was narrated from Abu Hurayrah that a man said: O Messenger of Allah, I have relatives with whom I try to keep in touch, but they cut me off. I treat them well, but they abuse me. I am patient and kind towards them, but they insult me.

He said: If you are as you say, then it is as if you are putting hot ashes in their mouths. Allah will continue to support you as long as you continue to do that.» (Muslim)

Commentary on the hadith

Knowing our lineage and keeping good ties of kinship is a moral virtue that is very much neglected in many societies, especially the Western society where the concept of family is narrowed down and confined to the 'nuclear family' of father, mother, and children. In Islam, as we can see from this hadith of Allah's Messenger (bpuh), learning our lineage facilitates keeping good ties of kinship with our extended families, which in turn brings about affection, love, understanding, and better family relationships.

Moreover, whenever there is a good relationship and understanding between extended family members, they tend to support and help each other financially and in other ways. When the more financially fortunate members of the family support and aid the less fortunate members by economically empowering them, this brings about a sense of harmony and satisfaction within the family structure.

Negative feelings of jealousy, hatred, anger, anxiety, contempt, pride, boastfulness, and the like do not crop up often in such a family. The absence of such negative feelings is a great blessing from Allah (the Exalted) that bears the three fruits mentioned by Allah's Messenger in the first hadith under discussion. Allah (the Exalted) mentioned this blessing in His final revelation to humankind, the glorious Qur'an, saying:

{Allah has made for you spouses of your own kind, and has made for you, from your wives, children and grandchildren and bestowed on you good provisions. Will you then believe in vain things and be ungrateful for Allah's favors?}

(Qur'an 16: 72)

As an individual, a woman may at one and the same time be a daughter, a mother, a grandmother, a wife, a sister, an aunt, and a niece. A man may at one and the same time be a son, a father, a grandfather, a husband, a brother, an uncle, and a nephew. However, many societies today tend to care little about the positions one hold within a family.

Our present secular societies have gone to many extremes with regard to family relations. For instance, in liberal Western societies, an individual is regarded as the basic unit of society, and the individual feels independent with the freedom to do whatever he or she wants, whenever he or she wants to. Men and women may choose to live together or have sexual relations without any bond of marriage between them. A man may be a father and know nothing about it – and he may not even care. Children may grow up without ever knowing their fathers, grandparents, or other relatives.

At the other extreme are experimental social systems where the individual counts for nothing and the needs of the community or the state take control of everything. In these cases, childrearing becomes a social industry where care, education, and the provision of all needs becomes a public affair, and being a parent carries few responsibilities or none at all. Even though such systems do promise material comfort and efficiency, the reality is that the love, compassion, and warmth expected between parents and their children is weak or missing. In fact, the human being is devalued and the natural bonds and needs of kinship are stifled and destroyed.

Clearly, the basic unit of society can be neither the individual nor the community. Both units are artificial; they produce much personal stress, distress, and consequently societal disorder for everyone in the society, especially the women and children. This is why the Prophet (bpuh) encouraged learning one's family lineage and connecting family ties and kinship.

«Abu Hurayrah (may Allah be pleased with him) narrated that the Messenger of Allah (bpuh) said: Allah created the creation, and when He had finished, the womb stood up and said: I seek refuge from those who sever the ties of kith and kin.

Allah said: Yes, would it please you if I were to take care of those who take care of you and cut off those who cut you off?

It said: Of course.

Allah said: Then your prayer is granted.

Then the Messenger of Allah (bpuh) said: Recite, if you wish:

{Would you then, if you were given the authority, do mischief in the land and sever your ties of kinship? Such are they whom Allah has cursed, so that He has made them deaf and blinded their sight. Do they not then think deeply on the Qur'an, or are their hearts locked [not open to understanding it]?}

(Qur'an 47: 22-24)» (Muslim)

In many passages in the noble Qur'an, Allah (the Exalted) has emphasized upholding the ties of kinship. He has commanded us to respect and honor family ties and treat blood relations with kindness, even if they are not Muslims, as long as we do not exceed the limits of the Sharia in what they ask us to do.

{O humankind! Be dutiful to your Lord, Who created you from a single person and created, of like nature, his spouse, and from the two of them scattered [like seeds] countless men and women [on the face of the earth]. Fear Allah, through Whom you demand your mutual [rights], and [revere] the wombs [that bore you and do not cut the ties of kinship]; for Allah ever watches over you.}

(Qur'an 4: 1)

In this passage, Allah (the Exalted) links God-consciousness and fear of Him with the respect due to kinship and blood relations, thereby emphasizing the significance of blood ties and their priority over all other relationships, as long as the laws of Allah (the Exalted) are not jeopardized. In another verse, Allah, the Exalted, says:

{The Prophet is closer [and dearer] to the believers than their own selves, and his wives are [pbuh] their mothers [in regard to respect and marriage]. Blood relations among them are closer personal ties, in the decree of Allah [regarding inheritance], than [the ties of brotherhood with other] believers and Muhâjireen. Nevertheless, do what is just and fair to your closest friends; such is the writing of the decree [of Allah].}

(Qur'an 33: 6)

In yet another two statements among the many made by Allah's Messenger (bpuh), he explained to us the high status of kinship and family ties, which will be means of entry into paradise for those who uphold them. In addition, he warned us of neglecting or undermining these bonds and of the consequence of doing so, which is being denied entry into paradise.

«Abu Ayyoob said: A man came to the Prophet (bpuh) and said: Tell me of a deed that I can do which will bring me closer to paradise and take me away from hell.

He said: Worship Allah and do not associate anything with Him, establish the prescribed prayers, pay the zakâh poor-due, and uphold ties of kinship.

When he left, the Messenger of Allah (bpuh) said: If he adheres to what is enjoined upon him, he will enter paradise.» (Muslim)

It was narrated that Jubayr ibn Muṭ'im (may Allah be pleased with him) heard the Prophet (bpuh) say:

«The person who severs bonds of kinship will not enter paradise.» (Bukhari and at-Tirmidhi)

Chapter Twenty-Six: Caring for the weak

Ṣafwân ibn Sulaym narrated that the Prophet (bpuh) said:

«The one who cares for (and looks after) a widow and a poor person is like a person performing jihad in the cause of Allah, or like one who fasts all the day and stands (in prayer) all the night.» (Bukhari, Muslim, at-Tirmidhi, and Ibn Mâjah)

Commentary on the hadith

Among the most vulnerable people in the society – with respect to the necessities of life such as food, shelter, clothing, water, and medical care – are the widows, the poor, and the orphans. That is why a person who makes it a prime concern to care for their continuous daily needs merits the same great rewards as a person who fasts all day and prays all night or a person who performs jihad in the path of Allah. Similarly, Abu Hurayrah (may Allah be pleased with him) narrated:

«The Messenger of Allah (bpuh) said: The one who sponsors an orphan, whether it is a relative of his or not, he and I will be like these two in paradise – and he pointed with his forefinger and middle finger together.» (Muslim)

Thus, it is a praiseworthy moral virtue to care for widows, orphans and the poor – so meritorious that it deserves the mercy of Allah and entry into paradise. This is because it involves sacrificing time, money, and other luxuries for the sake of the weak in society. Today, many people find it very hard to make such sacrifices, so they neglect or care little about such vulnerable and needy people.

It is a great sacrifice for a person to take care of an orphan as if the child were his or her own son or daughter and to provide all the facilities that make life worth living, including tender parental love and care, while knowing that the child is not his or her own. The intention of such a person should be to please Allah (the Exalted) and to make the orphan feel well taken care of, just as the father and mother would have done if they were alive. Thus, the person caring for him or her helps remove the feelings of loss felt by the orphan. It is reported that the Prophet (bpuh) said:

«Would you love for your heart to become soft and for you to be successful in what you seek? Be merciful to the orphan, stroke his or her head (gently, with feelings of love and compassion) and feed him or her with your food. Your heart will become soft, and you will be successful in what you do.»[70]

In the same spirit, Allah (the Exalted) admonishes those believers who are taking care of orphans to neither treat them harshly nor squander the wealth left behind by their parents, because orphans are in a weak and sensitive state from having lost their parents. Allah, the Exalted, says:

{Therefore, do not oppress the orphan.}

(Qur'an 93: 9)

{...They ask you concerning orphans. Say: The best thing to do is what is for their good. If you mix their affairs with yours, they are your brothers. Allah knows the person who means mischief from the person who means good; and if Allah had wished, He could have put you into difficulties. He is indeed Exalted in Power, Wise.}

(Qur'an 2: 220)

In fact, Allah (the Exalted) has reiterated the just and kind treatment of orphans in at least sixteen different places in the glorious Qur'an. Allah clarified the treatment of orphans and gave guidance on how to live with them. Without guidelines, some people are likely to take unfair advantage of orphan children whose parents have left them some inheritance, especially when they are too young to manage and take care of the wealth by themselves.

The widows and the poor are also in the same category as orphans since they too are among the most vulnerable people in society. Hence, those who take orphans, widows, or the poor to live with them, but then end up oppressing and mistreating them, are accountable to Allah (the Exalted) on the Day of Judgment – both for not taking their duties seriously and for forgetting that they will be held accountable for that. Allah (the Exalted) rebukes them in strong terms because they do not really believe in the Day of Recompense:[71]

{No! But you do not honor the orphans [you neither treat them well nor give them their exact right of inheritance]! And you do not urge one another to feed the poor! And you devour the inheritance with greed. And you love wealth with excessive love.}

(Qur'an 89: 17-20)

{Have you seen the one who denies the recompense? That is the one who drives away the orphan and does not encourage the feeding of the poor.} (Qur'an 107: 1-3)

Taking care of the needs of the weak and vulnerable in society is a moral virtue that earns us success in this world and the hereafter. As a result of the prayers and supplications of the weak, we are granted victory in all that we do. This means that whenever the weak and vulnerable are neglected and forgotten, then Allah (the Exalted) also neglects the needs of those who are considered better off, and thus we lose in all our endeavors. On the other hand, when the basic needs of the vulnerable are fulfilled, and they are happy and supplicate to Allah (the Exalted), then we are victorious, as reported in two narrations:

«Muṣ'ab ibn Sa'd narrated that his father thought he was better than other Companions of the Prophet (bpuh), but the Prophet (bpuh) told his father: On the contrary, Allah supports this Ummah because of its weak ones – because of their supplications, their prayers, and their sincerity.» (A sound hadith recorded by an-Nasâ'i)

Jubayr ibn Nufayr al-Ḥaḍrami narrated from Abu ad-Dardâ' (may Allah be pleased with him) that he heard the Messenger of Allah (bpuh) say:

«Bring me the weak, for you only receive provision and divine support by virtue of your weak ones.» (A sound hadith recorded by an-Nasâ'i)

May Allah (the Exalted) help us always to remember to take care of the needs of the weak in our society. Âmeen.

Chapter Twenty-Seven: Treating servants well

«Al-Ma'roor ibn Suwayd narrated: I saw Abu Dharr wearing a *burdâ* (type of garment) and his slave also wearing a burdâ (the same type of garment).

So I said to Abu Dharr: If you take this (burdâ of your slave) and wear it (along with yours), you will have a nice outfit, and you can give him another (different) garment.

Abu Dharr explained: Once, there was a quarrel between me and another man whose mother was not an Arab, and I called her bad names. The man complained about me to the Prophet (bpuh).

The Prophet (bpuh) asked me: Did you abuse So-and-so?

I said: Yes.

He said: Did you call his mother bad names?

I said: Yes.

He said: You still have the traits of (the pre-Islamic period of) ignorance.

I said: Do I (still have traits of ignorance) even now in my old age?

He said: Yes; they (your slaves or servants) are your brothers, and Allah has put them under your command. So the one under whose hand Allah has put his brother should feed him with what he eats, should dress him with what he himself wears, and should not ask him to do a task beyond his capacity. If he asks him to do a hard task, he should help him with it.» (Bukhari, Muslim, at-Tirmidhi, Abu Dâwood, Ibn Mâjah)

Commentary on the hadith

Servants or domestic workers, such as housekeepers, maids, gardeners, gatekeepers, guards, drivers, and the like are often looked upon as lowly. In our day and age, many of them are mistreated, especially by wealthy and well-to-do people.

In this hadith, Abu Dharr (may Allah be pleased with him) shared the advice he was given by Prophet Muhammad (bpuh) regarding the treatment of servants. Abu Dharr received this advice after he had the bad experience of abusing one of the Prophet's Companions, a black Abyssinian and former slave known as Bilâl ibn Rabâḥ (may Allah be pleased with him). Abu Dharr regretted his actions; he never repeated that kind of behavior and strictly followed the guidance he was given by the Prophet (bpuh). That is why his servant or slave was seen wearing the same garments as he himself was wearing.

The magnanimous moral teachings of Islam, as reported in the hadith under discussion, require that we treat our servants in the best manner. We should feed them with what we eat ourselves, clothe them with the same kind of clothes that we wear, and not overburden them with work. If we do give them too much work, then it is our duty to give them a helping hand.

Regardless of how wealthy and well-off we are, the moral teaching of Islam is that we cannot mistreat or mishandle those whom we have employed in our homes or our workplaces – those whom Allah (the Exalted) has made to be our servants. The sublime words of Prophet Muhammad (bpuh) in this regard are very precise and clear. We treat our servants as our brothers and sisters in faith, eating with them the same kinds of food and dressing with them in the same kinds of clothes.

This kind treatment that we give to our servants springs from our true faith in God. In essence, we are all equal in the sight of God regardless of our color, race, tribe, or socio-economic status. It is only that Allah (the Exalted) has favored us with being their employers. If Allah had willed, it could be the reverse; they could be our masters and we could be their servants. Allah (the Exalted) considers this favor a test to see whether we will humble ourselves, as discussed in Chapter 3, or whether we will puff ourselves up with pride over situations that can change in a moment's time. How many rich and wealthy people are there who used to be masters and employers but are now servants and laborers?

{It is He [Allah] Who has made you [His] agents, inheritors of the earth. He has raised you in ranks, some above others so that He may try you in the gifts He has given you. Your Lord is quick in punishment, yet He is indeed Oft-Forgiving, Most Merciful.}

(Qur'an 6: 165)

Even when our servants, whom the Messenger of Allah (bpuh) has called our brothers and sisters in faith, commit common mistakes in the performance of their duties, we should recognize that all human beings make mistakes. It is not befitting to shout at them, beat them, mistreat them or falsely accuse them of things they have not done and then go further and deny them food or deduct their salaries.

We should fear Allah (the Exalted), to Whom all of us are going to be accountable, with regard to the way we handle and treat our servants and those whom Allah has put under us, as the hadith under discussion says. In fact, in a number of statements from Prophet Muhammad (bpuh), he gave us clear moral instructions in this regard:

Abu Hurayrah (may Allah be pleased with him) narrated that Abul-Qâsim (bpuh) – Prophet Muhammad, the Prophet of repentance – said:

«If someone slanders his slave (by falsely accusing him of committing illegal sexual intercourse, stealing or other offences) and the slave is innocent of what he says, Allah will impose the punishment upon him (the person who made the false accusation) on the Day of Resurrection, unless it is (true) what he said about him.» (A sound hadith recorded by at-Tirmidhi)

«Abu Mas'ood al-Anṣâri said: I was beating a slave of mine, and I heard someone behind me saying: Beware, Abu Mas'ood! Beware, Abu Mas'ood!

I turned around and saw that it was the Messenger of Allah (bpuh).

He said: Allah has more power over you than you have over him.

Abu Mas'ood said: I have not beaten any slave of mine since then.» (A sound hadith recorded by at-Tirmidhi)

«'Abdullâh ibn 'Umar narrated: A man came to the Prophet (bpuh) and said: O Messenger of Allah, how many times should a servant be pardoned?

The Prophet (bpuh) was silent.

Then he asked again: O Messenger of Allah, how many times should a servant be pardoned?

He said: Seventy times a day.» (A reliable hadith recorded by at-Tirmidhi)

These are the lofty and beautiful practical teachings of Islam that have almost gone into oblivion in all other systems and ways of life besides Islam. In fact, many Muslims themselves are unaware of these teachings, and we all could use a 'refresher course' in manners!

Chapter Twenty-Eight: Hospitality

«Abu Shurayḥ al-Khuzâ'i (may Allah be pleased with him) reported: Allah's Messenger (bpuh) said: Hospitality is for three days, and full hospitality is one day and night. It is not permissible for a Muslim man to stay with his brother until he causes him to sin.

The people asked: O Messenger of Allah, how could he cause him to sin?

He answered: When he stays with him until there is nothing left with which to entertain him.» (Muslim)

Commentary on the hadith

Welcoming our guests is a highly commendable moral duty in Islam, as the Prophet (bpuh) insisted in this hadith. He explained that hospitality is for three days and nights, and full hospitality, or the guest's reward, is for one day and one night. According to Muslim scholars, complete hospitality means that when the guest departs, he should be given provisions for a day and a night's journey, to ease his travel. This was the view of Ibn Ḥajar al-'Asqalâni in his commentary on this part of the hadith.

Thus, we have a moral obligation to welcome our guests and visitors with a clean and open heart for three days and nights, to serve them the kind of food we eat, and to provide accommodation as good as our own accommodation. If we sincerely welcome our guests and visitors in this manner, on an equal footing without discrimination, then we fulfil our moral obligation, and our rewards are assured with Allah (the Exalted).

{Never will you attain righteousness until you spend [in the way of Allah] from that which you love; and whatever you spend, indeed Allah knows it well.}

(Qur'an 3: 92)

{Not yours [O Muhammad] is responsibility for their guidance. Allah guides whom He wills. Whatever good you [believers] spend is for [the benefit of] yourselves, and you do not spend except seeking the countenance of Allah. Whatever you spend of good [of your wealth, property, resources, time, effort, and so on], it will be fully repaid to you, and you will not be wronged.}

(Qur'an 2: 272)

Without discrimination means that one should not treat guests who seem to be in a higher socio-economic class differently from those who seem to be from a lower socio-economic class. As we indicated in the previous chapter, all children of Adam – all human beings – are equal in Allah's estimation.

{O humankind, indeed We created you from a male and a female, and made you into nations and tribes that you may know one another [not that you may despise or discriminate against each other]. Verily the most noble of you in the sight of Allah is the most righteous of you, and Allah has full knowledge and is Well-Acquainted [with all things].}

(Qur'an 49: 13)

Another important point in this hadith, as explained by Prophet Muhammad (bpuh), is that just as hospitality on the part of a host is a moral obligation, it is a moral obligation for guests to exemplify the best character and behavior while under the host's care. The guest should not be too demanding or choosy in terms of food and accommodation. He or she should not stay longer than the limits sanctioned by the Sharia or beyond the ability of the host, lest this create an inconvenience and a nuisance for the people of the house. The guest must show humility, gratitude and satisfaction for the hospitality accorded him or her.

It was the Sunnah of Prophet Muhammad (bpuh) to supplicate for the host before leaving.

«'Abdullâh ibn Busr from Banu Sulaym reported: The Messenger of Allah (bpuh) came to my father and stayed with him. My father offered him food (and he mentioned the type of food that he brought to him). He brought him something to drink, and he drank it; then he passed it to the person who was on his right (to drink from it also). He ate some dates and put the date stones on the back of his forefinger and middle finger.

When he stood up (to go), my father stood up, took hold of the reins of his mount and said: Supplicate to Allah for me.

He said: *Allâhumma bârik lahum feemâ razaqtahum, waghfirlahum wârhamhum.* (O Allah, bless them in what You have bestowed upon them, and forgive them, and have mercy on them.)» (A sound hadith recorded by Abu Dâwood)

Knowing the situation of the guest, the host may sincerely welcome him or her to stay for a period of more than three days and nights. In this case, anything beyond three days and nights is charity on the part of the host and not an obligation. Nevertheless, it is a commendable act of generosity in the sight of Allah (the Exalted).

Chapter Twenty-Nine: Protecting people's honor

It was narrated from Sa'eed ibn Zayd that the Prophet (bpuh) said:

«The most prevalent form of *ribâ* (usury or interest) is attacking a Muslim's honor without a right.» (A sound hadith recorded by Abu Dâwood)

Ṣafwân narrated from Rasheed ibn Sa'd and 'Abdur-Raḥmân ibn Jubayr that Anas ibn Mâlik reported:

«The Messenger of Allah (bpuh) said: When I was taken up (into heaven), I passed by some people who had nails of copper with which they were scratching their faces and chests.

I asked: Who are these, Gabriel?

He said: They are the ones who consumed the people's flesh (through backbiting) and impugned their honor.» (A sound hadith recorded by Abu Dâwood)

Commentary on the hadiths

One very common habit that many people are involved in – made easier with the revolution in information technology by way of telephones, the Internet, and other forms of media – is maligning other people's honor and integrity and attacking their character and reputations, particularly saying bad things about fellow human beings and looking for their faults. This habit has the consequence of destroying the unity and goodwill in any society. That is why in these two hadiths, the Prophet (bpuh) in very strong terms disapproved of attacking a Muslim's character and integrity, not only comparing it to usury and interest but calling it the worst kind of usury and interest. Moreover, we know how serious the taking of usury and interest is in Islam.[72]

In order to emphasize the serious nature of attacking a person's honor and dignity, Allah's Messenger (bpuh) stated, in another hadith narrated by Abu Hurayrah (may Allah be pleased with him):

«There are seventy degrees of usury, the least of which is equivalent to a man having intercourse with his mother.» (A reliable hadith recorded by Ibn Mâjah)

This implies that the highest degree of usury is reviling and attacking someone's honor without any justification. This understanding is based on the first hadith under discussion, as well as this hadith above. The second caliph of the Muslim state, 'Umar ibn al-Khaṭṭâb (may Allah be pleased with him), was an excellent judge of character; he is reported to have said:

> Do not be deceived by a man's eloquence; rather, whoever fulfils trusts and refrains from impugning people's honor is a real man.[73]

Many people take it lightly when they backbite, slander, and cast doubt on the honor and dignity of their fellow Muslims, whereas Allah (the Exalted) said:

> {O you who believe! Avoid suspicion as much [as possible], for suspicion in some cases is a sin. Do not spy on each other, and do not speak ill of each other behind one another's backs. Would any of you like to eat the flesh of his dead brother? No, you would abhor it. Therefore, fear Allah, for Allah is Oft-Returning, Most-Merciful.}

(Qur'an 49: 12)

It was narrated by Abu Barzah al-Aslami that the Messenger of Allah (bpuh) said:

> «O you who have believed with your tongues but faith has not yet entered your hearts! Do not slander Muslims or seek their faults, for if anyone seeks their faults, Allah will seek his faults; and if Allah seeks a person's faults, He will expose him, even in his own house.» (A reliable hadith recorded by Abu Dâwood)

This is a stern warning from Allah (the Exalted) and His Messenger Muhammad (bpuh) with regard to attacking the honor and integrity of our Muslim brothers and sisters for no good reason at all. It behooves us as Muslims to uphold the moral virtue of protecting our fellow human beings' honor and integrity. Indeed, one who attacks and destroys a fellow Muslim's character and honor for paltry material gain in this world should be sure that his or her character and honor will also be attacked, for the Prophet (bpuh) is reported to have said:

> «No Muslim forsakes a Muslim when his rights are being violated or his honor is being tampered with [or belittled] except that Allah will forsake him at a place in which he would love to have His help. And no person helps a Muslim at a time when his honor is being belittled or his rights are being violated except Allah will help him at a place in which he would love to have His help.» (A weak hadith recorded by Abu Dâwood)

Even though this hadith in *Sunan Abu Dâwood* has been declared weak, there is another hadith with a similar meaning that strengthens it. Abu ad-Dardâ' (may Allah be pleased with him) narrated that the Prophet (bpuh) said:

«If anyone protects his brother's honor, Allah will protect his face from the fire on the Day of Resurrection.» (A reliable hadith recorded by at-Tirmidhî)

In yet another narration, the Prophet (bpuh) is reported to have echoed the same principle: that as you do to others, so it will be done to you:

«Piety and good behavior is never lost, and evil conduct is never forgotten. Allah (the Exalted) does not sleep. So do as you wish, but as you do to others, so it will be done to you.»[74]

«It was narrated that 'Abdur-Raḥmân ibn 'Abdur-Rabb al-Ka'bah said: I entered the mosque and saw 'Abdullâh ibn 'Amr ibn al-'Âṣ sitting in the shade of the Kaaba (the House of Allah in Makkah), and the people were gathered around him.

I came to them and sat down with him, and I heard him say: We were with the Messenger of Allah (bpuh) on a journey, and we made a stop. Some of us began to repair tents, and some of us competed in shooting (arrows), and some of us let our animals graze.

Then the Messenger of Allah's caller for prayer called out: Prayer is about to begin.

We gathered around the Messenger of Allah (bpuh), and he said: It was the duty of every prophet before me to tell his Ummah the best of what he knew was good for them and the worst of what he knew was bad for them. The time of peace and security for this Ummah has been made in its first era, and its last era will be afflicted with trials and things that you object to. Tribulations will come in waves, one after another.

A tribulation will come, and the believer will say: This is going to cause my doom. Then when it ends, another tribulation will come, and the believer will say: This is the one.

If anyone would like to be delivered from hell and enter paradise, let him die believing in Allah and the Last Day, and let him treat people as he would like to be treated...» (Muslim)

The Prophet (bpuh) described a believer as a mirror of another believer. It is only fair and morally upright to protect and care for the honor of our fellow believers, because in essence we are protecting our own honor and integrity.

It was narrated from Abu Hurayrah (may Allah be pleased with him) that the Messenger of Allah (bpuh) said:

«The believer is the mirror of his fellow believer, and the believer is the brother of his fellow believer. He protects him from ruin and looks after him (and his honor).» (A reliable hadith recorded by Abu Dâwood)

'Abdullâh (may Allah be pleased with him) narrated that the Messenger of Allah (bpuh) said:

«The believer does not insult the honor of others, curse, or commit great sins (such as unlawful sexual intercourse), nor is he foul (in speech).» (Muslim and at-Tirmidhi)

Chapter Thirty: Trustworthiness

Al-Mugheerah ibn Ziyâd ath-Thaqafi narrated from Anas ibn Mâlik (may Allah be pleased with him) that Allah's Messenger (bpuh) said:

«The person who has no trustworthiness has no faith, and the person who does not fulfil promises has no religion.» (Recorded by Aḥmad; authenticated by al-Baghawi and Ibn Ḥibbân)

Commentary on the hadith

The above hadith is loud and clear with regard to trustworthiness and fulfilling promises. When people are not trustworthy, it does not matter what they may say or claim for themselves about their faith. They are bound to be judged by their words and actions, and according to this hadith, the Prophet (bpuh) clearly said that such people are not true believers. Moreover, as long as they do not fulfil their promises, then just as they have no complete or true faith, similarly, their religion is not complete. Their practice of religion is lacking in one way or another.

The Companion and caliph 'Umar ibn al-Khaṭṭâb (may Allah be pleased with him) used to say, "Do not look at a person's prayer and fasting; look at his reason and honesty."[75]

This is the reason why Allah (the Exalted) has strongly rebuked those who claim faith with their tongues but do not live according to their claims:

{O you who believe, why do you say that which you do not do? Most hateful it is with Allah that you say that which you do not do.}

(Qur'an 61: 2-3)

{...They say with their tongues what is not in their hearts. Say: Who then has any power at all [to intervene] on your behalf with Allah if His Will is to give you some loss or to give you some profit? Verily, Allah is Well-Acquainted with all that you do.}

(Qur'an 48: 11)

Allah (the Exalted) has directly commanded the rendering back of the trusts to their owners and made it a component of faith, and Allah warned us against betrayal of trust and its bad consequences:

{Allah commands that you should render back the trusts to those to whom they are due, and that when you judge between people, you judge with justice. Verily, how excellent is the teaching which He gives you! Truly, Allah is ever All--Hearing, All--Seeing.}

(Qur'an 4: 58)

{O you who have believed, do not betray Allah and the Messenger or betray your trusts while you know [the consequences].}

(Qur'an 8: 27)

Every promise will be accounted for, and we shall be questioned about them in front of Allah (the Exalted) on the Day of Resurrection:

{...Fulfil every promise, for every promise will be inquired into [on the Day of Resurrection].}

(Qur'an 17: 34)

Trustworthiness is a moral virtue that is directly linked to a person's faith and relationship with Allah (the Exalted). Linguistically, the Arabic word for faith, *eemân*, also has various connotations as it is used in the glorious Qur'an, which include, among others, keeping a trust, securing something, bearing a responsibility, volition or free will, moral choice, chastity, and religion itself as managed by human beings. It is for this reason that Prophet Muhammad (bpuh) said in this hadith that one who cannot be trusted with anything is not a true believer and that one who does not fulfil his or her promises is deficient in religion.

In another of his statements, the Prophet (bpuh) described his own generation and the two following ones as the best generations of all time. Then he foretold that after that, due to lack of faith, there would be people who would betray their trusts and not fulfil their promises:

«Then there will come after them people who will be dishonest and not trustworthy. They will make vows and not fulfil them, and obesity will become widespread among them.» (Muslim)

Similarly, Allah (the Exalted) explains that among the characteristics of true believers who will be successful on the Day of Resurrection is their fulfilment of trusts and promises. It is interesting to note that every time Allah (the Exalted) speaks of the fulfilment of trusts and promises, He links that directly with the strict establishment and guarding of the prescribed prayers:

{Those who faithfully observe their trusts and their promises and who [strictly] guard their prayers, those will be the inheritors, who will inherit the highest part of paradise. They will dwell in it eternally.}

(Qur'an 23: 8-11)

{Those who faithfully observe their trusts and their promises, and those who stand firm [and upright] in their testimonies, and those who [strictly] guard their prayers, such will be the honored ones in the gardens [of bliss in paradise].}

(Qur'an 76: 32-35)

From what Allah (the Exalted) has revealed in these two passages, it is clear and understandable why Allah's Messenger Muhammad (bpuh) described those who are not trustworthy and who do not fulfil their words and promises as lacking in both faith and religion. Indeed such people border on disbelief, or are much closer to disbelief than belief, as Allah (the Exalted) described them in yet another passage when He was exposing the hypocrites in the time of Prophet Muhammad (bpuh):

{And that He might make evident those who are hypocrites, for it was said to them: Come, fight in the way of Allah or [at least] defend yourselves. They said: If we had known [there would be] fighting, we would have followed you. They were nearer to disbelief that day than faith, saying with their mouths what was not in the hearts; and Allah is most knowing of what they conceal.}

(Qur'an 3: 167)

If we consistently fail to fulfil our trusts and promises, then we should realize that we are bordering on hypocrisy because we will have two of the four characteristics of hypocrites described by Prophet Muhammad (bpuh) in this well-known statement narrated by 'Abdullâh ibn 'Amr (may Allah be pleased with both of them):

«Whoever has the following four (characteristics) will be a pure hypocrite, and whoever has one of the following four characteristics will have one characteristic of hypocrisy unless and until he gives it up:

When he is entrusted, he betrays.

When he speaks, he tells a lie.

When he makes a covenant, he proves treacherous.

When he quarrels, he behaves in a very impudent, evil, and insulting manner.» (Bukhari)

Abu Hurayrah (may Allah be pleased with him) narrated that Allah's Messenger (bpuh) said:

«Two things will not be found together in a hypocrite: good manners and comprehension of the religion.» (Recorded by at-Tirmidhi)[76]

On the same note, 'Umar ibn al-Khaṭṭâb (may Allah be pleased with him), who was very worried about finding any sign of hypocrisy in himself, warned us:

There are two (types of) men I do not fear for you: a believer whose faith is obvious and a *kâfir* [disbeliever] whose *kufr* [disbelief] is obvious. Rather I fear for you the hypocrite who hides behind a show of faith but strives for some other purpose.[77]

Prophet Muhammad's Companion Abu Bakr aṣ-Ṣiddeeq (may Allah be pleased with him), in his inaugural sermon when he ascended to leadership after the death of Prophet Muhammad (bpuh), is reported to have said:

O people, I have been appointed over you, but I am not the best of you. If I do well, support me, and if I do wrong, correct me. Truthfulness is sincerity, and dishonesty is a betrayal....[78]

In other words, truthfulness is being trustworthy and lying is treachery. Thus, not keeping our words and promises is tantamount to lying and treachery. Allah (the Exalted) gave a wonderful comparison of the truthful and the trustworthy, promising them paradise, in contrast with the liars and the treacherous, who are given a wretched promise of hell.

{Allah presents an example of those who disbelieved: the wife of Nooḥ [Noah] and the wife of Looṭ [Lot]. They were under [the care of] two of Our righteous servants but betrayed them, so they [those prophets] did not avail them at all against Allah, and it was said to them: Enter the fire with those who enter.}

(Qur'an 66: 10)

{Allah sets forth as an example to those who believe the wife of Pharaoh. Behold, she said: O my Lord! Build for me, in nearness to You, a mansion in the garden, and save me from Pharaoh and his doings, and save me from those that do wrong. And Maryam [Mary], the daughter of 'Imrân, who guarded her chastity: We breathed into [her body] of Our spirit; and she testified to the truth of the words of her Lord and of His revelations, and was one of the devout [servants of Allah].}

(Qur'an 66: 11-12)

Muslim scholars' understanding of truthfulness & trustworthiness[79]

Ar-Râghib al-Aṣfahâni in his *Mufradât Alfâdh al-Qur'ân al-Kareem* noted, "Truthfulness is being consistent in your spoken and unspoken word."

This implies that if we are truthful, the words that we speak are consistent with what we are formulating in our hearts, and the tongue merely speaks for the heart.

We can draw an analogy of this if we consider that the tongue is like a loudspeaker for what a 'cassette tape' is playing in the heart. When we hear speech coming from the speaker of any electronic gadget, we do not conclude that the message is actually being uttered by the gadget; it is coming from what is recorded on a cassette tape or disc of some type. This is like the relationship between the heart and the tongue when a person is truthful. The heart contains the message, and the tongue only articulates what is in the heart.

Therefore, Imam ar-Râghib al-Aṣfahâni concludes that truthfulness occurs when what is in the heart is consistent with what manifests itself on the tongue. Truthfulness is also said to mean consistency between speech and action. For instance, if a man tells his wife that he loves her, yet he continuously does things that annoy her, then this shows that the man is obviously not being truthful with his wife.

Imam Khushari said in his *Risâlah*:

Truthfulness means there is no pollution in our inner states, and then there is no doubt in our beliefs, and there is no defect in our actions, that our actions are uprightly done strictly for Allah and that our actions are done to the best of our ability.

Imam al-Mâwardi in his *Adab ad-Dunyâ wad-Deen* said that there are four things that call us to be truthful in our words and deeds:

1.
    The Islamic Sharia;

2.
    The intellect;

3.
    Basic human decency;

4. Loving a good reputation (wanting to maintain integrity).

Imam Ibn al-Qayyim stated that truthfulness has three manifestations:

1. In our speech – and he explained that the uprightness of the tongue is like the uprightness demonstrated by the ears of the corn in the stalk.

2. In our actions – that is the uprightness of our actions in dealing with the commandments of Allah (the Exalted) and following His Messenger (bpuh), and he noted that this is like the uprightness of the head on the body.

3. In our internal state – that is the uprightness of our hearts in dealing with the commandments of Allah (the Exalted) and His Messenger (bpuh).

Thus, truthful men and women are trustworthy in both their words and deeds. Their word is their bond because they know and are fully convinced that they will be questioned about their truthfulness or their deception and then they will be rewarded or punished accordingly.

{That [Allah] may question the truthful about their truth, and He has prepared for the unbelievers a grievous penalty.}

(Qur'an 33: 8)

The truthful are never treacherous or hypocritical. They stand by what they say under all circumstances. They are straightforward in their lives, and as such, they merit great rewards from Allah (the Exalted), as He says:

{That Allah may reward the truthful for their truth and punish the hypocrites, if that be His will, or turn to them in mercy: for Allah is Oft-Forgiving, Most Merciful.}

(Qur'an 33: 24)

We pray to Allah (the Exalted) to help us all to be truthful and trustworthy in all our endeavors so that we can be among those who will benefit both in this life and the next life when we most need His mercy. Âmeen.

Chapter Thirty-One: Good neighborliness

'Â'ishah (may Allah be pleased with her) reported that she heard Allah's Messenger (bpuh) say:

«Angel Gabriel continued impressing upon me kind and polite treatment towards neighbors (to the extent) that I thought he would confer upon them (the right of) inheritance.» (Bukhari and Muslim)

Commentary on the hadith

Good neighborliness is such a high moral virtue that if it is practiced well, it is capable of creating peaceful coexistence among people of different faiths, religions, and cultures. Especially in this multi-religious and multi-cultural world we live in, which is turning into a global village, we are in need of such lofty moral values with respect to good treatment of our neighbors. That is why Allah (the Exalted) kept sending Angel Gabriel to impress upon Prophet Muhammad (bpuh) the rights of our neighbors until the Prophet (bpuh) thought that they might be included among those who would inherit from us when we die.

This hadith of Prophet Muhammad (bpuh) teaches us that we must at least know who our neighbors are and be concerned about their wellbeing. Nowadays in big cities, many people live in the same block of flats or on the same street for many years without knowing each other. Robbers or gangsters in the neighborhood may attack somebody without the person's neighbors caring or coming to help. However, in the Islamic sense of the word, a neighbor is not just the person who lives next door to you or in your own neighborhood. Rather, a fellow student, a colleague at work, or a fellow traveler on a journey are all regarded as neighbors, and treating them with care and kindness is considered part of worshipping Allah (the Exalted), according to the following verse in the noble Qur'an:[80]

{Worship Allah and associate nothing with Him [in worship], and do good to parents, and to relatives, orphans, the needy, the near neighbor, the neighbor farther away, the companion at your side, the traveler, and those [slaves] whom your right hands possess. Indeed, Allah does not like those who are self-deluding and boastful.}

(Qur'an 4: 36)

The moral high ground manifested by Islam is that neighbors must be given the best treatment in terms of mercy, kindness, and sympathy as mentioned in the Qur'an and as was practiced as a part of the lifestyle of Prophet Muhammad (bpuh), who is reported to have said:

«Whoever believes in Allah and the Last Day should not harm his neighbors.» (Muslim)

«Abu Dharr (may Allah be pleased with him) said: My beloved friend (Muhammad [bpuh]) advised me: Whenever you cook some soup, add extra water, and choose a family among your neighbors and give them some of it with courtesy.» (Muslim)

'Abdullâh ibn 'Amr (may Allah be pleased with both of them) narrated that the Messenger of Allah (bpuh) said:

«The companion who is the best to Allah is the one who is best to his companion, and the neighbor that is the best to Allah is the one that is best to his neighbor.» (A sound hadith recorded by at-Tirmidhi)

«'Â'ishah (may Allah be pleased with her) narrated: I asked: O Allah's Messenger, I have two neighbors; which of them should I give a gift to?

The Prophet (bpuh) replied: (Give) to the one whose door is nearer to you.» (Bukhari)

According to Abdulwahid Hamid:

In terms of preferential treatment, the neighbors who live closest to you have priority regardless of whether they are Muslims or non-Muslims because Islam does not distinguish between Muslims and non-Muslims as far as the human needs and rights of neighbors are concerned.[81]

Following the advice of Prophet Muhammad (bpuh) would solve many problems facing humanity today. We may well ask: Are these the teachings of terrorism, as portrayed by biased media propaganda, or are they the sublime and enlightened teachings that humanity urgently needs to enjoy peaceful co-existence in this short life?[82]

May Allah (the Exalted) open our eyes to see the benefit of these noble teachings of Islam as taught by Prophet Muhammad (bpuh) and to embrace them rather than ignoring or fighting them. Âmeen.

Chapter Thirty-Two: Having a good fragrance

'Abdur-Raḥmân ibn Abi Sa'eed al-Khudri narrated from his father that Allah's Messenger (bpuh) said:

«*Ghusl* (complete ablution) on Fridays is obligatory for everyone who has reached the age of puberty, as well as using siwâk and whatever perfume is available.

(Some of the narrators said: even if it is women's perfume.)» (Muslim)

Commentary on the hadith

Just as it is part of human nature to love beauty and hate ugliness, so it is with cleanliness and a good fragrance as opposed to filth and a bad smell. In light of this reality, Allah's Messenger (bpuh) highly recommended taking a complete bath on Fridays and brushing one's teeth, as well as using perfume that has a nice smell. This is especially important for the Friday congregational prayers, where a large number of Muslims meet to listen to the Friday sermon and perform prayers.

Cleanliness helps a person smell good, which makes those around him or her feel comfortable. To emphasize the importance of cleanliness and personal hygiene, Prophet Muhammad (bpuh) said, in a statement narrated by 'Â'ishah (may Allah be pleased with her):

«Ten things are a part of the *fiṭrah* (the innate, natural inclination of human beings): trimming one's moustache, letting one's beard grow, using the siwâk (or something else to clean the teeth), rinsing the nose with water, trimming one's nails (of fingers and toes), washing in between one's fingers, plucking one's underarm hair, shaving one's pubic hair, and cleaning the private parts (after relieving oneself) using water.» (Muslim)

In fact, it is considered an act of charity to apply a nice perfume that gives us a good smelling fragrance before mixing with our fellow Muslims and human beings. Perfume is an expense, but it is not considered wastefulness or extravagance because we are not putting the perfume on for our own sake but for the sake of those around us.

Muslim women are not allowed to apply perfume when they are going to be around men with whom they have no close relation (literally meaning those they could possibly marry if they were single). However, among other women and close family members, especially their husbands, they are allowed to use perfume. Al-Ash'ari narrated that the Messenger of Allah (bpuh) said:

«If a woman puts on perfume and then passes by people so that they can smell her fragrance, then she is an adulteress.» (An authentic hadith recorded by at-Tirmidhi and an-Nasâ'i)

On the other hand, having a bad odor is considered distasteful and offensive, be it from filth and dirt emanating from our bodies or a foul smell coming from things like cigarettes or raw garlic. Allah (the Exalted) and His Messenger (bpuh) urged the Muslims to behave well towards their Muslim brothers and sisters and not offend them with bad smells.

{Those who harm [and annoy] the believing men and women for other than what they deserve have certainly burdened themselves with a slander and manifest sin.}

(Qur'an 33: 58)

«It was narrated that Jâbir (may Allah be pleased with him) said: Allah's Messenger (bpuh) forbade eating (raw) onions and leeks, but we were overcome by need and we ate some of them.

He said: If anyone eats from these foul-smelling plants, let him not come near our mosques (until he or she has removed the smell), for the angels are offended by the same things that offend humans.» (Muslim)

Chapter 33: Forbearance and Deliberation

Ibn 'Abbâs (may Allah be pleased with both of them) narrated that the Prophet (bpuh) said to Ashajj 'Abdul-Qays:

«Indeed, there are two traits in you that Allah loves: forbearance and deliberateness.» (Muslim and at-Tirmidhi)

Commentary on the hadith

Two other moral virtues that are taken lightly, but which amazingly could solve many problems that cause a lot of regret in people's lives, are forbearance and deliberateness. This refers to thinking deeply and taking one's time over something, so as to consider all alternatives before making a decision. Allah's Messenger (bpuh) described these traits as ones that Allah (the Exalted) loves.

Acting wisely without haste is a most commendable attitude that brings about much good and benefit, in both individuals and society at large, and that makes human life enjoyable and pleasant. Acting wisely means acting with patience and a great deal of deliberation, thoughtfulness, and reflection, while at the same time praying to Allah (the Exalted) for guidance in making important decisions in life, as taught by Prophet Muhammad (bpuh).

It is for this reason that Allah's Messenger (bpuh) taught his Companions to always take their time before making decisions, to first seek sincere advice from honest and trustworthy fellow Muslims, and to seek Allah's guidance through a special prayer known as *istikhârah* before making any important decision in life.

«Jâbir (may Allah be pleased with him) said: The Prophet (bpuh) used to teach us to pray for guidance in making a decision for each and every matter, as he used to teach us chapters from the Qur'an.

He would say: If one of you intends to do something, he should offer a two-unit prayer, other than the obligatory prayer, and then say: O Allah, I seek the counsel of Your knowledge, and I seek the help of Your omnipotence, and I beseech You for Your magnificent grace. Surely, You are capable and I am not. You know and I know not, and You are the Knower of the unseen. O Allah, if You know that this matter (then mention the thing to be decided) is good for me in my religion, in my life, and for my welfare in the life to come (or say: in this life and the hereafter), then ordain it for me, make it easy for me, and bless me in it. And if You know that this matter is bad for me in my religion, in my life, and for my welfare in the life to come (or say: in this life and the hereafter), then distance it from me, and distance me from it, and ordain for me what is good, wherever it may be, and help me to be content with it. (*Allâhumma inni astakheeruka bi'ilmika, wa astaqdiruka biqudratika, wa as'aluka min faḍlikal-'adheem, fa innaka taqdiru wa lâ aqdiru, wa ta'lamu wa lâ a'lamu, wa anta 'allâmul-ghuyoob. Allâhumma in kunta ta'lamu anna hâdhal-amra khayrun lee fee deeni wa ma'âshi wa 'âqibati amri* [or say: *fee 'âjili amri wa âjilihî*] *faqdurhu lee thumma bârik lee feehi. Allâhumma wa in kunta ta'lamu anna hâdhal-amra sharrun lee fee deeni wa ma'âshi wa 'âqibati amri* [or say: *fee 'âjili amri wa âjilihî*] *faṣrifhu 'anni waṣ-rifni 'anhu wa aqdur liyal-khayra ḥaythu kâna, thumma raḍḍini bihi.*)» (Bukhari)

When we practice these noble habits of forbearance and deliberation before making critical decisions in most of our matters, we will get the benefit of not having regrets about the decisions that we make. Allah (the Exalted) advised us never to make hasty decisions, which we will regret afterwards when damage has been caused and it is irreversible.

{O you who believe! If a mischievous person comes to you with information, ascertain the truth, lest you harm people unwittingly and afterwards become full of regrets for what you have done.}

(Qur'an 49: 6)

Of course, it is not easy to acquire such traits except for true and sincere believers who strongly believe that nothing happens except by Allah's permission, especially since we know that Allah (the Exalted) said we human beings are hasty creatures:

{The supplication that people should make for good, they make for evil; for humankind is ever hasty.} (Qur'an 17: 11)

{The human being is a creature of haste...}

(Qur'an 21: 37)

True believers who have forbearance and deliberation learn from their past mistakes and rarely make the same mistakes twice. It was narrated from Abu Hurayrah (may Allah be pleased with him) that the Prophet (bpuh) said:

«A believer should not be bitten twice from the same hole.» (Bukhari and Muslim)

Chapter 34: Reconciliation

«Ḥumayd ibn 'Abdur-Raḥmân narrated from his mother that the Prophet (bpuh) said: A person is not lying when he makes up something between two people in order to reconcile between them.

Aḥmad ibn Muhammad and Musaddad said (in their version): The person is not a liar who reconciles between people and says something good, or conveys something good.» (A sound hadith recorded by Abu Dâwood)

Commentary on the hadith

Among the chronic problems in many parts of the world are disputes and trying to finding resolutions to these conflicts. Allah has given us beautiful moral teachings about how to reconcile between disputing parties, both in the Hadith of His Messenger Muhammad (bpuh) and in many verses of the glorious Qur'an.

The Prophet (bpuh) even said that if someone makes up good statements, even if they are not completely true, with an intention of bringing calmness and a sense of goodwill and reconciliation between contending and disputing parties to resolve their conflict, then such a person is not considered a liar.

«Ḥumayd ibn 'Abdur-Raḥmân ibn 'Awf narrated that his mother, Umm Kulthoom (may Allah be pleased with her) the daughter of 'Uqbah ibn Abu Mu'ayṭ, who was one of the first women of the Muhâjireen to swear allegiance to the Prophet (bpuh), told him that she heard Allah's Messenger (bpuh) say: The person is not a liar who reconciles between people, saying good things and conveying good things.

Ibn Shihâb said (in what he narrated from her that she said): I did not hear of any concession being granted concerning anything that people call lies except in three cases: war, reconciling among people, and what a man says to his wife or a woman says to her husband.» (Muslim)

Thus, the Prophet (bpuh) encouraged us to use any means possible to calm down a hotly disputed situation and make peace and reconciliation. The steps of conflict resolution were laid down in the noble Qur'an more than fourteen centuries ago when Allah (the Exalted) revealed:

{If two parties among the believers fall into a quarrel, make peace and reconciliation between them; but if one of them transgresses beyond bounds against the other, then fight against the one that transgresses until it complies with the command of Allah. If it complies, then make peace and reconciliation between them with justice. Be fair, for Allah loves those who are fair and just. The believers are but a single brotherhood, so make peace and reconciliation between your two [contending] brothers; and fear Allah, that you may receive mercy.}

(Qur'an 49: 9-10)

The beauty of the teachings of Islam is that they are natural and take into account human emotions. That is why we are not allowed to take sides when engaging in conflict resolution. We must face both parties, listen to both sides and make sure that our intentions are to make peace and reconciliation, while not forgetting to face the reality of the dispute without shying away from or hiding the facts. If one party is not ready for reconciliation and peace but instead transgresses against the other party during the reconciliation process, we are required to join efforts and fight the transgressing party until it returns to the command of Allah (the Sharia) for peace and reconciliation. Reconciliation, peace, and settling conflicts are always better than leaving the status quo, as Allah (the Exalted) says elsewhere in the Qur'an:

{The recompense for evil is an evil like it; but whoever forgives and makes reconciliation, his reward is with Allah. Verily, He [Allah] does not like oppressors.}

(Qur'an 42: 40)

{If a wife fears cruelty or desertion on her husband's part, there is no blame on them if they arrange an amicable settlement between themselves; and such settlement is best, even though human souls are swayed by greed; but if you do good and practice self-restraint, Allah is Well-Acquainted with all that you do.}

(Qur'an 4: 128)

The moral virtue of reconciling people sometimes surpasses the rewards of voluntary prayers and fasting. Abu ad-Dardâ' (may Allah be pleased with him) narrated:

«The Messenger of Allah (bpuh) asked: Shall I inform you of what is more virtuous than the rank of fasting, prayer, and charity?

They replied: But of course!

He said: Making peace and reconciliation amongst each other – for indeed, spoiling relations with each other is the razor (that severs or cuts relations).»

It has also been related that the Prophet (bpuh) said:

«It is the razor, and I do not speak of what cuts hair, but what severs the religion.» (at-Tirmidhi and Abu Dâwood)[83]

The above statement, although considered a weak hadith by some scholars, is strengthened by another statement of Prophet Muhammad (bpuh) in which he allowed and encouraged reconciliation on the condition that it did not make unlawful that which is lawful, and vice versa. Katheer ibn 'Amr ibn 'Awf al-Muzani narrated from his father and grandfather that the Messenger of Allah (bpuh) said:

«Reconciliation is allowed among Muslims, except for reconciliation that makes the lawful unlawful or the unlawful lawful. Muslims will also be bound to (fulfil) their conditions, except the conditions that make the lawful unlawful or the unlawful lawful.» (A sound hadith recorded by at-Tirmidhi)

The moral virtue and great rewards of facilitating reconciliation among people, as long as it is done with sincerity seeking only the countenance and pleasure of Allah (the Exalted), have also been mentioned in the Qur'an:

{There is no good in much of their private conversation, except among those who enjoin charity or that which is right [all the good and righteous deeds which Allah has ordained] or reconciliation between people; whoever does that seeking means to the approval of Allah, then to that person We are going to give a great reward.}

(Qur'an 4: 114)

Chapter Thirty-Five: Giving gifts

Abu Hurayrah (may Allah be pleased with him) narrated that the Prophet (bpuh) said:

«Give gifts, for indeed gifts remove bad feelings from the chest. Do not let a person look down upon (the gift given by his or) her neighbor, even if it be a sheep shank.» (Recorded by at-Tirmidhi)[84]

Commentary on the hadith

A true gift is something you are given by one who has thought about you and wishes to please you, even though you did not ask for it. Naturally, the recipient of a gift usually accepts it graciously with happiness and thanksgiving and gratitude to the giver. Consequently, he or she treats the gift preciously, takes care of it, and uses it for his or her own benefit.

Exchanging gifts and presents among friends and neighbors is a healthy way of promoting mutual love and consideration. When done with sincerity of heart, such interaction has the effect of healing rifts and removing the ill feelings and misunderstanding among people that normally occur due to natural human emotions, as mentioned in the above hadith.

In yet another hadith, the Prophet (bpuh) encouraged Muslim women to accept presents and gifts from their neighbors, even if it is as low in value as a sheep's hoof. Abu Hurayrah (may Allah be pleased with him) narrated that the Prophet (bpuh) used to say:

«O Muslim women! A neighbor should not look down upon the present of her (female) neighbor, even if the gift is the trotters of a sheep.» (Bukhari)

This natural tradition and custom of giving gifts to each other, however small in value the gifts may seem, is of great value and importance in the sight of Allah. That is why Allah's Messenger (bpuh) advised that one should not look down on or despise a gift even if it is of low monetary value and little use. Abu Hurayrah (may Allah be pleased with him) related that the Prophet (bpuh) said:

«Give each other gifts and you will love each other.» (Bukhari)

On the other hand, the Prophet (bpuh) forbade us from giving gifts and then taking them back. Ibn 'Umar and Ibn 'Abbâs (may Allah be pleased with all of them) narrated:

«It is not lawful for a person to give a gift and then take it back, except in the case of the father with what he gives to his son. The parable of the one who gives a gift and then takes it back is that of a dog that eats until he is full, and then vomits, then he returns to his vomit.» (A sound hadith recorded by at-Tirmidhi and Ibn Mâjah)

We should not give gifts and then go about telling others about the gifts we have given out to our friends or neighbors. That will embarrass those who received the gifts and make them feel small; furthermore, all of our rewards for this act, both in this world and the hereafter, will be nullified. Allah (the Exalted) discouraged and condemned this kind of behavior, which sadly has become quite common.

{Kind words and forgiving of faults are better than charity followed by injury. Allah is Rich [Free of all wants], and He is Most-Forbearing.}

(Qur'an 2: 263)

Giving gifts to show off and be seen by other people will only bring great loss, rather than good, to those who do so. They will be deprived of Allah's blessings for their good deeds, since they are done to show off and seek the praise of other people. It was narrated by Abu Hurayrah (may Allah be pleased with him) that Allah's Messenger (bpuh) said:

«Allah, Blessed and Exalted is He, said: I am the least in need of a partner. If anyone does any deed in which he associates someone else with Me, I will reject him and his deed.» (Muslim)

How could Allah (the Exalted), the Most Wise, accept these actions when the person who performed them did not do them for His sake? And how could Allah (the Exalted), the Most Just, give to the person who performed actions solely for His sake the same blessings as He does to the one who was doing deeds only to show off and to gain fame and the praise of fellow human beings? Allah (the Exalted) warns against doing actions only for show:[85]

{O you who have believed, do not invalidate your charity with reminders [of it] or injury, like the person who spends his wealth [only] to be seen by the people and does not believe in Allah and the Last Day. His example is like that of a [large] smooth stone upon which is soil, and then it is hit by a downpour that leaves it bare. They are unable [to keep] anything of what they have earned, and Allah does not guide the disbelieving people.}

(Qur'an 2: 264)

Chapter Thirty-Six: Sincerity

«Tameem ad-Dâri (may Allah be pleased with him) narrated that the Prophet (bpuh) said: Religion is sincerity.

The Companions asked: To whom?

He said: To Allah, to His Book, to His Messenger, to the imams (leaders and scholars) of the Muslims and to the common folk.» (Muslim)

Commentary on the hadith

In this very concise and comprehensive statement, the Prophet (bpuh) summarized for us the essence of religion. The more sincere we are, the more religion we have. The less sincere we are in our daily lives – with regard to Allah, His Divine Book, His Messenger, the leaders and scholars of the Muslims, and one's fellow Muslim brothers and sisters – the less religion we have in our lives, and of course, the less morality we possess. Consequently, people who have no sincerity or honesty in their hearts with respect to what the Prophet (bpuh) mentioned above have no religion in their lives, regardless of what they may claim with their tongues, as we have already discussed in Chapters 1 and 30.

Sincerity is a blessing that Allah (the Exalted) grants to those whom He loves among His servants, according to the state of their hearts. If a person's heart is clean and pure, and he or she dedicates all good deeds and actions to Allah (the Exalted) alone, then Allah (the Exalted) will bless that person with true faith and will plant sincerity in his or her heart; otherwise, He will not.

Honesty and sincerity are among the rarest moral virtues in our society these days. Perhaps it is for this reason that there is so much pain and unhappiness in many people's lives. Little wonder then that there is so much dishonesty and corruption in our modern society.

In this hadith, the Prophet (bpuh) has ordered us to be honest and sincere to Allah (the Exalted), His Book, His Messenger (bpuh), Muslim leaders and scholars, and to all other Muslims in general.

Sincerity to Allah (the Exalted)

The first and most important aspect of sincerity is with Allah (the Exalted), the One Who created us and sustains us. Sincerity to Allah (the Exalted) entails fulfilling the following conditions, without which we will not have been completely sincere to Allah (the Exalted):

1. To believe in Allah (the Exalted) without having any doubts in our hearts about His existence. *(Qur'an 49:15; 14:10)*

2. To worship Allah (the Exalted) without associating any partners with Him. *(Qur'an 2:21-22)*

3. To affirm all of Allah's perfect names and attributes as stated in the Qur'an and the Sunnah. *(Qur'an 7:180)*

4. To fulfil to the best of our ability all of Allah's commands and abstain from all that He has forbidden. *(Qur'an 4:69; 2:208)*

5. To do our best to remember, glorify, and praise Allah at all times and in all circumstances. *(Qur'an 62:10; 33:41-42)*

6. To love and hate for the sake of Allah, to befriend those who believe and support His cause, and to disown and oppose those who disbelieve in Allah and are fighting against His cause. *(Qur'an 60:1, 4)*

7. To be honorable for the sake of Allah and to be upset when the laws of Allah are ignored, trampled upon, and disrespected. *(Qur'an 63:8)*

8. To recognize Allah's blessings and to properly thank Him for those uncountable blessings. *(Qur'an 35:3; 16:81)*

9.

To sacrifice that which we love most – such as our money, time, family, energy, sleep, and so on, as we normally do in the month of Ramadan – for the sake of Allah and His religion. *(Qur'an 3:92; 6:162)*

10.

To purify our intentions in all our acts and deeds of righteousness, seeking only the pleasure of Allah (the Exalted). *(Qur'an 18:110; 39:3)*

Obviously when we worship Allah (the Exalted), it is only for our own benefit. Similarly, when we are sincere to Allah, it is also only we who are benefiting; Allah (the Exalted) is Self-Sufficient and is not in need of any of His creatures. It is we, the servants of Allah (the Exalted), who are in need of Him in every step of our lives. When we become sincere to Allah, it is for the good of our own souls because we are purifying ourselves and coming closer to Allah (the Exalted), thereby gaining His love and pleasure.

Sincerity to Allah's Book, the Qur'an

Sincerity to the Book of Allah (the Exalted) also requires the fulfilment of the following conditions:

1.

To believe without a doubt that the Qur'an is the final message of Allah to all of humankind and that it has been preserved and protected from any corruption. *(Qur'an 15:9; 41:41-42)*

2.

To believe that the Qur'an is the uncreated speech of Allah, which is not like the words of human beings. *(Qur'an 4:116)*

3.

To try to the best of our ability to recite, memorize, read, study, and act according to the Qur'an. *(Qur'an 29:45; 2:121)*

4.

To study the admonitions, lessons, and parables in the Qur'an in order to apply them properly in our daily lives. *(Qur'an 38:29)*

5.

To approach the Qur'an properly by seeking its proper interpretation and calling others to believe in it. *(Qur'an 14:1)*

6.

To believe in the Qur'an as the best book, revealed in the best night in the best month, given to the best prophet and the best community, in the best language, with the best of stories.

7.

To love the Qur'an by giving it true respect, treating it in the proper manner and not neglecting it. *(Qur'an 25:30; 20:24-27)*

8.

To rule, decide, and govern all our issues, whether individual or collective, according to the Qur'an. *(Qur'an 4:105; 5:44-47)*

Among the best statements from the Prophet's Companions with regard to sincerity to the Qur'an is this one by 'Ali ibn Abi Ṭâlib (may Allah be pleased with him), the fourth caliph of the Islamic state:

> Stick to the Book of Allah, which speaks of those who have gone before as well as those who will come later and tells the truth in clear and definite terms in matters about which you disagree. Whoever neglects it out of conceit or pride will be humiliated by Allah, and whoever looks for guidance elsewhere will be misled by Allah. It is the rope of Allah, which shall never break, the wise message and the right path, which shall never be distorted by evil minds nor corrupted by wicked tongues. Its mysteries shall never end, nor shall scholars ever be satisfied by the amount they know of it. Whoever speaks according to it has spoken the truth, whoever acts upon it shall be rewarded, whoever rules according to it does justice, and whoever calls [others] to it shows [them] the straight path.[86]

Sincerity to Allah's Messenger Muhammad (bpuh)

Similarly, sincerity to Allah's Messenger entails fulfilling the following conditions:

1.
    To believe that Muhammad (bpuh) is the last and final prophet and messenger, who was sent to all of humankind to guide them to the straight path. *(Qur'an 33:40)*

2.
    To believe that Muhammad (bpuh) is the best, greatest, and the most beloved of all the prophets and messengers. *(Qur'an 68:4)*

3.
    To follow Prophet Muhammad's teachings and obey him absolutely, without question, as long as what has been reported of his teaching is authenticated to be from him – for he is the true human judge and authority for all of humankind. *(Qur'an 4:59)*

4.
    To love Prophet Muhammad (bpuh) more than ourselves, and to love his family and Companions, who sacrificed so much for Islam. *(Qur'an 33:6)*

5.
    To honor, respect, and defend the personality of Prophet Muhammad (bpuh). *(Qur'an 3:31)*

6.
    To befriend those who love Prophet Muhammad (bpuh) and to disown those who are against him and his teachings. *(Qur'an 48: 29)*

7.
    To accept Prophet Muhammad (bpuh) as the sole and absolute human judge in all our affairs and disputes. *(Qur'an 4:65)*

8.
    To revive his Sunnah by learning, teaching, implementing, and conveying his teachings to humankind while at the same time fighting any innovations that go against or belittle his Sunnah. *(Qur'an 59:7)*

All this sincerity to the Messenger of Allah (bpuh) is not possible unless we study the biography of our beloved Prophet Muhammad (bpuh). It is indeed a false claim to say that we love our Prophet (bpuh) and that we are sincere to him when we know very little about his life, for indeed how can we love and be sincere to a person whom we do not know?

Sincerity to the leaders of the Muslims

There are two kinds of leaders in the Muslim community, according to the teachings of the hadith that we are analyzing: the religious leaders, or scholars, and the worldly leaders, or rulers. The importance of sincerity to our leaders is captured in the following statement from the Prophet (bpuh).

«There are three things that if a person adheres to them, they purify his heart from any form of treachery or evil: performing deeds purely for the sake of Allah, being sincere with those in authority, and sticking to the Muslim community, for (its members') supplications encompass each other.» (A reliable hadith recorded by Aḥmad, ad-Dârimi and Ibn Ḥibbân)

This clearly shows that there is no one above receiving and accepting good advice. Everyone is deserving of sincere conduct and sincere advice. Everyone is in need of such advice, and it must be given to everyone, no matter how high ranking or prestigious the person may be. With respect to submitting to Allah (the Exalted) and His Sharia, all are equal; no one is above the law. Indeed, rulers or scholars should be the first to accept sincere advice from others. At the same time, they are the first who deserve respect, honor, and sincere relations. Therefore, giving advice and being sincere to the leaders based on evidence from Qur'an and Sunnah includes:

1. Helping them when they are following the truth and judging justly

2. Obeying them in what is right according to the Sharia

3. Reminding them when they err or forget

4. Being patient with them when they do things that we dislike

5. Making jihad under their command and not rebelling against their proper authority

6. Praying for their guidance and piety, for this will benefit the community

7. Correcting them in the proper way when they make mistakes, but not searching for their errors in order to expose them, for they are human beings who are prone to make mistakes like the rest of us

The inaugural sermon of Abu Bakr aṣ-Ṣiddeeq, when he was given the pledge of allegiance as the first caliph after the death of Prophet Muhammad (bpuh), is evidence of how to show sincerity to our Muslim leaders as mentioned in the points above. Abu Bakr (may Allah be pleased with him) began by praising and glorifying Allah (the Exalted). He then said:

> O people, I have been appointed over you, but I am not the best of you. If I do well, support me, and if I do wrong, correct me. Truthfulness is sincerity, and dishonesty is a betrayal. The weak one among you is strong in my eyes until I restore his rights, if Allah wills; and the strong one of you is weak in my eyes until I take what is due from him, if Allah wills. If people abandon jihad for the sake of Allah, He will humiliate them. If immorality becomes widespread among the people, Allah will send His punishment upon them all. Obey me as long as I obey Allah and His Messenger; if I disobey Allah and His Messenger, you have no duty to obey me. Get up and pray, may Allah have mercy on you.[87]

In this sermon of Caliph Abu Bakr aṣ-Ṣiddeeq (may Allah be pleased with him), we can clearly see the humility, sincerity, open-mindedness, courage, sense of responsibility, motivational principles, spirit of participatory policy, correct understanding of obedience, and drive towards team building offered by the Commander of the Faithful. He gives an excellent masterpiece of comprehensive advice to his fellow Muslims, whom he considers equal members of the Muslim community. If only our modern leaders could adopt the advice and example of such truthful and God-fearing leaders, then all the seemingly complex tribulations that have befallen the Muslim Ummah could be easily simplified and quickly solved.

Sincerity to ordinary Muslims

Being sincere to other Muslims includes:

1. Guiding each other as Muslims to what is good for us in this world and in the hereafter.

2. Not harming each other.

3. Teaching each other Allah's religion and religious duties, about which some of us may be ignorant or neglectful.

4. Aiding and supporting each other in times of difficulty as brothers and sisters in faith.

5. Concealing each other's personal faults.

6. Encouraging each other to perform good deeds and forbidding each other from evil deeds.

7. Being merciful, kind, and gentle to the young among us and being respectful to the elderly.

8. Feeling joy when the Muslims are in a good state and feeling sadness when the Muslims are suffering.

9. Cooperating and helping each other in good works but not in sin or transgression.

10. Fulfilling the six rights of a Muslim from another Muslim, according to the hadith of Prophet Muhammad (bpuh):

«When you meet him, offer him greetings; when he invites you to a meal, accept the invitation; when he seeks your sincere advice, give it to him; when he sneezes and says: *Alḥamdulillâh* (All praise is for Allah), say to him: *Yarḥamuk Allâh* (may Allah have mercy on you); when he falls ill, visit him; and when he dies, follow his funeral bier.» (Muslim)

11.

Helping our fellow Muslims whether they are the oppressed or the oppressors.

«Anas (may Allah be pleased with him) narrated that Allah's Messenger (bpuh) said: Help (or assist) your brother, whether he is an oppressor or is oppressed.

A man enquired: Allah's Messenger, I help him when he is oppressed, but how can I help him when he is an oppressor?

He said: You can prevent him from committing oppression. That will be your help to him.» (Bukhari)

12.

Acting sincerely towards the Muslims when one is in a position of authority over them and doing what is in their best interests according to the Sharia. Ma'qil narrated that he heard the Prophet (bpuh) say:

«Any person to whom Allah has given the authority of ruling over people who does not look after them in an honest (and sincere) manner will never have even the fragrance of paradise.» (Bukhari and Muslim)

May Allah (the Exalted) bless us with soft and tender hearts full of sincerity in all our endeavors. Âmeen.

Chapter Thirty-Seven: Visiting the sick

It was narrated from Abu Asmâ' from Thawbân, who is also called Abu ar-Rabee', and also narrated from Abu Sa'eed that Allah's Messenger (bpuh) said:

«The one who visits the sick is in an orchard of paradise (or harvesting the fruits of paradise) until he returns.» (Muslim)

Commentary on the hadith

Sick people are some of the most vulnerable people because of the test and trial of illness that Allah (the Exalted) has given them. As such, they need constant encouragement as well as reassurance that whatever they may be going through, however painful it may seem, is only temporary and is bound to pass, and is hoped to be followed by good health and ease, as Allah (the Exalted) says:

{So, verily, with every difficulty, there is relief. Verily, with every difficulty there is relief.}

(Qur'an 94: 5-6)

Allah (the Exalted) never tests or burdens a soul with more than it can bear. This is the understanding of illness that we should give to sick people when we visit them.

{Allah does not burden a soul except with that which it can bear. It will have [the consequence of] what [good] it has gained, and will bear [the consequences of] what [evil] it has earned...}

(Qur'an 2: 286)

{But those who believed and did righteous deeds – We charge no soul except [within] its capacity. Those are the companions of paradise; they will abide therein eternally.}

(Qur'an 7: 42)

Taking time from our very busy schedules to go and visit the sick, whether in the hospital or in their homes, is a great moral virtue that deserves great rewards, as the Prophet (bpuh) indicated in the hadith under discussion. The reward is as if we are walking in the orchards of paradise until we return home. This is very true, because even visiting healthy fellow Muslims and friends for the sake of Allah causes a person to deserve the love of Allah (the Exalted), so how about going to visit one who is sick and very vulnerable? Certainly by visiting the sick (with the intention of seeking Allah's pleasure), we deserve the love of Allah (the Exalted) even more. It was narrated from Abu Hurayrah (may Allah be pleased with him) that the Prophet (bpuh) said:

«A man visited a brother (in faith) in another town, and Allah sent an angel to wait for him on the road.

When he came to him, the angel asked: Where are you headed?

The man replied: I am headed to a brother of mine in this town.

The angel asked: Have you done him any favor for which you hope to be recompensed?

He replied: No, but I love him for the sake of Allah.

The angel said: I am a messenger from Allah to you, to tell you that Allah loves you as you love him (your brother in Islam) for His sake.» (Muslim)

Abu Hurayrah (may Allah be pleased with him) narrated that Allah's Messenger (bpuh) said:

«If anyone visits the sick or his brother in (faith in) Allah, a caller calls out to him: May you have goodness and your livelihood be good, and certainly you have gotten for yourself a palace in paradise.» (Recorded by at-Tirmidhi)[88]

Abu Moosâ al-Ash'ari (may Allah be pleased with him) narrated that the Prophet (bpuh) said:

«Feed the hungry, visit the sick, and set captives free.» (Bukhari)

When we go to visit the sick, we must purify our intentions so that we are doing it for the sake of Allah (the Exalted). If that is the case, it is encouraged to carry some fruit or some other token gift for the sick person to show our concern for his or her health and wellbeing. Furthermore, Allah's Messenger taught us to give warm and welcoming greetings to the sick person with a face full of hope and reassurance, while saying to the sick person:

«It is not bad; may Allah make (the illness only) a purification (for you) if He wills. (*La ba's, ṭuhoorun in shâ' Allâh.*)»[89]

For indeed, the Prophet (bpuh) is reported to have said:

«If a Muslim who is afflicted with sickness or anything else (is patient with it), Allah will cause the person's bad deeds to fall away like leaves fall from a tree.» (Muslim)

We should also not forget to supplicate for Allah (the Exalted) to give good health and a quick recovery to the sick person whom we have gone to visit, as was taught by the Prophet (bpuh):

«'Â'ishah (may Allah be pleased with her) narrated that when the Messenger of Allah (bpuh) visited a sick person, he would pray for him and say: Take away the pain, O Lord of humankind, and grant healing, for You are the Healer, and there is no healing but Your healing, a healing that leaves no trace of sickness. (*Adh-hibil ba's rabbin-nâs, wa'shfi anta ash-shâfi, lâ shifâ' illâ shifâ'uka shifâ'an lâ yughâdiru saqaman.*)» (Muslim)

We should also request that the sick person pray and supplicate for us, since a sick person is very close to Allah (the Exalted) in the sense that he or she is always remembering and glorifying Allah (the Exalted) and supplicating to Him because of the pain the person feels, and most, if not all, of the person's sins are forgiven, as the hadith quoted above said. Abu Hurayrah (may Allah be pleased with him) narrated that the Messenger of Allah (bpuh) said:

«Allah, Glorified and Exalted is He, will say on the Day of Resurrection: O son of Adam, I fell sick and you did not visit Me.

It will be asked: O Lord, how could we visit You when You are the Lord of the Worlds?

He will say: Did you not know that My slave So-and-so was sick, but you did not visit him? Do you know that if you had visited him, you would have found Me with him...?» (Muslim)

This does not mean that Allah (the Exalted) is physically present with the sick person. It means that the sick person is close to Allah (the Exalted) in the sense that Allah (the Exalted) covers the sick person with His gracious mercy and sends angels of mercy to bless the person and ask forgiveness for the person and thus purify the person of sins. This understanding is taken from another hadith in which 'Ali ibn Abi Ṭâlib (may Allah be pleased with him) narrated that he heard the Messenger of Allah (bpuh) say:

«Whoever comes to his Muslim brother and visits him (when he is sick), it is as if he is walking among the harvests of paradise reaping its fruits, until he sits down; when he sits down, he is covered with (Allah's) mercy. If it is in the morning, seventy thousand angels will send blessings upon him until evening; if it is in the evening, seventy thousand angels will send blessings upon him until morning.» (A reliable hadith recorded by Ibn Mâjah)

Therefore, visiting our sick brothers and sisters in faith and humanity is a moral virtue that should not be taken lightly. We ask Allah (the Exalted) to grant us merciful hearts that are concerned about other people's suffering. Âmeen.

Chapter 38: Thinking well of people

It was narrated from Abu Hurayrah (may Allah be pleased with him) that the Prophet (bpuh) said:

«Thinking well of people is part of worshipping properly.» (A reliable hadith recorded by Abu Dâwood)

Commentary on the hadith

All human beings have been created with a natural inclination to do good, even though there is some inclination, from the whispers of Satan, to do evil.

{...[Adhere to] the *fitrah*[90] of Allah with which He has created [all] people. No change should there be in the creation of Allah...}[91]

(Qur'an 30: 30)

{We have certainly created human beings in the best of stature.}[92]

(Qur'an 95: 4)

Similarly, Abu Hurayrah (may Allah be pleased with him) narrated that Allah's Messenger (bpuh) said that every human child is born with the fitrah, in a natural state of goodness:

«No child is born except with the fitrah (of pure Islamic monotheism), and then his parents convert him into a Jew or a Christian or a Magian (fire-worshipper), just as an animal gives birth to a perfect baby animal. Do you find any among them that are mutilated[93] (at birth)?» (Bukhari and Muslim)

As such, we should always look at the positive qualities of our fellow human beings and think well of them. After all, we are all human beings and in that respect all equal in the sight of Allah (the Exalted).

{O humankind! We created you from a single [pair of a] male and a female, and made you into nations and tribes, that you may know each other [not that you may despise each other]. Verily the most honored of you in the sight of Allah is [the person who is] the most righteous of you, and Allah has full knowledge and is Well-Acquainted [with all things].}

(Qur'an 49: 13)

Therefore, there is no good in being overly suspicious or spying on one another. In most cases, suspicion only leads to backbiting, gossiping, rumor mongering, jealousy, and envy, all of which consequently lead to enmity of each other and the weakening and breakup of the community. That is why these actions were forbidden by Allah's Messenger (bpuh) in a narration by Abu Hurayrah (may Allah be pleased with him):

«Beware of suspicion, for suspicion is the falsest of speech. Do not seek out one another's faults, do not spy on one another, do not compete with one another (in material wealth), do not envy one another, do not hate one another, and do not turn away from one another. Be, O slaves of Allah, brothers (and sisters to one another).» (Muslim)[94]

It is really counterproductive to seek out people's private faults and afterwards spread news of them in public, since no one is perfect. Allah's Messenger Muhammad (bpuh) is reported by his Companion Anas (may Allah be pleased with him) as saying:

«All of Adam's descendants are prone to error, and the best of the error-prone are those who repent often.» (A reliable hadith recorded by Ibn Mâjah)

«A Muslim is a brother to a Muslim. He does not wrong him or let him suffer (nor does he forsake him when he is in need). If anyone takes care of his brother's needs, Allah will take care of his needs (too). If anyone relieves a Muslim of some distress in this world, Allah will relieve him of some distress on the Day of Resurrection, and if anyone conceals a Muslim's (faults), Allah will conceal (his faults) on the Day of Resurrection.» (A sound hadith recorded by Abu Dâwood)

According to the main hadith under discussion, if we concentrate on having good thoughts about people and cease looking for their faults, we will benefit from the good that Allah (the Exalted) has placed in them through the mutual cooperation in good works that will naturally develop among us. Ibn 'Umar (may Allah be pleased with both of them) narrated that the Messenger of Allah (bpuh) said:

«You will find that people are like a hundred camels among whom a man cannot find one that is fit for riding.» (Muslim and at-Tirmidhi)

With this approach of looking for the good side of others, we will not waste much of our precious time on useless idle talk about our fellow human beings, which can eat up our righteous deeds. Instead, we will reflect on our own selves and how we will fare in our graves and in front of Allah (the Exalted) for our own judgment on the Day of Resurrection.

{O you who believe, fear Allah and let every soul look to what it has put forth for tomorrow – and fear Allah. Indeed, Allah is acquainted with all that you do. Do not be like those who forgot Allah, so He made them forget themselves; such are the rebellious transgressors.}

(Qur'an 59: 18-19)

'Abdullâh ibn Mas'ood (may Allah be pleased with him) reported that the Prophet (bpuh) said:

«On the Day of Resurrection, the feet of the son of Adam will remain firmly planted, and he will not be able to move from Allah until he answers five questions: how he spent his lifetime, where and how he spent his youth, how and where he acquired his wealth, how and where he spent his wealth, and what he did with the knowledge he acquired.» (An 'odd' hadith recorded by at-Tirmidhi; graded reliable by al-Albâni)

Dear brothers and sisters in humanity and in Islam, may Allah (the Exalted) have mercy on you and me. Let us weigh what we think about our fellow human beings and be especially careful about what we say about them, for indeed good thoughts about people join hearts together, which in itself is part of proper worship of Allah (the Exalted).

Privacy of people's personal affairs is as highly regarded in Islam as it is in most man-made systems of government, if not more so, because it is a part of man's nature to regard certain things as personal and confidential. Hence... the invasion of human privacy is opposed by Islam from every conceivable angle. The last Prophet of Islam (bpuh) advised his followers to stay out of other people's business by describing the practice of minding one's own business as being among the qualities which complete a Muslim's Islam. It was reported by Abu Hurayrah (may Allah be pleased with him) that the Prophet (bpuh) said, "Among the things which complete a person's Islam is his leaving that which is of no concern of his."[95,96]

The only things we will be excused for regarding negative or prying thoughts about others are thoughts that come into our minds which we do not put into speech or action. Allah (the Exalted) has excused us from blame for these because we are not able to completely control thoughts that pass through our minds. Abu Hurayrah (may Allah be pleased with him) reported that the Prophet (bpuh) said:

«Allah (the Exalted) overlooks the evil thoughts of the Muslim nation as long as they do not speak about them or act on them.» (Bukhari)

Chapter Thirty-Nine: Observing the rights of the street

«It was narrated from Abu Sa'eed al-Khudri (may Allah be pleased with him) that the Prophet (bpuh) said: Beware of sitting in the street.

The Companions said: Messenger of Allah, we have no other choice but to sit there and engage in conversation there.

The Messenger of Allah (bpuh) said: If you must sit there, then give the street its rights.

They asked: What are its rights?

He said: Lowering the gaze, refraining from causing annoyance, returning the greeting, enjoining what is good, and forbidding what is evil.» (Bukhari, Muslim, Abu Dâwood, and Aḥmad)

Commentary on the hadith

There is so much talk about human rights, women's rights, and even children's rights – but based on people's own wishes rather than Allah's will. However, instead of the modern society becoming a better place in which to live, in which to enjoy Allah's bounties and unlimited favours, and in which to worship Allah (the Exalted) and obey His commands, the earth has become a most insecure place to live in, replete with corruption, immorality, and disobedience of Allah (the Exalted), because of the oppression and injustices that prevail in society.

The essence of moral values in Islam as taught by Prophet Muhammad (bpuh), as we have seen in all these hadiths discussed so far, is fundamentally to enable us to do good to others. We should give other human beings their due rights, and we should prevent human beings from harming and usurping other people's rights.

In this amazing hadith, Prophet Muhammad (bpuh) taught us how to guard the rights of the streets and byways and, in the process, give the rights due to all those passing by. In the same way, Allah (the Exalted) also directed the people in the time of Prophet Shu'ayb (pbuh) not to sit on every roadside threatening and hindering people from the path of Allah:

{Do not sit on every path, threatening and averting from the way of Allah those who believe in Him, seeking to make it [seem] crooked. Remember when you were few and He increased you [in numbers]; and see how the end was for those who did mischief.}

(Qur'an 7: 86)

Lowering the gaze

The first right of the street mentioned by Allah's Messenger (bpuh) is lowering the gaze. Neglect of this right has become one of the biggest problems facing the world today. In addition, there is the problem of near nudity, especially among women, which is increasing day by day. These problems are becoming compounded, leading to increasing immorality in all its forms in society.

> Feelings of shyness and modesty are natural and instinctive in humans. Their expression is the natural shyness one feels in exposing one's private parts to anyone else.
>
> On the other hand, the sexual instinct is the greatest weakness of the human race. Satan, indeed, selected this weak spot for his attack on his adversaries and devised a scheme to strike at their modesty. The first step he took in this direction was to expose their nakedness to them so as to open the door of indecency before them and beguile them into shameless sexuality.
>
> To this day Satan and his disciples adopt the same scheme of depriving women of feelings of modesty and shyness. They convince them that exposing and exhibiting themselves to all and sundry is part of what it means to be 'liberated'.[97]

Satan, the greatest enemy of humankind, is always keen to tempt and seduce people into committing forbidden acts by making those acts fair-seeming and attractive. This is exactly how he promotes the promiscuous intermingling of sexes under the name of freedom. He entices pleasure-loving, misguided men and women to disregard the restrictions laid down by their Creator so they will ignore their natural instincts of modesty:[98]

{O you who believe! Do not follow the footsteps of Satan. Whoever follows the footsteps of Satan, then certainly, he commands indecency and all that is evil and wrong and forbidden in Islam...} (Qur'an 24: 21)

Prophet Muhammad (bpuh) also informed us that Satan moves through the human being like blood runs through the veins. (Muslim) One of the most 'innocent' ways through which he induces people into committing indecent acts is by leading a man to be alone with a non-*mahram*[99] woman. It was reported that the Prophet (bpuh) said:

«If a man is alone with a (non-mahram) woman, Satan will be the third with them.» (A sound hadith recorded by at-Tirmidhi)

It is an admitted fact that the eyes are the messengers that carry the messages to the minds and hearts of the one looking. It is the attraction of the face and shape of the body of the opposite sex that arouses feelings of desire and stirs emotions in one's heart. Islam therefore segregates the sexes and enjoins that the believing men and believing women keep their eyes down and avoid staring at the opposite sex as much as possible, to avoid unlawful arousal. Muslims are forbidden from casting evil and critical glances at members of the opposite sex, but today the temptation and provocation has gone beyond the limit, and that is especially apparent in the way many modern women dress.[100] Many women today go about in the weirdest manner, without hijabs, displaying their beauty and their costly outfits, and with strong scented perfume, all in a blatant way that naturally attracts the attention of men. These unhealthy conditions coupled with the poisonous habit of free mixing in almost every place in our society, including public transport, schools, hospitals, private companies and government offices, have created situations where males and females alike are exposed to moral degeneration and chaos.[101]

Hence, the first right of the street or public place is that we lower our gaze and safeguard ourselves from the sexual immorality that has plagued the society and is threatening to completely destroy it from within. Allah, the Exalted, says:

{Say to the believing men that they should lower their gaze and guard their modesty; that will make for greater purity for them; and Allah is well acquainted with all that they do. And say to the believing women that they should lower their gaze and guard their modesty; that they should not display their beauty and adornment except that which is [necessarily] apparent of it...}

(Qur'an 24: 30-31)

Refraining from causing annoyance

The second right of the street mentioned by Allah's Messenger (bpuh) is to avoid causing annoyance in the streets and roads. This right is comprehensive and includes everything that would bother or irritate other people, such as the following:

- Spitting on the roadside

- Smoking or being drunk on the roadside

- Throwing filth and rubbish on the streets

- Blocking the pathways where people need to pass

- Laughing in a very loud and disturbing manner

- Hugging, kissing, and other public displays of sexual affection

Allah (the Exalted) and His Messenger Muhammad (bpuh) have forbidden us from causing any form of annoyance to our fellow Muslims and other human beings, either by our speech or our actions with any kind of unbecoming behaviour, as mentioned above.

{Those who harm [and annoy] the believing men and women for other than what they deserve have certainly burdened themselves with slander and manifest sin.}

(Qur'an 33: 58)

Jâbir (may Allah be pleased with him) reported that he heard Allah's Messenger (bpuh) say:

«The Muslim (or true believer) is the one from whose tongue and hand (other) Muslims are safe.» (Muslim)

Returning the greeting

Another right of the street is to reply to greetings which are given, for indeed returning a greeting joins hearts together and creates a sense of love and friendliness between people, thus increasing their faith. Allah (the Exalted) expressly commanded the returning of greetings:

{When a [courteous] greeting is offered to you, reply to it with a greeting even more courteous, or [at least] of equal courtesy. Indeed, Allah takes careful account of all things.}

(Qur'an 4: 86)

Thus, it is sinful for us to ignore greetings and not reply accordingly whenever they are offered to us. We are held accountable for returning greetings, for Allah (the Exalted) said in the above verse: {Allah takes account of all things} – even the seemingly simple reply to greetings offered.

Furthermore, Prophet Muhammad (bpuh) expressly indicated that the act of spreading greetings of peace among ourselves brings about love of each other in our hearts and strengthens our faith. Abu Hurayrah (may Allah be pleased with him) narrated that the Messenger of Allah (bpuh) said:

«You will not enter paradise until you (truly) believe, and you will not (truly) believe until you love one another. Should I not guide you to something which, if you do it, will cause you to love one another? Spread the greetings of peace (As-salāmu 'alaykum [peace be with you]) among you.» (Muslim)

Enjoining good and forbidding evil

The last right of the roadway enjoined by Allah's Messenger (bpuh) in the hadith under discussion is: enjoining what is good and pleasing to Allah (the Exalted) and forbidding each other from evil. This is a very important matter that helps to reform both individuals and society so that good character and moral values permeate the society. Otherwise, if evil is left to continue in society without being checked, then we run the risk of heading towards total destruction. As discussed in Chapter Fifteen, an-Nu'mân ibn Basheer (may Allah be pleased with him) narrated that the Prophet (bpuh) said:

«The situation of the person abiding by Allah's orders and limits, in comparison to the one who does wrong and violates Allah's orders and limits, is like the example of people drawing lots for seats in a boat. Some of them get seats in the upper part, while the others get seats in the lower part. Those in the lower part have to pass by those in the upper one to get water, and that troubles the latter.

One of the people (in the lower part) takes an axe and starts making a hole in the bottom of the boat.

The people of the upper part come and ask him: What is wrong with you?

He replies: You have been troubled much by me (coming up to your section), and I have to get water.

Now if the people of the upper part prevent him from doing what he is doing, they will save him and themselves, but if they leave him (to do what he wants), then they will all be destroyed.» (Bukhari)

Ḥudhayfah ibn al-Yamân (may Allah be pleased with him) narrated that the Prophet (bpuh) said:

«By the One in Whose Hand is my soul! Either you command good and forbid evil, or Allah will certainly soon send upon you a punishment from Himself; then you will call upon Him, but He will not respond to you.» (A reliable hadith recorded by at-Tirmidhi)

Allah (the Exalted) reminds us about this situation in the Qur'an so that we may take heed:

{Evil has appeared on land and sea because of what the hands of humans have earned [by their oppression and evil deeds], that Allah may make them taste a part of that which they have done, in order that they may return [by repenting to Allah and begging His pardon].}

(Qur'an 30: 41)

To be safe from these calamities in the community, we must always have people who are enjoining good and forbidding evil. Without such people, immorality becomes more widespread in society, and the punishment of Allah (the Exalted) follows. Then we will try to supplicate to Allah (the Exalted) to remove the calamities and punishment, but our supplications will not be answered, as we saw in the preceding hadith.

{Let there arise out of you a band of people inviting to all that is good, enjoining what is right, and forbidding what is wrong. They are the ones that will [ultimately] be successful.} (Qur'an 3: 104)

Commanding good and forbidding evil is a condition for being safe from all kinds of afflictions and trials, and it is a sure way to succeed in this life and the hereafter. Allah, the Exalted, says:

{When some of them said: Why do you preach to a people whom Allah will destroy or visit with a terrible punishment? The preachers answered: To discharge our duty to your Lord, and perchance they may fear Him. When they disregarded the warnings that had been given them, We rescued those who forbade evil; but We visited the wrongdoers with a grievous punishment, because they were given to transgression.}

(Qur'an 7: 164-165)

Abu Sa'eed al-Khudri (may Allah be pleased with him) reported that he heard Allah's Messenger (bpuh) say:

«If anyone of you sees an evil action (taking place), let him change it with his hand; and if he is not able to do so, then with his tongue; and if he is not able to do so, then with his heart – and that (last option) is the weakest of faith.» (Muslim and Abu Dâwood)

The duty of commanding good and forbidding evil on the roadside, or any other public place, is one of the rights of the street. It will invite the mercy of Allah (the Exalted) and save us from all the disasters and calamities plaguing humanity today. Allah, the Exalted, says:

{The believing men and believing women are allies [helpers, supporters, and protectors] of one another. They enjoin what is right, forbid what is wrong, establish prayer, give zakât, and obey Allah and His Messenger. Those are the ones upon whom Allah will have mercy. Indeed, Allah is Exalted in Might and Wise.}

(Qur'an 9: 71)

Chapter Forty:
Listening and obeying

«'Irbâḍ ibn Sâriyah (may Allah be pleased with him) said: Allah's Messenger led us in the dawn prayer, and then he delivered a concise admonition that reached our inner selves; it made our eyes tearful and our hearts fearful.

One of us said: O Messenger of Allah, it is as if it is a farewell admonition, so advise us.

He said: I advise you to have taqwâ of Allah and to listen and obey (your leader), even if it is an Abyssinian slave. Certainly, the ones among you who will live after me will see lots of differences. So stick to my Sunnah and the Sunnah of the rightly-principled and rightly-guided successors. Cling to that (as if) with your molars, and avoid newly-introduced matters. Verily, every newly-introduced heresy leads to going astray.» (A sound hadith recorded by at-Tirmidhi, Abu Dâwood, Ibn Mâjah, ad-Dârimi)

Commentary on the hadith

The first piece of advice given by Allah's Messenger (bpuh) in this concise admonition, which made his Companion's eyes tearful and their hearts fearful, was for them to have taqwâ of Allah: to always be conscious of Allah, to fear and love Him, and to keep one's duty to Him, as He deserves.

Muslim scholars explain that taqwâ of Allah was the first thing Allah's Messenger (bpuh) advised because taqwâ is the heart of all advice in the glorious Qur'an. It is by fearing Allah (the Exalted) that people become obedient to Allah and keep away from evil. It is by having taqwâ that we become good-hearted, kind, polite, sympathetic, well-behaved, and dutiful, not only to Allah (the Exalted) but also to our parents and to other human beings.

Taqwâ, or the fear of Allah, is the beginning of wisdom. Because of the importance and significance of having taqwâ, Allah (the Exalted) mentioned it, together with its derivatives, more than one thousand times in the glorious Qur'an. Taqwâ is a defence against evil and temptations; it keeps a person within the boundaries of his or her pure and natural state.[102]

The scholars have described taqwâ as 'the single most important quality that a person should develop in relation to good and evil'.[103] The great scholar Safi-ur-Raḥmân al-Mubârakpuri (may Allah have mercy on Him) calls taqwâ 'the foundation of the religion'. Allah's Messenger's concise admonition to have taqwâ of Allah is so important that the Prophet (bpuh) gave this advice to Muslims in numerous hadiths. In fact, all of the prophets were sent to admonish people to have fear and consciousness of Allah. Allah, the Exalted, says:

{The people of Nooḥ [Noah] denied the messengers when their brother Nooḥ said to them: Will you not fear Allah? Indeed, I am to you a trustworthy messenger. So fear Allah and obey me. I do not ask you for any payment for it. My payment is only from the Lord of the worlds. So fear Allah and obey me.}

(Qur'an 26: 105-110)

{To Allah belong all that is in the heavens and all that is in the earth. We have advised the People of the Scripture before you and you also [Muslims] to have taqwâ of Allah [to fear Allah and keep your duty to Him]...}

(Qur'an 4: 131)

The great philosopher and Muslim scholar Abu Ḥâmid al-Ghazâli discussed the importance of having taqwâ of Allah; he commented on the preceding Qur'anic verse:

If there were any characteristic that is better for humans, more comprehensive in its goodness, greater in its reward, more important for worship, weightier in its measure, more important in its substance, more rescuing in the long-run than this characteristic of taqwâ of Allah, then Allah would have ordered His servants to have that other characteristic. Allah has advised His most dear servants to have this characteristic out of His Perfect Wisdom and Encompassing Mercy. When he advised this one characteristic, and combined together His previous and later servants upon that characteristic, and mentioned that characteristic only, you then know that it is the final goal beyond which there is none other and for which there is no other purpose. ...Also you know by that fact that this one characteristic of taqwâ of Allah combines together all the good of this life and the hereafter, that is sufficient for all the important matters that lead one to the highest ranks [in paradise].[104]

Definition of *taqwâ*

In order to understand any subject in life, we must understand the true meaning of what is being discussed. Most Muslim scholars always begin any subject by giving the complete definition of what is being discussed, in order to remove and avoid any misunderstanding or misconception in the minds of their audience. In Arabic Islamic scholarship, definitions come in five different shades: a word may be defined according to the language of its origin, according to its technical usage, according to its customary and traditional usage, or according to the Islamic Sharia – which is the meaning that was adopted after the Qur'an and Sunnah were revealed to Prophet Muhammad (bpuh), or a word can be understood figuratively.[105]

For our purposes (and with respect to the scope of this short commentary), we are going to look at:

- The literal meaning of having taqwâ of Allah as it is used in the Arabic language, since it is originally an Arabic term, and

- The definition of the term from the Sharia point of view, since it is mentioned many times both in the Qur'an and the Sunnah, as we have seen in the admonitions given by Allah's Messenger (bpuh) to his Companions and the Muslims in general.

Literally, the word taqwâ, as in 'taqwâ of Allah', means to be conscious of Allah and to be careful and watchful enough not to overstep the limits set by Him. Among Arabic language dictionaries, *Lane's Lexicon* defines a person who has taqwâ in the following way:

> He preserved or guarded himself exceedingly or extraordinarily; he put something between himself and another to preserve himself or guard himself. In the conventional language of the law, *He preserved or guarded himself exceedingly or extraordinarily from sin of commission or omission...* It may often be rendered, *He was pious, or he was careful of his religious duties.* (He guarded himself against them in an extraordinary degree and was cautious or wary.)[106]

The meaning implied in this Arabic understanding of the word taqwâ is that the essence of taqwâ is 'putting a barrier or guard between oneself and that which one fears in order to protect oneself from what is feared'. In other words, one should fear or protect himself or herself from Allah's anger and punishment. This can only be done by obeying Allah without any disobedience. This is the minimum aspect of taqwâ, according to the scholar Jamâl al-Din Zarabozo.

Furthermore, if one puts some kind of distance between himself or herself and disobedience of Allah (the Exalted), then the person has fulfilled what this admonition of taqwâ really implies. The Companions Abu ad-Dardâ' and al-Ḥasan (may Allah be pleased with both of them) both stated that people who have taqwâ even leave off permissible deeds out of fear that there might be something harmful in them. Consequently, these doubtful or permissible acts are the barriers that they have put between themselves and the acts of disobedience.

Sometimes the word taqwâ is directly followed by mentioning the place of Allah's punishment, such as hell, or the time of Allah's punishment, such as the Day of Resurrection. Again, the meaning in the Arabic usage of the word is the same, in the sense that one must protect himself or herself from the harm related to those times and places. Three examples from the Qur'an will suffice to show that the verb derivative of taqwâ means to fear and guard oneself:

{Then guard yourselves against a Day [of Judgement] when one soul will not avail another, nor will intercession be accepted for it, nor will compensation be taken from it, nor will anyone be helped [from outside].}

(Qur'an 2: 48)

{Fear the day when you shall be brought back to Allah. Then shall every soul be paid what it earned, and no one shall be dealt with unjustly.}

(Qur'an 2: 281)

{Fear the fire, which is prepared for those who reject faith. So obey Allah and the Messenger in order that you may obtain mercy.}

(Qur'an 3: 131-132)

Allah (the Exalted) and His Messenger (bpuh) also explicitly defined to us the meaning of taqwâ and noted the characteristics of people who have taqwâ, as we find in the following very comprehensive verse and hadith:

{It is not righteousness that you turn your faces towards the east or west [in prayers]. Righteousness is to believe in Allah, the Last Day, the angels, the Book [the Qur'an], and the messengers; and to give of your wealth, out of love for Him, to your kinsfolk, the orphan, the needy, the wayfarer, and those who ask, and to ransom [the freedom] of slaves; to establish the prayer and practice regular charity; to fulfil the contracts which you have made; and to be firm and patient, in pain [or suffering] and adversity, and throughout all periods of panic. Such are the people of truth; such are the God-fearing.}

(Qur'an 2: 177)

An-Nawwâs ibn Sam'ân (may Allah be pleased with him) narrated that the Prophet (bpuh) said:

«Righteousness is good character (or morality), and wrongdoing is that which wavers in your heart and which you dislike people finding out about.» (Muslim)

In other words, having taqwâ of Allah is not merely claiming it with one's tongue; it is not only establishing prayers, nor is it how long a man's beard is or how high above the ankles his trousers are. Although they are important aspects of the Sunnah of Allah's Messenger (bpuh) that cannot be neglected, these things contribute towards the fear of Allah but in and of themselves do not constitute taqwâ of Allah. Rather, taqwâ, as we have seen, is an important quality and characteristic of piety and God-consciousness, a longing for His pleasure and a fear of His displeasure, all of which creates a real and lasting improvement in human habits and good conduct. It is an inner quality that we have to struggle to develop and maintain in our daily lives, and it is supported by righteous actions.

Consequently the place of taqwâ is not in our faces, our appearances or our socio-economic status but rather in our hearts. This is exactly as Prophet Muhammad (bpuh) taught us.

«The Messenger of Allah said: Piety is here – and he pointed to his chest three times.» (Muslim)

He also said:

«Allah does not look at your outward forms and your wealth. Rather, He looks at your hearts and your deeds.» (Muslim)

Saying that the place of taqwâ is the heart means that a heart which is infected with common spiritual diseases may not attain taqwâ of Allah. Therefore, we must strive to rid ourselves of the ailments of the heart that prevent it from being conscious of its Lord, such as disbelief in Allah's favours, associating partners with Allah, hypocrisy, envy and jealousy, arrogance and boastfulness, nationalism and tribalism, greed and miserliness, doubtfulness, hatred, backbiting, showing off, and the like.[107]

Like faith, taqwâ of Allah has different levels to it. There is the minimum level that is required to save oneself from eternal punishment in the hellfire, and there is the higher level of those who deserve the title of *muttaqeen*, or the righteous. Al-Âloosi, a famous commentator on the Qur'an, wrote:

> Linguistically, *wiqâyah* means seeking protection or guarding oneself in general. In the Sharia, it is for a person to guard himself from what is harmful in the hereafter. It is of different levels that correspond to the different levels of possible harm. The first level is to protect and keep oneself away from *shirk* [or associating any partners with Allah]. The second level is to refrain from the great sins, and this includes committing a minor sin on a daily basis. The third level is what is alluded to in what is recorded by at-Tirmidhi from the Prophet (bpuh):

> «A person will not reach the level of the Muttaqeen until he leaves something in which there is no harm out of fear that it may contain some harm.»[108]

How to develop *taqwâ* in one's heart

Among the requirements necessary to develop and gain taqwâ are: correct Islamic knowledge, true and correct Islamic faith and beliefs, and the worship of Allah as taught in the Qur'an and the Sunnah.

With regard to correct Islamic knowledge as a foundation for building taqwâ, Allah, the Exalted, says:

{...Those among Allah's servants who truly fear Him are those who have knowledge, for Allah is Exalted in Might, Oft-Forgiving.}

(Qur'an 35: 28)

{Is one who is devoutly obedient during periods of the night, prostrating and standing [in prayer], fearing the hereafter and hoping for the mercy of his Lord [like one who is not]? Say: Are those who know equal to those who do not know? It is only people of understanding who will remember [and get a lesson from Allah's signs and verses].}

(Qur'an 39: 9)

As for having strong faith in Allah and other pillars of faith and increasing faith as a way of developing taqwâ, Allah (the Exalted) says in the Qur'an:

{O you who believe! Believe in Allah and His Messenger and the scripture which He has sent to His Messenger and the scripture which He sent to those before [him]. Anyone who denies Allah, His angels, His Books, His messengers, and the Day of Judgement has gone far, far astray.}

(Qur'an 4: 136)

{The believers are those who, when Allah is mentioned, feel a tremor in their hearts; and when His verses are recited to them, the verses increase their faith; and in their Lord they put their full trust.}

(Qur'an 8: 2)

In the case of the various acts of worship which are pleasing to Allah, Allah (the Exalted) directed all humankind to worship Him devoutly in order to attain taqwâ:

{O people! Worship your Lord, Who created you and those who came before you, that you may become righteous.}

(Qur'an 2: 21)

{Worship Allah and do not join any partners with Him. Do good to parents, kinsfolk, orphans, those in need, neighbours who are near, neighbours who are strangers, the companion by your side, the wayfarer [you meet], and [the slaves] that your right hands possess: for Allah does not love those who are arrogant and vainglorious.}

(Qur'an 4: 36)

There are many acts of worship that, if sincerely and devoutly directed to Allah (the Exalted), will increase and strengthen our faith and consequently help us to develop taqwâ. The following eight are especially effective:

(1) Knowing with certainty that no good or harm can befall a person except by the will of Allah

{If Allah touches you with affliction, no one can remove it but He; and if He touches you with happiness, He has power over all things.}

(Qur'an 6: 17)

{The believers are only those who have believed in Allah and His Messenger, and have never since doubted, but have striven with their belongings and their selves in the cause of Allah. Such are the sincere ones.}

(Qur'an 49: 15)

Ibn 'Abbâs (may Allah be pleased with both of them) narrated:

«I was (riding) behind the Prophet (bpuh) one day when he said: Son, I will teach something (important). Be mindful of Allah,[109] and He will protect you. Be mindful of Allah, and you will find Him before you.[110] When you ask, ask Allah; when you seek aid, seek Allah's aid. Know that if the entire creation were to gather together to do something to benefit you, you would never get any benefit unless Allah had written it for you, and if they were to gather to do something to harm you, you would never be harmed unless Allah had written it for you. The pens have been lifted, and the pages are dried.» (A reliable hadith recorded by at-Tirmidhi)

(2) Constant remembrance of Allah (*dhikr*)

{O you who believe! Remember Allah with much remembrance, and glorify His praises morning and afternoon.}

(Qur'an 33: 41-42)

{Verily, in the creation of the heavens and the earth, and in the alternation of night and day, there are indeed signs for people of understanding, those who remember Allah [always, and in prayers] standing, sitting, and lying down on their sides, and who think deeply about the creation of the heavens and the earth [saying]: Our Lord! You have not created [all] this without purpose, glory to You! Give us salvation from the torment of the fire.}

(Qur'an 3: 190-191)

{O you who believe! When the call to prayer is proclaimed on Friday [the Day of Assembly], hasten earnestly to the remembrance of Allah and leave off business; that is best for you if you but knew! When the prayer is finished, then you may disperse through the land and seek of the bounty of Allah; and celebrate the praises of Allah often [and without stint], that you may prosper.}

(Qur'an 62: 9-10)

{Remember Me [Allah], and I will remember you. Be grateful to Me; do not be ungrateful to Me and reject the faith.}

(Qur'an 2: 152)

{...For men and women who guard their chastity, and for men and women who engage much in Allah's praise, for them Allah has prepared forgiveness and great reward.}

(Qur'an 33: 35)

{Recite what has been revealed to you of the Book [the Qur'an] by inspiration, and establish regular prayer, for prayer keeps one away from shameful and unjust deeds; and the remembrance of Allah is the greatest [thing in life] without doubt; and Allah knows what you do.}

(Qur'an 29: 45)

Abu Moosâ (may Allah be pleased with him) narrated that the Prophet (bpuh) said:

«The example of the one who celebrates the praises of his Lord (Allah) in comparison to the one who does not celebrate the praises of his Lord is that of a living creature compared to a dead one.» (Bukhari)

Abu Hurayrah (may Allah be pleased with him) narrated that he heard Allah's Messenger (bpuh) say:

«Indeed the world is cursed and what is in it is cursed, except for remembrance of Allah, what is conducive to that (or those acts which Allah loves that bring one nearer to Him), the knowledgeable person, and the person who is trying to learn.» (A reliable hadith recorded by at-Tirmidhi)

«Abu ad-Dardâ' (may Allah be pleased with him) narrated that the Prophet (bpuh) said: Should I not inform you of the deeds that are best, the deeds that are purest with your Lord, the highest of your deeds in rank, and what is better for you than spending gold and silver, and better for you than meeting your enemy while you strike their necks and they strike your necks?

The Companions said: Yes, of course.

He said: It is the remembrance of Allah.

Muʿâdh ibn Jabal (may Allah be pleased with him) said: There is nothing that brings more salvation from the punishment of Allah than the remembrance of Allah.» (A reliable hadith recorded by at-Tirmidhi)

It was narrated from Abu Hurayrah (may Allah be pleased with him) that the Messenger of Allah (bpuh) said:

«If anyone says: None has the right to be worshipped but Allah alone, with no partner or associate; His is the dominion, to Him is all praise, and He has power over all things (*Lâ ilâha illâ Allâhu waḥdahu lâ shareeka lahu; lahul-mulk wa lahul-ḥamd, wa huwa ʿalâ kulli shay'in qadeer*) one hundred times in a day, it will be equivalent to freeing one hundred slaves, and one hundred good deeds will be recorded for him, and one hundred bad deeds will be erased for him, and it will be a protection for him against Satan all day until evening comes, and no one will do anything better than what he has done except one who does more than that. If anyone says: Glory and praise be to Allah (*Subḥân Allâhi wa biḥamdihi*) one hundred times in a day, his sins will be erased, even if they are like the foam of the sea.» (Muslim)

The remembrance of Allah that will help us increase our faith and consequently develop taqwâ of Allah includes the following:

- Establishing the five daily prescribed prayers *(Qur'an 20: 14)*

- Supplicating to Allah (the Exalted) at all times *(Qur'an 40: 60; 2: 186; 59: 10)*

- Glorifying, sanctifying, praising, and exalting God Almighty[111]

- Reciting the Qur'an, especially in the morning after the dawn prayer *(Qur'an 17: 78; 8: 2-4)*

- Enjoining what is good and right and forbidding what is wrong and evil *(Qur'an 9: 71)*

(3)

Recognizing Satan as our avowed enemy and being watchful by keeping away from him and his companions

Satan took a vow in front of Allah (the Exalted) that he would try to make us deviate from the straight path and make us ungrateful to Allah (the Exalted). Both of these go directly against taqwâ of Allah, Who says:

{He [Satan] said [to Allah]: Because You have thrown me out of the way [due to my ingratitude and transgression], I will lie in ambush for them on Your straight path. Then I will assault them from in front of them and from behind them and from their right and their left sides so that most of them will not be grateful [for Your mercy].}

(Qur'an 7: 16-17)

The commentators of the Qur'an explain that when Satan said he was going to assault us 'from in front', it means he will make us doubt the hereafter; and when he said he will assault us 'from behind', it means he will make us crave the worldly life. When he said he will assault us from our right, it means he will confuse us in our religion by causing us to be divided on minor issues and by making us introduce innovations in Islam; when he said he will assault us from the left, it means he will make us rebel against Allah's commandments. Alas, this is exactly what is happening today! So Allah (the Exalted) warned us against following the footsteps of Satan and told us unequivocally that Satan is our great enemy:

{O people! Eat of what is on earth, lawful and good; and do not follow the footsteps of Satan, for he is to you an avowed enemy.}

(Qur'an 2: 168)

{O people! Certainly the promise of Allah is true. So do not let this present life deceive you, and do not let the chief deceiver [Satan] deceive you about Allah. Verily Satan is an enemy to you, so treat him as an enemy. He only invites his followers that they may become companions of the blazing fire.}

(Qur'an 35: 5-6)

{O Children of Adam! Do not let Satan seduce you in the same manner as he got your parents [Adam and Eve] out of the garden, stripping them of their raiment to expose their shame; for he and his tribe watch you from a position where you cannot see them. We made the devils friends [only] to those without faith.}

(Qur'an 7: 27)

If we listen to and respond to the whispers of Satan and follow him, then our faith will be affected. Consequently, there will be no taqwâ of Allah in our hearts, and on the Day of Judgement, Satan will only forsake us and laugh at us. Allah, the Exalted, said:

{Satan will say when the matter is decided: It was Allah Who gave you a promise of truth. I too promised, but I failed in my promise to you. I had no authority over you except to call you, but you listened to me. So do not reproach me; instead, reproach your own souls. I cannot listen to your cries, nor can you listen to mine. I reject your former act in associating me with Allah. For wrongdoers there must be a grievous penalty.}

(Qur'an 14: 22)

(4) Constant remembrance of death

Remembering that we will one day die and appear before Allah (the Exalted) for judgement also increases our faith and helps us to develop taqwâ in our hearts. This is because when we remember death, we tend to repent and ask Allah to forgive our sins. Allah, the Exalted, says:

{Every soul shall have a taste of death, and only on the Day of Judgement will you be paid your full recompense. Whoever is saved far from the fire and admitted to paradise, he is indeed successful, for the life of this world is but the enjoyment of deception [a deceiving thing].}

(Qur'an 3: 185)

{From the [earth] We created you, and into it We will return you, and from it We will bring you out once again.}

(Qur'an 20: 55)

{Every soul shall have a taste of death, and We test you by evil and by good by way of trial, and to Us you will be returned.}

(Qur'an 21: 35)

{O you who believe! Let not your riches or your children divert you from the remembrance of Allah. If any do so, the loss is their own. Spend something [in charity] out of the substance which We have bestowed on you before death comes to any of you and he says: O my Lord! Why did you not give me respite for a little while? I would then have given [a large amount] in charity, and I would have been one of the good-doers. Allah grants respite to no one when the time appointed [for death] has come, and Allah is Well-Acquainted with all that you do.}

(Qur'an 63: 9-11)

Abu Hurayrah (may Allah be pleased with him) narrated that the Messenger of Allah (bpuh) said:

«Increase your remembrance of the severer of pleasures (meaning death).» (A reliable hadith recorded by at-Tirmidhi and Ibn Mâjah)

«Hâni' (may Allah be pleased with him), the freed slave of 'Uthmân (may Allah be pleased with him), said: When 'Uthmân stopped at a grave, he would cry until his beard was soaked (in tears).

It was said to him: Paradise and the fire were mentioned, and you did not weep, yet you weep because of this?

So he said: Indeed Allah's Messenger (bpuh) said: The grave is the first stage among the stages of the hereafter, so if one is saved from (punishment in) it, then what comes after it is easier. If one is not saved from it, then what comes after it is worse. And Allah's Messenger (bpuh) said: I have never seen any scene more horrible than the grave.» (A reliable hadith recorded by at-Tirmidhi)

This is why Prophet Muhammad (bpuh) encouraged visiting graveyards, washing the dead, burying the dead, and visiting the sick – so that we could continuously prepare ourselves for the hereafter and thus strengthen our faith and increase our obedience to Allah (the Exalted).

«Al-Barâ' ibn 'Âzib (may Allah be pleased with him) narrated that Allah's Messenger (bpuh) ordered us to do seven things and forbade us from doing seven other things... He ordered us to accompany funeral processions, visit the sick, and extend the greeting (of peace) to everyone...» (Bukhari)

(5)
Increasing one's voluntary acts of worship

People who depend on obligatory acts of worship (done ritualistically without devotion and consciousness) and who do not do any voluntary acts of worship beyond the basic requirements are likely to be losers in the long run. They may not develop the quality of taqwâ in their lives, as Allah (the Exalted) says:

{Among humankind are some who worship Allah negligently. If good befalls them, they are well contented; but if a trial comes to them, they turn their faces [away from Allah] and lose both this worldly life and the hereafter. That is indeed a manifest loss!}

(Qur'an 22: 11)

The Prophet (bpuh) encouraged us to increase voluntary acts of worship as a way of improving our faith and developing the quality of taqwâ in our hearts. Abu Hurayrah (may Allah be pleased with him) narrated that Allah's Messenger (bpuh) said:

«Allah said: I will declare war against the person who shows hostility to a pious worshipper of Mine. The most beloved things with which My slave comes nearer to Me are what I have enjoined upon him, and My slave keeps on coming closer to Me through performing extra deeds of worship until I love him. So I become his sense of hearing with which he hears, and his sense of sight with which he sees, and his hand with which he grips, and his foot on which he walks; and if he asks Me, I will give him. If he asks for My protection (and refuge), I will protect him.» (Bukhari)

According to Muslim scholars, the meaning of Allah (the Exalted) becoming our eyesight by which we see, our hearing by which we hear, our hands by which we grasp, and our feet by which we walk is that He will assist and help us in doing only those things that are pleasing to Him. Hence, obligatory acts of worship should be followed by voluntary acts of worship that might include the following:

- Extra sunnah prayers

- Fasting, such as on Mondays and Thursdays and on the three 'white' days (the 13th, 14th, and 15th) of every month according to the lunar calendar

- Giving charity to the poor

- Reciting and memorizing the Qur'an

(6) Keeping good company

Keeping away from bad companionship and bad friends will help a person to avoid all types of sins, and having good friends and companions will help a person to increase his or her faith and consequently to develop taqwâ. This is why Allah, the Exalted, says:

{Close friends, that day, will be enemies to each other except for the righteous [to whom Allah will say]: O My servants! No fear will there be concerning you this day, nor will you grieve.

[You] who believed in Our verses and were Muslims, enter paradise, you and your spouses, rejoicing and delighted.}

(Qur'an 43: 67-70)

Allah (the Exalted) also advised us to keep good company, such as the companionship of righteous people, scholars, students of knowledge, those who command what is good and right and forbid what is evil and wrong, those who encourage the giving of charity, and those who facilitate reconciliation between people. Allah, the Exalted, says:

{There is no good in most of their secret talks except (for) the person who orders charity, or the good and righteous deeds which Allah has ordained, or reconciliation among people. He who does this, seeking the good pleasure of Allah, We shall give him a great reward.}

(Qur'an 4: 114)

Abu Hurayrah (may Allah be pleased with him) reported that the Prophet (bpuh) said:

«A person follows the religion of his (or her) friend; so look (and be careful about) whom you befriend.» (A reliable hadith recorded by at-Tirmidhi and Abu Dâwood)

Abu Sa'eed reported that the Prophet (bpuh) said:

«Do not accompany anyone except a believer, and do not let anyone eat your food but a person of taqwâ.» (A sound hadith recorded by Abu Dâwood)

Allah (the Exalted) further warned us to keep away from evil companionship and stick with the people of the Sunnah of Allah's Messenger (bpuh) to avoid regrets on the Last Day.

{The day that the wrongdoer will bite at his hands, he will say: Oh! Would that I had taken a [straight] path with the Messenger! Woe is me! Would that I had never taken such a one for a friend! He did lead me astray from the Message [of Allah] after it had come to me! Ah! The Evil One [Satan] is but a traitor to humankind!}

(Qur'an 25: 27-29)

(7) Purification of the soul

As we have seen, our hearts can get 'rusted' with diseases of the heart just as iron gets rusted. As such, a heart that has rusted over a period of time cannot attain the fear of Allah. Therefore, one of the acts of worship recommended for cleansing the heart and ridding it of all rust is purification of the soul. Allah, the Exalted, says:

{In their hearts is the stain of the evil which they [continuously] do.}

(Qur'an 83: 14)

{By the soul, and the proportion and order given to it, and its enlightenment as to its wrong and its right, truly he succeeds who purifies it, and he has failed who corrupts it.}

(Qur'an 91: 7-10)

{...Verily Allah loves those who turn to Him constantly in repentance, and He loves those who keep themselves pure and clean.}

(Qur'an 2: 222)

This purification of the soul increases our faith and helps in developing taqwâ of Allah. Purification of the soul involves, among other things:

- Avoiding all forms of intoxicants

- Avoiding all forms of music with musical instruments, otherwise described by the Messenger of Allah (bpuh) as 'instruments of Satan'

- Keeping away from movies and other forms of media, including all forms of vulgar literature and pornographic materials, that promote or glorify acts which are forbidden

- Ingesting permissible foods and drinks, as well as avoiding all that is not permissible to eat or drink, and avoiding extravagance

- Waking up for night prayers and frequently asking for Allah's forgiveness and thanking Allah (the Exalted) for His uncountable blessings

Along with the above efforts to purify our souls, we should also endeavour to supplicate with the words that the Prophet (bpuh) used in beseeching Allah's pardon and purification of the heart:

«It was narrated that Zayd ibn Arqam (may Allah be pleased with him) said: I do not tell you anything but that which the Messenger of Allah (bpuh) said.

He used to say: O Allah, I seek refuge with You from helplessness, laziness, cowardice, miserliness, old age, and the torment of the grave. O Allah, grant my soul piety and purify it;

You are its Guardian and its Lord. O Allah, I seek refuge with you from knowledge that is not beneficial, a heart that is not humble (before You), a soul that is never satisfied, and a prayer that is not answered. (*Allâhumma, inni a'oodhu bika minal-'ajzi wal-kasali, wal-jubni wal-bukhli, wal-hazami wa 'adhâbil-qabri. Allâhumma, âti nafsi taqwâhâ, wa-zakkihâ anta khayru man-zakkâhâ; anta waliyuhâ wa mawlâhâ. Allâhumma inni a'oodhu bika min 'ilmin lâ yarfa'u wa min qalbin lâ yakhsha'u, wa min nafsin lâ tashba'u wa min da'watin lâ yustajâbu lahâ.*)» (Muslim)

(8) Loving Allah and His Messenger (bpuh) together with the believers, and hating the enemies of Islam

Loving Allah (the Exalted) and His Messenger Muhammad (bpuh) is manifested by our obedience to them. Allah, the Exalted, said:

{Say [Muhammad (bpuh) to humankind]: If you do love Allah, then follow me. Allah will love you and forgive your sins, for Allah is Oft-Forgiving, Most Merciful.}

(Qur'an 3: 31)

{There are some among men who take [for worship] others besides Allah, as equal [with Allah]. They love them as they should love Allah, but those of faith are overflowing in their love for Allah. If only those who do wrong could see, when they will see the torment, that to Allah belongs all power and that Allah is severe in punishment.}

(Qur'an 2: 165)

{O you who believe! If any from among you turn back from his religion, soon will Allah produce a people whom He will love and they will love Him, humble towards the believers, mighty against the unbelievers, fighting in the way of Allah, and never afraid of the censure of any censurer. That is the grace of Allah, which He will bestow on whom He pleases, and Allah is All-Encompassing, All-Knowing.}

(Qur'an 5: 54)

Anas (may Allah be pleased with him) narrated that the Prophet (bpuh) said:

«I swear by the One in Whose Hands is my soul, none of you will be a complete believer until I am more beloved to him than his father, his children, and all of humankind.» (Bukhari)

Anas (may Allah be pleased with him) also narrated that the Prophet (bpuh) said:

«There are three characteristics, and whoever attains them has found the sweetness of faith: that Allah and His Messenger are dearer to him than all others, that he loves a person only for the sake of Allah, and that he hates to return to disbelief after Allah has saved him from it, as he hates to be thrown into the fire.» (Bukhari and Muslim)

The benefits of *taqwâ*

Perhaps we can by now comprehend why the first piece of advice that Allah's Messenger (bpuh) gave to his Companions and to the Muslim Ummah, in his admonition contained in this hadith under discussion, was to have taqwâ of Allah. Taqwâ is the single most important quality that a person should have for success in this world and the hereafter.

{So fear Allah as much as you can: listen and obey, and spend in charity for the benefit of your own souls. Those who are saved from the covetousness of their own souls, they are the ones that achieve prosperity.}

(Qur'an 64: 16)

When we know the benefits of something in life, we will strive and do our best to gain it. Similarly, once we realize the benefits of taqwâ in our lives we will definitely do something about it so that we develop it in ourselves. Abu Dharr (may Allah be pleased with him) reported that the Prophet (bpuh) said to him:

«Fear Allah wherever you are, follow a bad deed with a good one – it will wipe it out – and treat the people with good behaviour.» (A reliable hadith recorded by at-Tirmidhi)

The benefits of taqwâ of Allah, both in this life and the hereafter, are too numerous to count. Among those mentioned by Allah (the Exalted) in the glorious Qur'an are the following:

1.
   Taqwâ is a sure means of entry into paradise.

   {Verily for the *muttaqeen* [literally, those who have taqwâ] are gardens of delight, with their Lord.}

   (Qur'an 68: 34)

2.
Taqwâ is a means of gaining Allah's protection and support.

{...Allah is the protector and ally of the muttaqeen.}

(Qur'an 45: 19)

3.
Taqwâ is a way of attracting Allah's provisions.

{...For he who fears Allah, ...He will provide for him from [sources] he never could imagine...}

(Qur'an 65: 2-3)

4.
Taqwâ is a means of finding beneficial solutions and a way out of difficulty and confusion.

{...For he who fears Allah, He will make a way for him to get out [of every difficulty].}

(Qur'an 65: 2)

5.
Taqwâ is also the means of acquiring Allah's mercy and abundant blessings.

{If the people of the towns had only believed and feared Allah, We should indeed have opened up to them [all kinds of] blessings from heaven and earth; but they rejected [the truth], and We overtook them for their misdeeds.}

(Qur'an 7: 96)

6.
Taqwâ helps one to make true and accurate judgements and attracts Allah's forgiveness for one's sins.

{O you who believe! If you fear Allah, He will grant you a criterion [to judge between right and wrong], and will expiate for you your sins and forgive you, for Allah is the Owner of great bounty.}

(Qur'an 8: 29)

7.
Taqwâ increases one's knowledge, because knowledge is a light that Allah puts in the hearts of His righteous servants.

{...So fear Allah; for it is Allah Who teaches you; and Allah is Well-Acquainted with all things.}

(Qur'an 2: 282)

8. Taqwâ is a means of gaining Allah's aid in all affairs.

{...Fear Allah, and know that Allah is with those who fear Him.}

(Qur'an 2: 194)

9. Taqwâ is a means of gaining the love of Allah (the Exalted).

{...Whoever fulfils his pledge and fears Allah, verily Allah loves those who have taqwâ.}

(Qur'an 3: 76)

10. Taqwâ is a means of making one's life easier.

{...For whoever has taqwâ, He will make his affairs easy for him.}

(Qur'an 65: 4)

11. Taqwâ is a means of gaining guidance from the Qur'an.

{This is the Book concerning which there is no doubt, a guidance for the muttaqeen.}

(Qur'an 2: 2)

12. Taqwâ is a sure way of gaining Allah's forgiveness of our sins and great rewards.

{...Whoever has taqwâ, He will remit his sins from him and will enlarge his rewards.}

(Qur'an 65: 5)

13. Taqwâ is a means of Allah (the Exalted) accepting our good deeds.

{...Allah only accepts deeds from the muttaqeen.}

(Qur'an 5: 27)

14.

Taqwâ is a means of receiving Allah's glad tidings in this world and the hereafter, and that is indeed the greatest of rewards.

{For those who truly believed and had taqwâ are glad tidings in the worldly life and in the hereafter. [That is the word of Allah] and verily there is no changing the word of Allah; that is the great success.}

(Qur'an 10: 63-64)

15.

Taqwâ is a means of salvation from hellfire.

{There is not one of you but will pass [across the bridge] over it [hellfire]. This is a decree with your Lord which must pass. Then We will save those who had taqwâ and leave the wrongdoers [humbled] to their knees in it [hellfire].}

(Qur'an 19: 71-72)

The second piece of advice given by Allah's Messenger (bpuh) in the main hadith under discussion in this chapter was to listen and obey. It is by listening with our ears, minds, and hearts that we may gain some understanding of the teachings of our beloved Prophet (bpuh). If we are not ready to listen to Allah's commands in the glorious Qur'an; or Prophet Muhammad's statements known as the Hadith, as discussed in this treatise or any other book of Hadith; or the teachings of the Prophet's Companions; or the teachings of our great scholars; then it will not be easy to attain any truly useful guidance. We must listen to them and obey in order to get any understanding during our life in this world, as Allah (the Exalted) says:

{Those who listen to the Word and follow the best [meaning] in it, those are the ones whom Allah has guided, and those are the ones imbued with understanding.}

(Qur'an 39: 18)

Those who refuse to listen to and obey Allah (the Exalted), His Messenger Muhammad (bpuh), the Prophet's Companions, and the classical Muslim scholars as well as the leaders appointed among the Muslims, regardless of their tribes, races, or languages, they are the ones who will lose most – both in this world and in the hereafter. Theirs will be a great regret. Allah, the Exalted, says:

{They will say: Had we but listened or used our intelligence, we would not have been among the dwellers of the blazing fire! They will then confess their sins, but far will be [forgiveness] from the dwellers of the blazing fire!}

(Qur'an 67: 10-11)

{If only you could see when the guilty ones will hang their heads before their Lord, [saying]: Our Lord, we have now seen and heard, so send us back [to the world] and we will do righteous good deeds. Verily, we now believe with certainty. If We had willed, surely, We could certainly have brought every soul its true guidance, but the Word from Me took effect, that I will fill hell with jinn and humankind [the evildoers and the ungrateful ones] together. So taste [the torment of the fire] because you forgot the meeting of this day of yours. Surely, We too will forget you, so taste the abiding torment for what you used to do!}

(Qur'an 32: 12-14)

{Then leave Me alone with those who reject this teaching [the Qur'an]. We will punish them gradually from directions they do not perceive. A respite will I grant them; truly powerful is My plan. Or is it that you ask them for a reward, so that they are burdened with a load of debt? Or that the unseen is in their hands, so that they can write it down?}

(Qur'an 68: 44-47)

As for those who listen, obey and implement Allah's commands and the guidance of Prophet Muhammad (bpuh), they are the successful ones both in this world and the hereafter. They are the true believers and will have for their companions the best of humankind, as Allah, the Exalted, says:

{All who obey Allah and the Messenger are in the company of those on whom is the grace of Allah, the company of the prophets, the sincere [lovers of truth], the witnesses [who testify], and the righteous [who do good]. What a beautiful companionship and fellowship! Such is the bounty from Allah, and sufficient is Allah as the All-Knower.}

(Qur'an 4: 69-70)

Conclusion

All praise be to Allah (the Exalted) Who has given us such beautiful moral teachings through His beloved prophets and messengers, especially the last and final Prophet and Messenger, Muhammad (bpuh). Allah (the Exalted) subsequently enabled the Prophet's Companions and their students to memorize, preserve and convey these invaluable moral values through their conduct and through the various books of Hadith and other Islamic sciences, books which the learned have compiled from the end of the first century of Islam until today.

What has been compiled and discussed in this small treatise is a tiny part of the vast knowledge of the hadiths which teach moral values that humanity urgently needs for healing, happiness, and prosperity in this world and the hereafter.

The virtuous moral values discussed here are practical, simple, and straightforward. They are not utopian or imaginary philosophical fancies that are portrayed in beautiful terms but are impractical in real life. They are part of the ideal and practical lifestyle of all the prophets and messengers of God, who were all human beings sent as examples and role models to be followed and emulated. They are also teachings that were put into practice by Prophet Muhammad's Companions (may Allah be pleased with all of them) and the righteous Muslims who followed them.

If human beings would only go back to these beautiful moral teachings and strive to implement them, then they would be able to lead the same kind of lifestyle – full of serenity, simplicity, peace of mind, and happiness – that was enjoyed in the era of Prophet Muhammad's generation and the three generations that followed; they were able to coexist with people of all other faiths.

Yes, even with the seemingly complex socio-moral problems plaguing humanity today, problems that have made human beings harm and kill each other and made it nearly impossible for them to coexist peacefully, these noble, practical, and timeless moral teachings can still illuminate peoples' lives and bring back long lost rays of hope.

As we saw in the introduction, moral values are practical teachings that either prevent people from injuring the life, property, and honour of others or prompt them to do good to others. The people who practice religion superficially in their lives but lack moral values will be the most bankrupt people on the Day of Judgement. They will come to Allah's court of absolute justice with a mountain of good deeds, such as prayers, fasting, charity, and the like, but they will be thrown into the hellfire because they trampled on the rights of other people.

«Abu Hurayrah (may Allah be pleased with him) narrated that Allah's Messenger (bpuh) said: Do you know what bankruptcy means?

The Companions of the Prophet (bpuh) said: Among us, the one who has no money and no goods is the one who is bankrupt.

The Prophet (bpuh) said: The one who is bankrupt in my Ummah is the one who will come on the Day of Resurrection with prayers, fasting, and charity, but he will come having insulted this person, slandered that one, consumed the wealth of this one, shed the blood of that one, and beaten this one. They will each be given from his good deeds, and if his good deeds run out before the scores have been settled, some of their bad deeds will be taken and cast upon him. Then he will be thrown into the fire.» (Muslim)

On the other hand, the ones who will be the closest to the prophets and messengers in paradise are those who sincerely worshipped Allah (the Exalted) alone, without associating partners with Him, and who combined both religion and good moral values in their lives. Allah (the Exalted) will be well pleased with them, and they will be well pleased with Allah (the Exalted), and that will be the greatest and truest success. Jâbir (may Allah be pleased with him) narrated that Allah's Messenger (bpuh) said:

«Indeed the most beloved among you to me, and the one who will sit nearest to me on the Day of Judgement, is the best of you in character...» (A reliable hadith recorded by at-Tirmidhi)

We must be more conscious of our character than our reputation, because our character represents who we really are, whereas our reputation is only a reflection of what people think we are.

{Say: O people, the truth has come to you from your Lord, so whoever is guided is only guided for [the benefit of] his own soul, and whoever goes astray only goes astray to his own loss; I am not responsible for you [to force you to do what is right].}

(Qur'an 10: 108)

This book is what Allah (the Exalted), by His grace and bounty, allowed to be written as a reminder first to my own self and then as a reminder to others. We pray and hope that people with better understanding and insight will improve on what has been compiled here and do an even better job at spreading the important messages found in this short compilation.

{Verily in this is a message for any that has a heart and understanding or who gives ear and earnestly witnesses [the truth].}

(Qur'an 50: 37)

I close with final words that are in accordance with the noble Qur'an and the Sunnah of Prophet Muhammad (bpuh):

{...My success [in my task] can come only from Allah. Upon Him I have relied, and to Him I return.}

(Qur'an 11: 88)

All praise is for Allah, by Whose favour all good works are accomplished.[112]

Notes

1. Hadith: the collected statements and actions of Prophet Muhammad (bpuh) that with the Qur'an form the basis of Islamic law

2. Sunnah: the practice and collected sayings of Prophet Muhammad (bpuh) that together with the Qur'an forms the basis of Islamic law

3. hadith: a statement or action of Prophet Muhammad (bpuh) that was remembered and recorded by his Companions and followers

4. *Hadith of Al-Nawawi*, 1:61.

5. Quran 23:8

6. Rahbar, *Raising Children According to Qur'an and Sunnah*, 29.

7. at-Tirmidhi, *Abwâb al-Birr*, hadith no. 2005,

8. The translators of *Sunan Ibn Mâjah* made the following comments about this hadith:

    a. Due to immodesty and impudence many dangerous diseases like syphilis and gonorrhoea emerged, and thereafter AIDS and hepatitis came to existence. The more the society is free from immodesty, the less is the prevalence of these diseases.

    b. Cheating in weighing or measuring results from greediness. It usurps the rights of others, so its punishment also inflicts them in the form of financial loss and famine.

    c. Zakâh brings blessings to wealth. If those who pay zakâh in any society stop doing so, then their livelihood is stopped, as a punishment for them.

    d. Allah showers His mercy upon those who have compassion for others. Conversely, the one who causes harm to others, abstains from helping them, or exploits them, does not deserve His mercy.

    e. Included in the covenant of Allah and His Prophet (bpuh) is protecting the lawful rights of non-Muslims who live under an Islamic government. Moreover, the one who accepts Islam promises to worship Allah and to obey the Prophet (bpuh). Breaking this promise also entitles people to the punishment of Allah.

f.
>
> To protect the health of the nation from diseases, all means of obscenity should be eradicated (such as, indecent literature, musical instruments, dance, films, mixing of men and women, lewd programs on radio and television, and so on).

9

Taqwâ of Allah means fulfilling one's duty towards Allah by obeying His commandments and refraining from His prohibitions, whereas good character implies behaving well towards one's fellow human beings and other creatures.

10

Quran (23:8)

11

A blister seems to be an important thing seen from the outside; yet when popped, one sees that it does not contain anything. Similarly, some people seem religious and pious from the outside, but their hearts are empty and devoid of any goodness.

12

Quran(2:12)

13

Quran (9:112)

14

The scholars of Hadith have declared that the hadith in *Jâmi' at-Tirmidhi* is reliable and that the one in *Sunan Ibn Mâjah* is sound.

15

at-Tirmidhi 4:464

> A sense of shyness or modesty is a natural human trait that plays an important part in building a person's character. It is modesty that prevents him from indulging in acts that are lewd and evil. Only those who can guard their minds against evil thoughts, protect their bellies from unlawful food and drink, and are mindful of what conditions await them in their graves after death could truly have shyness. And only those people can have real modesty who put no value on the ostentations and luxuries of the world, and reject the temptations of this world in favour of a happier life in the Hereafter.

16

This implies that one should not use the senses in the head (including the brain, eyes, ears, tongue, and so on) in a way that is not pleasing to Allah. See this author's series, *God's Blessings to Humanity* for the correct use of these senses.

17

The stomach and what is close to it, which includes the heart, the private parts, and the legs and arms. One should not use these parts in any act of disobedience to Allah.

18

Bukari authenticated this hadith, even though others said it is weak.

19

Al-Nawawi, 2:807

[20]

 Al-Nawawi, 807

[21]

Because of the lack of ḥayâ' in many parts of the Western world, people have gone as far as conducting same-sex marriages in the church, and some homosexual men and women have even been ordained as pastors and priests!

[22]

 jinn: non-human, rational beings created by Allah

[23]

 Al-Nawawi, 817.

[24]

Even though other scholars of Hadith have declared this hadith to be weak, al-Albâni has declared it a sound hadith in his *Ṣaḥeeḥ Sunan ibn Mâjah*, 2:406

[25]

 Al-Nawawi, 819.

[26]

Allah (the Exalted) eased the way for each human being into this world by his or her birth. This may also refer to life itself, which has been made easier by Allah's guidance.

[27]

 at-Tirmidhi commented on this hadith:

> Allah loves the act of a Muslim who, though well-to-do and rich, avoids wearing ostentatious garments out of modesty. However, not to wear fine garments because of the fear that those, who thinking him to be rich, would beg money from him or wearing shabby clothes in order to impress the people with one's piety and abstinence is plain hypocrisy unbecoming of a true believer.

[28]

Remember Allah always, and obey His orders, and He will save you from every evil and will take care of you in all aspects of your life.

[29]

Be loyal and obedient to Allah, and He will respond to your requests and needs.

[30]

Similar narrations are also reported by Muslim, Imam Aḥmad, Ibn Ḥibbân, al-Bayhaqi, and others.

[31]

Accepting Allah as our only true Lord is only done by understanding this statement's true and deep meanings, as well as its implications, and then acting upon it.

[32]

 Muslim 2:104

[33]

 Quran (6:39)

[34]

 Al-Nawawi, 834-835

35

Al-Nawawi, 835.

36

The basic greeting of peace, or *salâm*, is *as-salâmu 'alaykum* (peace be with you). The fullest greeting is *as-salâmu 'alaykum wa raḥmatullâhi wa barakâtuhu* (peace be with you, and the mercy of Allah and His blessings). The full reply is *wa 'alaykum as-salâm wa raḥmatullâhi wa barakâtuhu* (and with you be peace, and the mercy of Allah and His blessings).

37

Muslim, *Kitâb al-Birr*, hadith no. 6601.

38

Quran 2:223

39

Quran 2:223

40

'Minor faults' is a term mentioned in the Qur'an (53: 32).

41

It is striving for lawful earning, but not becoming completely engaged to the extent that he or she becomes heedless of the hereafter. It is adopting a balanced manner in earning worldly gain.

42

Wastefulness includes spending on that which is unlawful or in disobedience to Allah.

43

This means that you do not have the means to give them assistance at present.

44

Quran (6:141)

45

Quran (3:152)

46

Quran (2:120)

47

When the Muslims first migrated from Makkah to the city of Madinah (formerly known as Yathrib), Allah's Messenger (bpuh) paired up each Muhâjir (immigrant) with one of the Anṣâr (the local Muslims who received and welcomed the immigrants) in a brotherly-like relationship.

48

at-Tirmidhi 4:472.

49

He will wish that his death from this life would be the very end of all life rather than being the gateway to eternal life.

50

Abu Dâwood, *Kitâb al-Adab*, hadith no. 5090; it is also in the *Musnad* of Imam Aḥmad and *Sunan an-Nasâ'i*. The scholars of Hadith have declared this hadith weak, even though Ibn Ḥibbân authenticated it.

51

Quran 2:59

52

In a variety of cultures and languages, the right hand is associated with strength and positive qualities, while the left hand is associated with weakness and negative qualities. This statement precludes any possible mistaken transfer of such ideas of deficiency to an attribute of Allah.

53

Degrees of kinship are as follows according to the Qur'an and the Sunnah: first of all, parents and grandparents; then offspring; then brothers and sisters; then paternal uncles and aunts; then maternal uncles and aunts; and then other relatives.

54

They are those who, when they weigh or measure, short-change people by giving them less than they deserve or less than what they paid for. Often, the amount shortchanged is be so little as to hardly be noticed.

55

Quran 16:90

56

They submit obediently to the laws of Allah.

57

at-Tirmidhi 4:408.

58

Quran (2:165)

59

Quran (33:19)

60

al-Ghazâli, *Fiqh-us-Seerah*, 147-148.

61

The literal definition of a muhâjir is a person who emigrates from a land of disbelief to a land of belief, but as this hadith points out, the true definition includes all those who turn away from evil deeds and sins and turn instead toward obedience to Allah.

62

Quran 2:9

63

Sahih Muslim 2749

64

Bukhari, *Kitâb ad-Du'â'*, hadith no. 6308.

65

al-Ghazzali

66

Sahih al-Bukhari 7376

67
Scholars of Hadith have declared the version of this hadith in *Jâmi' at-Tirmidhi* to be sound, and the version in *Sunan Abu Dâwood* to be reliable.

68
Muslim 7434

69
Muslim 6475.

70
al-'Awâyishah, *The Prayer: Its Effects in Increasing Eemân & Purifying the Soul*, 20. He says that the hadith is reported by aṭ-Ṭabarâni and others from Abu ad-Dardâ' and also found in *Ṣaḥeeḥ ul-Jâmi'*.

71
Quran (5:60)

72
Quran (2:275)

73
Umar ibn al-Khaṭṭâb

74
al-Albâni stated that this hadith is weak but added that the meaning is correct.

75
Umar ibn al-Khaṭṭâb

76
Some scholars of Hadith have declared this hadith to be weak, while others have said it is sound.

77
Umar ibn al-Khaṭṭâb

78
Abu Bakr as-Siddeeq

79
Quran (2:11)

80
Quran 4:36

81
Quran (4:36)

82
Quran 4:94

83
Some scholars of Hadith have declared this hadith to be weak

84

Scholars of Hadith have said this hadith is weak, Bukhari, in his *al-Adab al-Mufrad* hadith no. 594, has recorded a hadith that says:

«Give each other gifts and you will love each other.»

Muslim also recorded the second part of the above hadith that says:

«O Muslim women, no woman should look down on a gift given by her neighbour, even if it is the meat from a sheep's hoof.»

in *Kitâb az-Zakâh*, hadith no. 2379. So the least that can be said about the hadith collected by Imam at-Tirmidhi is that it may be reliable due to other supporting evidence, and Allah knows best.

85

Quran (2:112)

86

at-Tirmidhi hadith no. 2906

87

Abu *Bakr as-Siddeeq*

88

Though some scholars of Hadith have declared this hadith weak

89

Cited by Bukhari

90

fiṭrah: the natural inborn inclination of humans to worship their Creator prior to the corruption of this nature by external influences. Islamic monotheism is described as the religion of fiṭrah and part of the inherent good nature of humankind.

91

Let people remain true to their fiṭrah within the religion of Islam.

92

Humankind is created in the best of moulds: upright, symmetrical, and balanced in form and nature with physical, intellectual, psychological and spiritual components.

93

This mutilation likely refers to the branding, slitting of ears, and other marks which some of the Muslims and non-Muslims of the time used to do their animals.

94

Quran (3:154)

95

See Ibn Kathir Tafsee *Soorah al-Ḥujurât (ISBN 9781512266573)*

96

at-Tirmidhi hadith no. 2318; also recorded by Ibn Mâjah.

97

Quran (24:31)

98

Quran (23:5)

99

maḥram: relatives who are so closely related that marriage would never be permitted between them; for a man this would include his mother, grandmother, daughters, granddaughters, sisters, aunts, and nieces

100

With the barely-covering, skin-tight, and see-through types of clothes that many women put on today, the situation is worse than ever, as Prophet Muhammad (bpuh) predicted. In *Ṣaheeḥ Muslim*, it is reported that the Prophet (bpuh) said:

«There are two types of the people of hell whom I have not yet seen (present among us): people with whips like the tails of cattle, with which they beat the people, and women who are clothed yet naked, misguided and leading others astray, with their heads like the humps of camels, leaning to one side. They will not enter paradise or even smell its fragrance, although its fragrance may be detected from a great distance.»

101

Paraphrased from Siddiqi, *Islam Forbids Free Mixing of Men and Women*, 65.

102

Quran (30: 30)

103

Quran (2:83)

104

Al-Nawawi, 699-700

105

The corresponding Islamic terms are *ma'nâ lughah* – definition according to the language of its origin; *ma'nâ iṣṭilâhi* – definition according to its technical usage; *ma'nâ 'urfi* – definition according to its customary and traditional usage; *ma'nâ shari'i* – definition according to the Islamic Sharia; and *majâz* – figurative definition.

106

Al-Nawawi, 700-701.

107

Quran (49:12)

108

Al-Nawawi, 704.

109

Remember Him always, and obey His orders. He will save you from every evil and will take care of you in all the spheres of life.

110

Be loyal and obedient to Him, and He will respond to your requests and needs.

111

Such as saying *Subḥân Allâh* (Glory be to Allah); *Lâ ilâha illâ Allâh* (There is none worthy of worship other than Allah); *Alḥamdulillâh* (All praise is for Allah); and *Allâhu akbar* (Allah is the Greatest).

112

Quran (2:110)

For example, in the First book of Samuel 15: 1-3, Samuel said to Saul:

I am the one the LORD sent to anoint you king over his people Israel; so listen now to the message from the LORD. 2 This is what the LORD Almighty says: I will punish the Amalekites for what they did to Israel when they waylaid them as they came up from Egypt. 3 Now go, attack the Amalekites and totally destroy everything that belongs to them. Do not spare them; put to death men and women, children and infants, cattle and sheep, camels and donkeys.

According to Deuteronomy 20:10-18, God said:

10 When you march up to attack a city, make its people an offer of peace. 11 If they accept and open their gates, all the people in it shall be subject to forced labor and shall work for you. 12 If they refuse to make peace and they engage you in battle, lay siege to that city. 13 When the LORD your God delivers it into your hand, put to the sword all the men in it. 14 As for the women, the children, the livestock and everything else in the city, you may take these as plunder for yourselves. And you may use the plunder the LORD your God gives you from your enemies. 15 This is how you are to treat all the cities that are at a distance from you and do not belong to the nations nearby. 16 However, in the cities of the nations the LORD your God is giving you as an inheritance, do not leave alive anything that breathes. 17 Completely destroy them—the Hittites, Amorites, Canaanites, Perizzites, Hivites and Jebusites—as the LORD your God has commanded you. 18 Otherwise, they will teach you to follow all the detestable things they do in worshiping their gods, and you will sin against the LORD your God.

In Numbers 31:17-18, Moosâ said, "17 Now kill all the boys. And kill every woman who has slept with a man, 18 but save for yourselves every girl who has never slept with a man."

And in Joshua 6: 21, "They devoted the city to the LORD and destroyed with the sword every living thing in it-men and women, young and old, cattle, sheep and donkeys."

Appendix 1: Jihad

This appendix appears in
'Umdat al-Fiqh Explained
(Volume 2) authored by
Dr. Hatem al-Haj
and published by IIPH

Jihad is the struggle against all forms of evil and injustice, both within one's own self (*nafs*) and against others. Thus, jihad is not limited to the use of military force, although such armed struggle is one form of it, and in that sense, jihad has been practiced and sanctioned by all nations since the beginning of time. After all, there is no nation in our world that does not have an army, and in all nations, martyrdom is seen as the ultimate sacrifice. War, then, may be good or bad, depending on the motives of those who engage in it and their conduct during and after the campaign. We believe that armed struggle was prescribed in Islam to defend not only Muslims but also non-Muslims who suffer from oppression, as well as to support God's cause of justice on Earth. It was also meant to protect the right to worship God, Who created us, in complete security; it is natural that He would want that right granted to His servants.

There are, however, certain Qur'an verses that may be taken out of context and wrongly described as a declaration of endless war against the unbelievers. For example, Allah (the Exalted) says:

{…and fight against the polytheists collectively as they fight against you collectively…}

(at-Tawbah 9: 36)

And:

{And when the sacred months have passed, then kill the polytheists wherever you find them…}

(at-Tawbah 9: 5)

While the vast majority of Muslims do not think that we should be fighting perpetually against the rest of humanity, a fringe minority of mostly youth, inflamed by the real and perceived injustices committed against Muslim peoples, use these verses and others to wage jihad against all of their opponents, both Muslims and non-Muslims.

Lacking any means to wage conventional wars, they resort to terrorism to pursue their agenda or to avenge themselves against the enemies who fight them. Such is the dilemma that Muslims are facing nowadays and that mars the name of jihad.

It is true that the verses cited are the words of Allah, Most High. He also said:

{Fight those who do not believe in Allah or in the Last Day and who do not consider unlawful what Allah and His Messenger have made unlawful and who do not adopt the religion of truth [that is, Islam] from those who were given the Scripture – [fight] until they give the jizyah [poll tax] willingly while they are humbled.}

(at-Tawbah 9: 29)

He also said:

{Fight them until there is no [more] fitnah and [until] religion [that is, worship] is [acknowledged to be] for Allah. But if they cease, then there is to be no aggression except against the oppressors.}

(al-Baqarah 2: 193)

And the Prophet (bpuh) said:

«I was commanded to fight the people until they testify that none is worthy of worship except Allah, and (until) they believe in me and what I came with. If they do that, then they have safeguarded their blood and wealth from me, except according to it (Islam), and their judgment is upon Allah.» (Agreed upon, on the authority of Abu Hurayrah)

Not only that, but in previous scriptures, namely the Bible, much more than this is attributed to God, including the killing of infants and children, referred to in the books of Deuteronomy, Joshua, and others.[113] Certainly, we do not believe that those statements about children and infants are from God, because it would be too hard to provide context that could explain them. However, in Islam, there is an explanatory context for all of these verses. First, it is important to note that Allah (the Exalted)(the Exalted)also says:

{And if they incline to peace, then incline to it [also] and rely upon Allah. Indeed, it is He Who is the Hearing, the Knowing.}

(al-Anfāl 8: 61)

{...So if they remove themselves from you and do not fight you and offer you peace, then Allah has not made for you a cause [for fighting] against them.}

(an-Nisâ' 4: 90)

Allah's Messenger (bpuh) said:

«O people, do not wish to meet the enemy, and ask Allah for pardon. But if you meet them, be patient and know that paradise is under the shade of the swords.» (Agreed upon, on the authority of 'Abdullâh ibn Abi Awfâ)

Who should be connecting the dots and reconciling the seemingly conflicting reports? The scholars well-grounded in the tradition. One of them, namely Imam Ibn Taymiyah, wrote a treatise on *Qitâl al-Kuffâr wa Muhâdanatuhum* [War and peace (treaties) with the disbelievers], in which he showed conclusively that the *'illah* (effective cause) for fighting them is their aggression, not their disbelief. He pointed out that the texts implying an open fight against them can never be used as proof for fighting the people at large, because they appear to contradict other evidences (some of which is mentioned above), the consensus, and even the life of the Messenger (bpuh) himself. Some of them appear to suggest fighting the people at large until there is no religion on Earth except Islam – yet this is contrary to the consensus. Do you not see that the Messenger of Allah (bpuh) made peace and truces with non-Muslims? In fact, he said:

«Leave the Abyssinians alone so long as they leave you (alone), and leave the Turks (alone) as long as they leave you alone.» (Abu Dâwood, and deemed ḥasan by al-Albâni in *Ṣaheeh al-Jâmi'*)

This clearly indicates that the command to fight does not apply to the people at large. Rather, Ibn al-Qayyim (may Allah bestow mercy upon him) said in *Hidâyat al-Hayârâ* [Guiding the bewildered]:

When Allah sent His Messenger [bpuh], most of the religions willingly submitted to him and to his caliphs after him. He never forced the religion upon anyone, and he would only fight those who fought and warred against him. As for those who made peace with him, he did not fight them or compel them to embrace his religion, out of compliance with the command of his Lord [the Exalted], Who says:

{There is no compulsion in religion; truth has been made clear from falsehood...} (al-Baqarah 2: 256)

These verses and hadiths, which appear to enjoin fighting the people at large, were referring to specific peoples during the Prophet's time, or to fighting in specific circumstances – such as defending the oppressed in accordance with the words of the Most High:

{And what is [the matter] with you that you fight not in the cause of Allah and [for] the oppressed among men, women, and children...}

(an-Nisâ' 4: 75)

– or to prevent tyrants from forcing those who embraced Islam to abandon worshipping Allah, the One and Only, as in the words of the Most High:

{And fight them until there is no [more] fitnah...}

(al-Baqarah 2: 193)

– or preemptively against (genuine, not imaginary) enemy aggression, as the Muslims did when the Persians sent troops to arrest the Messenger of Allah (bpuh), or when the Romans incited their allies, the Christians of Shâm, against the Muslims. The Christians blocked the Muslims' roadways and surrounded their trade caravans, and the ally of the Romans, Shurahbeel ibn 'Amr al-Ghassâni, killed al-Ḥârith ibn 'Amr al-Azdi, who was the Prophet's messenger to the ruler of Busra.

Scholars in the past entertained the following question: Is the default in international relations peace or warfare? The majority viewed peace as the default, while others believed it was warfare, although some of the latter may have been referring to the situation at their time, when they had no stable borders or statehood as we know it. Empires were constantly fighting against others to expand their territories (as can be seen in any infographics showing the changes in the map of Europe over the last one thousand years). If we pose this question to them again, using different wording, asking, "Do we prefer peace or warfare?", perhaps all of them would answer in favor of peace. Did not the Messenger of Allah (bpuh) say, in addition to all of the aforementioned?

«Indeed, Allah is gentle and loves gentleness, and He grants because of gentleness what He does not grant because of harshness, nor what He grants because of anything else.» (Agreed upon, on the authority of 'Â'ishah, and this is the wording of Muslim)

If a nation that essentially rules with justice makes peace with us, grants security to the Muslims within its borders, and does not persecute us, then why should we fight them? If our objectives are that no one is deprived of the right to worship their Lord in peace, that no tyrant subjugates any of the creation of Allah, and that no one threatens the interests of our Ummah, and we can attain all that peacefully, is fighting still justified? Would choosing it in these circumstances embody the gentleness that Allah loves in all matters?

Even after all this discussion, we have still not looked at the essence of the matter in question: war. Was war one thousand years ago the same as war today? This is not an insignificant inquiry because applying the legislative rulings correctly is contingent upon understanding the current reality in the place where these specific rulings are to be applied. In our age, the structure of nations has become stabilized and the borders of these nations have become distinct, in contrast to previous ages when nations did not rule themselves. Instead, they were ruled by dynasties and factions whose sovereignty would expand and then contract, only to be occupied by another.

In the past, the ruling factions fought on the battlefield, but this fighting rarely harmed ordinary people, farmers, women, or the weak. Furthermore, the masses would enjoy the rule of a just nation that replaced the tyranny that they had lived under for decades or centuries. This would bring them joy, just as the Christians of Shâm were overjoyed when the Muslims liberated them from Rome and its allies. But nowadays, the price of warfare is widespread chaos, corruption, and tragedy that do not differentiate between soldiers and civilians – for bombs and rockets are not like arrows and spears. Most scholars have said that a catapult could not be used except for the necessary jihad (to repel the enemy), what would he say about modern weapons of war?

In the past, jihad was sometimes necessary to secure the deliverance of *da'wah* to the entire creation, for it removed the obstacles, such as the tyrants and their oppressive regimes, that were preventing it. In our times, the deliverance of the da'wah is possible through the jihad of articulation and the tongue, via broadcasts, satellite channels, and especially the Internet, which delivers written, audible, and visual statements alike. Furthermore, the *du'ât* can travel to distant lands, mix with their people, and invite them, while enjoying security throughout.

To conclude this point, we can never deny the virtue of jihad and martyrdom in Islam and its raising its people upon courage, dignity, honor, and sacrifice. However, we must also be confident that Islam decisively prefers peace over war.

Any Muslim state that signs peace is acceptable in Islam and makes all the world, by default, a land of *muwâda'ah* (peace). There is a difference of opinion on this issue among the Shâfi'i and Ḥanbali schools, but Ibn al-Qayyim (d. 751 AH/ 1350 CE), the famous Ḥanbali jurist and disciple of Ibn Taymiyah (d. 728 AH/ 1328 CE), made a strong case for the validity of such treaties. Imam Muhammad ibn Idrees ash-Shâfi'i (d. 204 AH/ 820 CE) has himself explicitly stated that such a treaty is valid if the parties are given the option to terminate the treaty at will. 'Uthmân ibn 'Affân made a treaty with the Nubians that stated:

> We (Muslims) shall not wage war against you, prepare for war against you, or attack you, as long as you observe the conditions of the treaty between us and you… But it will not be incumbent upon the Muslims to drive away any enemy who may encounter you, or to prevent him from you, between the limits of the territory of Ulwah and Aswan.

There is another pertinent discussion here, which is that the war that Islam deems justifiable, at times, is an ethical war that must also be Sharia-complaint. It is a war where the civilians, or to be more precise, all non-combatants, are spared. Abu Dâwood reported from Anas that when they had to go to war, the Prophet (bpuh) would instruct them not to kill "an older man, a child, or a woman," and he would say, "Do righteousness and show kindness, for Allah loves those who are kind." Ibn Mâjah added that the Prophet (bpuh) forbade killing the *'aseef*, which is best translated as a non-combatant attachment to the army.

May Allah bring peace, justice, and security to the distressed and suffering among humankind.

Appendix 2: Slavery

This appendix appears in
'Umdat al-Fiqh Explained
(Volume 2) authored by
Dr. Hatem al-Haj
and published by IIPH

The issue of slavery may be one of the hardest issues to discuss. Our collective conscience as a global community is extremely averse to the discussion because of a variety of factors, not least of which is the cruel treatment that slaves suffered for centuries. Many preachers find it difficult to talk about the issue, particularly when they are asked why Islam's stance did not mandate the immediate and absolute abolition of slavery. Furthermore, classical books of Islamic law contain extensive discussions of the rulings pertaining to the slaves, causing discomfort to many educators who must address them. In the following discussion, I will attempt to highlight some of the facts about Islam's stance on slavery.

A Historical Matter

To begin with, any discussion of slavery in Islam that does not put the issue in its proper historical context will be flawed. No heavenly religion sought to eliminate the institution of slavery more than Islam did. It would welcome the current state of abolishment of slavery worldwide, and it would certainly be keen on all the nations of the world maintaining this state. A central credo of conduct for Muslims is that when they engage in any agreement, they must comply with it, for Allah (the Exalted)(the Exalted)says:

{O you who have believed, fulfill [all] contracts...}

(al-Mā'idah 5: 1)

This defense of the Islamic stance on slavery, and its description of the excellent treatment of the slaves in Islam is, therefore, only a topic of theological and historical importance, not a practical matter.

Never Racist

The second important point to highlight is that slavery in Islam was never a racist practice. In the early history of the Muslim state, there were slaves from all nations, and even before Islam, the Arabs had slaves of all races. The most famous slaves in the history of Islam were the Prophet's esteemed Companions Salmân the Persian, Bilâl the Abyssinian, and Ṣuhayb the Roman (may Allah be pleased with all of them). Indeed, as British historian S. H. Leeder writes, the issue of color was irrelevant to the early Muslims.

> "TAKE away that black man!" exclaimed the Christian Archbishop Cyrus. "I can have no discussion with him!" when the Arab conquerors had sent a deputation of their ablest men to discuss terms of surrender of the capital of Egypt, headed by the negro Ubâdah, as the ablest of them all. To the scared archbishop's astonishment, he was told that this man was commissioned by the General Amr; that the Moslems held negroes and white men in equal respect – judging a man by his character and not by his colour.

This is not to claim that there have never been racist Muslims. Racism is a human condition that arises from egoism and is manifested in different forms, such as tribalism, groupism, classism, nationalism, and so on. The closer and more devoted you become to Allah, the less egoistic you will be. The information here is about the institution of slavery in its theory, governing laws, and communal legal practice. Throughout the history of Islamic states, slaves came from all backgrounds; in fact, through most of Islamic history, they were from non-African nations, since there were not many conquests in sub-Saharan Africa. As in the Far East, those nations mostly came into the fold of Islam without war.

Slavery before Islam and in Other Religions

Slavery existed before Islam, and it spanned nearly every culture, nationality, and religion. While it may not have been known among hunter-gatherer populations, it was a part of every ancient civilization. In both a socio-geographic and religious context, slavery was normalized and tolerated worldwide, including in pre-Columbian America. Slavery was also common in Africa; in non-Muslim Africa, it was associated with pagan practices such as burying one or two young slaves alive next to the body of their deceased master. The spread of Islam is credited with ending this practice.

Research shows that no religion encouraged the ending of the practice as much as Islam did; likewise, no religion encouraged the beneficent treatment of the slaves as much as Islam did.

Here are some mentions of slavery in the Bible. (Note that the newer translations have changed the word 'slave' to 'servant'.)

Numbers 31: 17-18, NIV

Now kill all the boys. And kill every woman who has slept with a man, but save for yourselves every girl who has never slept with a man.

This statement, attributed to Moosâ (pbuh), clearly allows capturing, enslaving and having sex with young women.

Leviticus 25: 44-46, NIV

Your male and female slaves are to come from the nations around you; from them you may buy slaves. You may also buy some of the temporary residents living among you and members of their clans born in your country, and they will become your property. You can bequeath them to your children as inherited property and can make them slaves for life, but you must not rule over your fellow Israelites ruthlessly...

Exodus 21: 2-11, GNB

If you buy a Hebrew slave, he shall serve for six years; but on the seventh he shall go out as a free man without payment. If he comes alone, he shall go out alone; if he is the husband of a wife, then his wife shall go out with him. If his master gives him a wife, and she bears him sons or daughters, the wife and her children shall belong to her master, and he shall go out alone. But if the slave plainly says, "I love my master, my wife and my children; I will not go out as a free man," then his master shall bring him to God, then he shall bring him to the door or the doorpost. And his master shall pierce his ear with an awl; and he shall serve him permanently.

American historian and philosopher Will Durant describes the position of the Church as follows:

The Church did not condemn slavery. Orthodox and heretic, Roman and barbarian alike assumed the institution to be natural and indestructible; a few philosophers protested, but they too had slaves... Pagan laws condemned to slavery any free woman who married a slave; the laws of Constantine ordered the woman to be executed, and the slave to be burned alive. The Emperor Gratian decreed that a slave who accused his master of any offense except high treason to the state should be burned alive at once, without inquiring into the justice of the charge.

Islam's Answer to the Dilemma of Slavery

It may be said that Islam did not take an absolute abolitionist stance on the institution of slavery, and this is true to some extent. One must remember, though, that during the time of the ministry of the Prophet (bpuh), not only was the immediate abolitionist approach not proposed by any religious or secular order, but it would have been infeasible. Furthermore, it might have resulted in social and economic turmoil, not only for the larger communities, but firstly for the many slaves who would have been unable to fend for themselves.

In addition, the issue of how to handle war captives made slavery the surest path to saving their lives. In the past, armies could not keep the captives in prison and provide for them due to the scarcity of resources. Freeing them was not always possible because they could regroup and go back to fighting.

Finally, since the enslavement of captives was a common practice of all armies, it would have been unexpected for the Muslims to free all the captives when they won a battle but still be taken as captives when they lost.

Islam's answer to the dilemma of slavery can be summarized in two major points:

1. Gradual diminishment of the institution by simultaneously cutting off its tributaries and widening its runoffs

2. Enjoining the excellent treatment of slaves for as long as the institution survived

In the following paragraphs, I will address these two points.

The Gradual Diminishment of the Institution of Slavery

When one wishes to drain a river of its water, there are two methods: cutting off its tributaries (sources) and increasing its runoffs. Before Islam, a person could be condemned into slavery through various means, including a man selling his own wife or child, child abandonment, debt-slavery, captivity in war, kidnapping, and as a punishment for certain crimes. Islam cut off all of those tributaries that fed into the river of slavery except for one: captivity in war, for, as mentioned previously, it was a logistical necessity at times and, more importantly, enslavement helped protect the captives' lives. Despite that, Islam recommended freeing those captives. The Prophet (bpuh) said:

«Free the captives, feed the hungry, and visit the sick.» (Bukhari)

Islam's Encouragement of the Emancipation of Slaves

Evidence from the Qur'an and the Sunnah makes it clear that the emancipation of slaves is considered one of the greatest virtues and ways to earn the Lord's pleasure.

Allah (the Exalted)(the Exalted)said:

{And have shown him [humankind] the two ways [of good and evil]? But he has not broken through the difficult pass [to righteousness]. And what can make you know what is [breaking through] the difficult pass? It is the freeing of a slave.}

(al-Balad 90: 10-13)

{Righteousness is not that you turn your faces toward the east or the west, but [true] righteousness is [in] one who believes in Allah, the Last Day, the angels, the Book, and the prophets and gives wealth, in spite of love for it, to relatives, orphans, the needy, the traveler, those who ask [for help], and for freeing slaves...}

(al-Baqarah 2: 177)

Abu Hurayrah narrated that the Prophet (bpuh) said:

«Whoever frees a Muslim slave, Allah will save all the parts of his body from the (hell) fire as he has freed the body parts of the slave.»

Sa'eed ibn Marjânah said that he narrated this hadith to 'Ali ibn al-Ḥusayn, who then freed his slave, even though 'Abdullâh ibn Ja'far had offered him ten thousand dirhams, or one thousand dinars, for that slave. (Bukhari)

Abu Hurayrah also narrated that the Prophet (bpuh) said:

«Whoever frees his portion of a jointly-owned slave should free the slave completely by paying the rest of his price if he has enough money; otherwise, the price of the slave is to be estimated, and the slave should be helped to work, without hardship, until he can pay the rest of his price.» (Bukhari)

Islam also specified the freeing of slaves as the expiation for many sins.

Yet the best system Islam legislated was to give the slaves control over their own passage into the world of the free, by allowing them to purchase their own freedom with the help of the community members whom Allah ordered to support their cause. Allah (the Exalted)(the Exalted) says:

{...And those who seek a contract [for eventual emancipation] from among whom your right hands possess – then make a contract with them if you know there is within them goodness and give them from the wealth of Allah which He has given you...}

(an-Noor 24: 33)

This was beneficial for the slaves who had to be weaned from depending on their masters for provisions, for they would have faced problems if they were suddenly required to provide their own food, clothes, and shelter. (We must not underestimate the potential impact on the stability and security of the society if it had been mandated that all the slaves be immediately freed.) Of course, it was also beneficial for the masters, who were, to a great extent, dependent on the slaves for their businesses.

This was also favorable for the community, for they would see responsible people, who knew the value of work and labor, moving from the ranks of the slaves to those of the free.

It is worth noting that the Prophet (bpuh) led by example. According to the books of *seerah* (the Prophet's noble history), he emancipated all the slaves he had before Islam was revealed to him, as well as those given to him after Islam. In the most authentic book of Hadith, 'Amr ibn al-Ḥârith (may Allah be pleased with him), the brother of the Mother of Believers, Juwayriyah (may Allah be pleased with her), reported from her that when he died, the Messenger of Allah (bpuh) left neither a dinar nor a dirham, neither a male nor a female slave, nor anything else except his white riding mule, his weapons, and the land which he had given in charity to wayfarers. (Bukhari: Book 1, Hadith 475)

Finally, in attestation to the Islamic plan for eliminating slavery, C. Snouck Hurgronje writes:

> Setting slaves free is one of the most meritorious pious works, and, at the same time, the regular atonement for certain transgressions of the sacred law. So, according to Mohammedan principles, slavery is an institution destined to disappear.

Islam's Enjoinment of the Excellent Treatment of the Slaves

The excellent treatment of slaves in Islam is a fact that I will try to highlight by proofs from the textual and historical accounts, including testimonies by non-Muslim historians and thinkers.

In the Qur'an, there are several verses commanding the good treatment of slaves, including:

{Worship Allah and associate nothing with Him, and to parents do good, and to relatives, orphans, the needy, the near neighbor, the neighbor farther away, the companion at your side, the traveler, and those whom your right hands possess. Indeed, Allah does not like those who are self-deluding and boastful.}

(an-Nisâ' 4: 36)

The Messenger of Allah (bpuh) repeatedly commanded people to treat the slaves with mercy and compassion. One of his last recommendations to the Muslims before he died was to fear Allah regarding their slaves. A quick review of the following hadiths will further testify to his instructions regarding the excellent treatment of slaves:

«None of you should say: My slave ('*abdi*) or: My slave woman – for you are all (Allah's) slaves, and the Lord is Allah, Most High.» (A sound hadith recorded by Abu Dâwood)

Al-Ma'roor ibn Suwayd narrated:

«I saw Abu Dharr al-Ghifâri wearing a cloak, and his slave was wearing a cloak (like it). We asked him about that.

He replied: Once I abused a man, and he complained of me to the Prophet (bpuh).

The Prophet (bpuh) asked me:

O Abu Dharr! Did you abuse him by slighting his mother? You are a man who has *jâhiliyah* (pre-Islamic ignorance and disbelief).

(He added:) Your slaves are your brethren, upon whom Allah has given you authority. If you have your brethren under your control, you should feed them with the like of what you eat and clothe them with the like of what you wear. You should not overburden them with what they cannot bear, and if you do so, help them (in their hard job).» (Bukhari 3:46:721)

The Prophet (bpuh) unequivocally prohibited the separation of a mother from her slave child. Abu Moosâ reported that he said:

«May he be cursed, he who separates a mother from her child, or a brother from his sibling.» (A weak hadith recorded by Tirmidhi)

And for one who humiliates his slave by beating him or slapping him, the Prophet (bpuh) said:

«He who slaps his slave or beats him, there is no expiation for this but to free him.» (Muslim)

The Messenger of Allah (bpuh) was always concerned about the wellbeing of the slaves, and he would always mention them at the times when he expected the greatest attention from his audience, such as the time of his death and during the Farewell Pilgrimage, where he had the largest audience in his lifetime. "As for your slaves, male and female," he exhorted them during the Farewell Pilgrimage, "feed them with what you eat yourself and clothe them with what you wear. If you cannot keep them or they commit any fault, discharge them. They are God's people like unto you and be kind unto them."

No other nation or religious group in the world treated slaves better than the Muslims did, as demonstrated by the aforementioned examples of instructions from Allah and His Messenger (bpuh). The following are the testimonies of non-Muslim historians and leaders regarding this very fact:

On the attitude of the Muslim master towards his slaves, American historian and philosopher Will Durant writes:

…he handled them with a genial humanity that made their lot no worse – perhaps better, as more secure – than that of a factory worker in nineteenth-century Europe… It is astonishing how many sons of slaves rose to high place in the intellectual and political world of Islam, how many, like Mahmud and the early Mameluks, became kings.

At the end of the eighteenth century, Mouradgea d'Ohsson (an Armenian historian and diplomat who wrote extensively about the Ottoman Empire) declared:

There is perhaps no nation where the captives, the slaves, the very toilers in the galleys are better provided for or treated with more kindness than among the Muhammedans.

Napoleon Bonaparte, a military leader who was Emperor of France from 1804 to 1814, is recorded as saying about the condition of slaves in Muslim countries:

In the East, slavery never had the same characteristics as in the West. The slavery of the East is that which is seen in the Holy Scripture: the slave inherits from his master and marries his daughter. Most of the Pashas had been slaves; a great number of grand viziers, all the Mamluks, Ali Bey al-Kabir, and Murad Bey had all been slaves. They started by performing the most menial services in the house of their master and subsequently rose in status because of their merit or through favours. In the West, on the other hand, the slave was always below the domestic servant; he occupied the lowest rank...

With regard to the question of concubines and having sex with the slave girls, we must first say that the Prophet (bpuh) encouraged the masters to free their female slaves and marry them. He said:

«He will be doubly rewarded… the man who had a slave girl, and he fed her well, taught her manners and educated her, and then freed her and married her.» (Bukhari and Muslim)

Secondly, this system was not new, nor was it introduced by Islam; all the prophets before Islam acknowledged it and used it. There is no argument among the Jews, Christians, and Muslims that Hâjar was the concubine of Prophet Ibrâheem, and the Old Testament contains countless stories about concubines, including those of the Prophets Dâwood and Sulaymân (peace and blessings be upon them).

We can never view sexual relations with a female slave nowadays from the same perspective of those who lived during those times. It is illogical to deal with historical matters without understanding their context; judging a practice as good or bad cannot be done in the abstract, separate from its context and the norms of the time. Prostitution refers to sex outside of the socially acceptable context, but in ancient times, the concubine (like the wife) was allowed to have sex with the master as a legitimate partner. No woman would ever be allowed to have two sexual partners at the same time, so this concubine was not a sex tool to be enjoyed by the master and his relatives and friends.

She could be wed to only one person, and her rights, along with the rights of her children, were guaranteed. Ultimately, sex with the female slave provided a way to fulfill her needs, and she also gained a special status once she delivered a child, who had the same rights as the master's other children. After bearing his child, she could not be sold and was freed upon the death of the master.

I would conclude by emphasizing that Islam was keen on the emancipation of slaves, and it enjoined this throughout its teachings. The original and natural state in which God created his servants is the state of freedom, and He desires a return to that freedom. Let us all pray for the deliverance of all people from all forms of disguised slavery that exist in our world today and for the end of all manifestations of subjugation of people by others.

www.ingramcontent.com/pod-product-compliance
Lightning Source LLC
Chambersburg PA
CBHW081354070526
44583CB00020B/2554